A Quilter's Christmas

A Quilter's Christmas

Marti Michell

Rodale Press, Emmaus, Pennsylvania

Our Mission

We publish books that empower people's lives.

RODALE BOOKS

Notice

The author and editors who compiled this book have tried to make all the contents as accurate and as correct as possible. Illustrations, photographs, and text have all been carefully checked and cross-checked. However, due to the variability of materials, personal skill, and so on, neither the author nor Rodale Press assumes any responsibility for any damages or other losses incurred that result from the material presented herein. All instructions and diagrams should be carefully studied and clearly understood before beginning any project.

Projects on the Front Cover

On the tree: Quilted Diamond Ornaments (page 219), Heart Ornaments (page 84), No-Sew Miniature Ornaments (page 151)

On the table: Holiday Tablecloth with Star Topper (page 103)

On the couch: Temperance Tree Quilt (page 48)

On the rocking chair: Christmas Pinwheels Doll Bed Quilt (page 166)

Printed in the United States of America on acid-free ∞, recycled paper

Executive Editor: Margaret Lydic Balitas
Senior Editor: Suzanne Nelson
Senior Associate Editor: Mary V. Green
Copy Manager: Dolores Plikaitis
Copy Editor: Patricia A. Sinnott
Administrative Assistant: Susan Nickol
Editorial Assistance: Cyndi Hershey
Office Manager: Karen Earl-Braymer
Art Director: Anita G. Patterson
Design Director: Denise M. Shade
Book Designer: Darlene Schneck
Cover Designer: Denise M. Shade
Cover Photographer: Mitch Mandel
Interior Photographer: Bread and Butter Studios
Illustrator: Ann Davis Nunemacher
Technical Illustrator: Jack Crane
Technical Illustrator and Labeler: Robin M. Hepler

If you have any questions or comments concerning this book, please write to:

Rodale Press
Book Readers' Service
33 East Minor Street
Emmaus, PA 18098

Library of Congress Cataloging-in-Publication Data

Michell, Marti.
    A quilter's Christmas / Marti Michell.
        p.   cm.
    Includes index.
    ISBN 0–87596–565–2 hardcover
     1. Quilting–Patterns. 2. Appliqué–Patterns. 3. Christmas decorations. I. Title.
TT835.M5112 1993
745.594′12–dc20   93–19683
                                        CIP

Distributed in the book trade by St. Martin's Press

2 4 6 8 10 9 7 5 3 1 hardcover

CONTENTS

ACKNOWLEDGMENTS

It is always fun to complete a book and have your name listed as author, but it would be impossible to do any book alone. I would like to acknowledge the people who have made it possible for this book to be done.

All of the people at Rodale Press, especially my editor, Mary Green, who worked through a very tight editorial schedule, and Maggie Balitas, who kept everyone on track to meet the objective.

While the design concepts are mine unless acknowledged otherwise, Ann Davis Nunemacher interpreted my sketches and verbal descriptions into the pleasing shapes you see here, as well as provided most of the illustrations for the book.

Studio associates Martha Dudley, Ann Cookston, Sheri Gravel, Ellen Rosintoski, Mary Frances Hebert, and Camellia Pesto all contributed to the sewing,

while Jenny Lynn Price and Sally Cutler assisted editorially.

Without the projects designed and made by Kathryn Jones and the Boone Slick Quilters (Cardinals in the Pines Quilt on page 59), Sally Paul (Quilter's Greeting Cards and Gift Tags on page 226), and Iris Lee (the Crazy Quilting by Machine projects beginning on page 250), the book would not have been complete.

Stacy Michell, with a keen eye and decorative flair, assisted in the photo styling, while Steve Rucker of Bread and Butter Studios was the technical expert with the lens and lights. Scott and Barrie Alexander graciously allowed us to photograph many items in their home. The Storehouse, Lenox Square, Atlanta, was also an inspiring place to photograph "on location."

Thank you, everyone.

INTRODUCTION

It would be easy to wonder, "What is a 'quilter's Christmas?' " But first, it would be necessary to ask, "What is a quilter?" A recent letter to the editor of a quilting magazine asked, "What is the difference between a quilter and a person who makes quilts?" The drift of the editor's response was that a person who makes quilts goes out and buys a pattern and the fabric for a quilt and makes it. A quilter, on the other hand, buys fabric all the time, "just in case" it might be needed; likewise, books and tools. That sounded like a good explanation to me, and there is no question in my mind: I'm a full-blooded quilter.

My goal in putting together these projects, however, was to create a book that you don't have to be a full-blooded quilter to enjoy. A wide variety of subjects, styles, and techniques are included. Many people who aren't even half-blooded quilters enjoy quilts and quilting motifs as Christmas decorating themes. There are projects appropriate for sewers who are just starting to quilt, and some projects that are even suitable for nonsewers.

For years I tried not to let my love for quilts and quilted things overrun every nook and cranny of our home. When I started quilting, I said, "We are not going to have a quilt on every bed." After we had a quilt on every bed, I said, "Well, we aren't going to have a quilt on every wall." I felt it just wasn't very sophisticated to let a single interest show up everywhere. Now, however, I understand that quilting is not a *single* interest. First, there is patchwork, then appliqué, then the actual quilting by hand or machine. Count Seminole patchwork, reverse appliqué, crazy quilting, antique quilts, alternate uses of quilting de-

signs, and quilted clothing, and you're up to ten topics. And there are even more. So pardon me if it sounds as if I think congratulations are in order, but I have just discovered how many different interests I have.

Because Christmas is a time for celebrating and decorating and entertaining and family gatherings, it seems the perfect time to express my newfound freedom. It is common for people to decorate exuberantly at Christmastime. That makes it a logical time for spreading quilts and quilting motifs all through the house. From now on, I won't worry if people know the minute they walk into our house that I love quilting! I hope you feel the same.

It is my hope that many of the projects in this book will inspire you to action. It is not uncommon for those of us who love making things to start more Christmas projects than we can finish. In fact, at our house, that could be called a Christmas tradition. I learned a long time ago that it's better not to get a project completed by the intended Christmas than to finish it at all cost. The great thing about Christmas projects is that there is always another Christmas, and what doesn't get done this year will get done another.

Please join in and celebrate "A Quilter's Christmas" with me. Then, for year-round enjoyment of this book, please note that on many of the projects, it is only the color selection that makes it a Christmas design. Fabricate the designs in different colors, and they are suitable anytime.

Marti Michell

START WITH SOME BASICS

How to Use This Book

There are two people who think you should read every word of this book and make every project: my mother and me. However, recognizing that everyone may not accomplish that task, please consider these tips. There are some basic instructions in this chapter that are appropriate to read before starting any project. And, while there are also instructions that apply to only some of the projects, I recommend reading the entire chapter. The information is helpful, and in most cases, it is general enough to be applied to any quilting project you do.

In some of the project directions, you'll find cross-references that direct you back to this chapter for details. This was done to avoid repeating extensive directions and to allow space for more projects.

There is also a glossary with simple definitions of quilting-related words and phrases that might be unfamiliar. If you come across such a word or phrase, look in the glossary for a definition and information as to where there are complete instructions on that technique.

Different Investments of Time

Most of the designs in this book aren't either easy or hard; rather, the question is, "Do they take a little time or a lot of time or something in between?" While the instructions given are for the items as shown, please feel free to simplify or embellish them to make them more appropriate for your life-style or abilities; you might even want to interpret the designs in completely different ways.

Just as not everything we do for Christmas has to become a tradition, not everything we make has to be considered an heirloom. We can make things for the

enjoyment of the moment, too!

There are several places in the book where the same design is interpreted different ways, with different levels of time commitment. As a simple example, look at the Quilted Diamond Ornaments on page 219. These ornaments, featuring gold lamé mock bindings and purchased tassel trim, illustrate the point beautifully. You can spend a little time or a lot of time on them: either way, the result will be pleasing. Of the four diamonds shown in the photo, the one on the bottom left is hand quilted and took the most time, and the one at the top is painted and took the least amount of time. The ornament in the center is machine quilted, and the one on the bottom right is an enhanced machine-quilted version; the amount of time invested in these two falls somewhere between the hand-quilted version and the painted version. The machine stipple quilting that covers the entire background of the last ornament took less time than the hand quilting on the first ornament.

It's entirely up to you to decide how much time you want to spend and how much detail work you want to do. The projects presented are designed to be easily adaptable.

Using the Patterns in This Book

Almost all of the patterns in the book are printed full size. To accomplish that, it was sometimes necessary to divide pieces. If the patterns are divided, make sure you find all the correct pieces, and join them carefully where indicated.

To trace patterns, lay tracing paper or other lightweight paper on top of the patterns and trace carefully. The smaller or more intricate a project, the more accurate you need to be. If you are using a copy machine to reproduce patterns, be aware that there is sometimes a slight discrepancy in the copies and be sure to compare them with those in the book to insure accuracy.

You can also trace from the book directly onto template plastic. The plastic is transparent enough to allow you to see the lines of the pattern, and it makes a stiff pattern piece that can be used again and again.

For projects using paper-backed fusible material, you can either make a template of the pattern and trace around it onto the paper side of the material or trace the pattern from the book directly onto the paper. Be aware, however, that you cannot trace directly onto the fusible material if the pattern piece is directional. Letters, for example, have to be traced onto the paper in reverse to be facing the right way in the finished fused project.

Seam Allowances

The best piece of advice I can give you is to be sure to double-check the required seam allowance before you start any of the projects in this book. Because there are clothing projects mixed with quilting projects, the allowances vary. Please pay close attention to seam allowances on pattern instructions.

Most projects have a ¼-inch seam allowance. If you are new to patchwork and quilting, ¼ inch may seem narrow, but it is the seam allowance of choice, and once you become accustomed to it, the ⅝-inch seam allowance of dressmaking looks gigantic.

Watch for pattern pieces with no seam allowances. If the pattern has no seam allowance, it is not an attempt to save space. It means that the recommended construction method does not use a seam allowance, or at least not in the first step of the project. For example, fusing is the recommended process for the designs in the "Sew or No-Sew Miniatures" chapter on page 151. The small pieces are cut without a seam allowance. You could, of course, piece them rather than fuse them. If you decide to do so, be sure to include a seam allowance when cutting out the pattern pieces.

And then there is the ⅝-inch seam allowance on My Ladies' Vest on page 87. Because people who make garments are more accustomed to the ⅝-inch seam allowance, it seemed right for that project.

Grainline Designation on Patterns

Grainline arrows appear on some of the pattern pieces. Whenever possible, those arrows should be placed on the lengthwise grain of the fabric, parallel to the selvage.

Enlarging Patterns with a Grid

There are a few patterns in the book that were simply too large to be included full size. These are drawn so that you can enlarge them. Any pattern meant to be enlarged is drawn on a grid, with information included for the scale of enlargement.

1. From the scale given with the pattern, draw the appropriate size and number of squares for your grid. Use paper large enough to accommodate the full-size pattern, and with a ruler and pencil, draw horizontal and vertical lines to create the necessary squares. For example, the pattern for the Merry Chris-Moose Wallhanging on page 181 gets enlarged four times. So, while the squares in the original grid are ½ inch, those in the enlarged grid will be 2 inches.

2. Square by square, draw the original grid design onto the larger grid, as shown in **Diagram 1**.

ORIGINAL

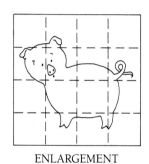
ENLARGEMENT

Diagram 1
Scale: 1 square = ½″

3. Smooth out curves and refine lines, and stand back and look at the newly enlarged design from a distance. When the design consists of several elements or pieces, it's a good idea to leave the new full-size original intact as a guide to placement of the pieces, as opposed to cutting it apart to use as patterns. You can trace the individual pattern pieces needed from the original.

You can use this same system to enlarge any pattern. For example, the block designs in the "Sew or No-Sew Miniatures" chapter, beginning on page 151, are 3 inches square. These are full-size patterns for the projects in that chapter. However, you may want to use the same patterns in a larger size. To do so, simply trace the original onto graph paper to create a grid. Determine the desired ratio for enlarging, draw your enlarging grid, and continue with Steps 2 and 3 above.

Fabric Selection

Most quilters use 100 percent cotton fabrics most of the time, but there are always exceptions. Cotton has been the fiber of choice for quiltmakers because it is easy to use, comfortable to wear or sleep under, and at this time, readily available in a wide range of colors and designs. The main reason for selecting other fibers is for specific characteristics, such as the glitter of lamé or satin or the texture of wool, that are not available in cotton.

Most quiltmakers collect fabrics for their regular sewing palette, but don't necessarily think of adding Christmas fabrics to their collection each year. Even if you don't have a specific project in mind, it's very useful to collect Christmas prints and Christmas-suitable fabrics when they're available. Nearly every project is more interesting if it isn't overmatched, and having a good collection on hand gives you more options. A good variety of colors, scales, and types of designs will make it much easier to find just the right fabric. Besides, the poinsettia print or the Teddy bears you fell in love with last year may not be available next Christmas.

Cotton fabrics are generally sold in 45-inch widths, although they are occasionally as narrow as 36 inches. Muslin is often available in widths up to 108 inches, which can be very useful if you want a quilt back without seams. In this book, fabric is assumed to be 45 inches wide, unless stated otherwise. Be aware, however, that even fabric marked as 45 inches wide sometimes comes off the bolt at 43 or 44 inches and can be as narrow as 42 inches after washing and drying. This is not meant to alarm you, but to prepare you if you find your fabric is narrower than you expected it to be. The materials lists for all the projects in this book allow sufficient yardage to cover these possibilities; most quilters will purchase a little extra fabric anyway just to be on the safe side.

Fabric Preparation

Standard doctrine is to prewash everything, but since I myself don't do that, it doesn't seem right to dictate it to others. Personally, I like to work with unwashed fabrics whenever possible. I machine piece and machine quilt, and the crispness makes the fabrics easier to use. However, many hand quilters say that they like to prewash because they think it makes the fabrics easier to quilt. Fabric color and appearance are never quite as great after washing, and since Christmas items may not have to be washed soon, I would rather not lose that fresh appearance any sooner than necessary.

Even if I don't prewash, I do test fabrics for shrinking and bleeding. It makes more sense to test fabrics first than to put them in a quilt and find out later that they bleed. Because I work from quite a stockpile of fabrics, I wait until I am actually ready to use the fabrics, then I test them. In a bowl, thoroughly wet a small piece of fabric of known size, for example, a 3-inch square or a 2 × 12-inch strip. During this process you can observe if you have any bleeding of color.

If the fabric bleeds, set the dye by soaking the entire piece of fabric in a solution that is three parts cold water to one part white vinegar. Rinse the fabric two or three times in warm water, and test it again. If the fabric still bleeds, you have two choices: Either don't use it, or use it in a project you know you will never wash.

Iron all your fabric samples dry. It is the heat on the wet fibers that shrinks cotton fabric. When the fabrics are completely dry, measure the pieces and compare those measurements with the original dimensions. If all of the fabrics are the same size or only slightly smaller, meaning that they have the same shrinkage, I don't do anything. If a fabric shows excessive shrinkage, I will either preshrink it or choose another fabric.

To preshrink, thoroughly wet the entire piece of fabric in the rinse cycle of the washing machine, and spin it dry. I don't add soap or go through extra cycles, as that just adversely affects the colors and finish but doesn't make the fabric shrink more effectively. Dry the fabric in the dryer. Press it, if necessary.

Remember to trim the selvages from fabric before using it. If there will be excess shrinkage, it will usually be in the selvages.

Batting Selection

One thing I have learned is that no one can decide for you what kind of quilt batting you will like best, and probably no one can change your mind once you decide. The purpose of this section is only to provide a brief introduction to the batting materials available. While the most basic decision appears to be choosing between polyester and cotton, it is really more complex. In reality, most quilters use different battings for different reasons.

I'm going to pass on some of my preferences, which vary with the end use. If you have not developed a personal preference, my preferences are as good a starting place as any. My recommendation, however, is to talk with as many people as possible who are using the same quilting method as you and ask them why they like a particular batting. Talk to salespeople at quilt and fabric stores for the latest information about batting.

There are so many new battings becoming available, I may have a new favorite by the time you read this. Also, there are many regional brands of batting that might be perfectly fine, but that I am just not familiar with. The shipping cost on batting is very high, and not all brands are available in all areas. This listing is not meant to be all-inclusive.

- **Generic Description:** Bonded polyester, medium-weight batting
  Brands: Fairfield Processing's Poly-fil Extra-loft; Hobbs Polydown. Many of the battings sold by the yard from rolls also fit this description. Hobbs also has a dark, almost black, Polydown that is especially nice on dark quilts. As an added feature, it seems to intensify the dark colors in fabrics.
  Uses: This is my favorite kind of batting for minimal machine *or* hand quilting on bed-size quilts. The polyester is very lightweight and easy care. The bonding helps minimize fiber migration. For a tied quilt, use a thicker version of bonded polyester or layer two batts for a puffier look.

- **Generic Description:** "New age" cotton batting. I added the "new age" part to distinguish it from the cotton batting in antique quilts. Until very recently, cotton batting meant lots of quilting—as close as every inch to hold the fibers in place and keep them from clumping. Several of these battings are not 100 percent cotton, but are actually 80 percent cotton and 20 percent polyester.
  Brands: Fairfield's Cotton Classic; Hobbs Heirloom; Warm and Natural
  Uses: More and more, as I am doing more complete coverage with machine quilting, I am using the flatter cotton battings. I also like cotton batting in garments. It molds to the body shape better than polyester and does not puff. It is, however, much heavier than polyester batting.

- **Generic Description:** Very lightweight polyester batting
  Brands: To my knowledge, Hobbs Thermore is unique in this category.
  Uses: It is the only polyester batting I currently use in vests. I like it in small quilts because the flatness seems more in scale and it has a softer drape. Sometimes I use a layer of Thermore or fleece to line things that are to be stuffed. The

lining will camouflage any bumps that might appear after stuffing.

- **Generic Description:** Fleece
  Brands: Dritz Craft-Fleece; HTC Armo Fleece; Pellon Quilter's Fleece and Thermolamb
  Uses: At this time, I use fleece only as a lining for stuffed cotton toys and pillows, in place mats, and in some Christmas ornaments. Fusible fleece is also available; some brands include Dritz Fusible Craft Fleece, HTC Armo Fusible Fleece, and Pellon Fusible Fleece. You can make your own fusible batting or fleece. Fuse a paper-backed fusible web or film to one side of the batting or fleece, using a pressing cloth and following the directions on the fusible product.

- **Generic Description:** Loose polyester fiberfill
  Brands: Fairfield's Poly-fil and Poly-fil Supreme; Hobbs Polydown fiberfill
  Uses: Stuffing pillows, dolls, and other dimensional items

Batting Sizes

One of the more interesting examples of the tail wagging the dog is the way packaged batting is sized. The sizes of batting were developed early this century based on the maximum width of manufacturing equipment. The sizes have little to do with the popular quilt sizes, but they have become standard in the industry. So, quiltmakers must either go up a size—for example, buy a king-size batt for a queen-size quilt—or cut some of the batt off the end and sew it on the side, a tedious experience at best. My recommendation is to always have the approximate finished size of the quilt with you and buy a batting that exceeds those measurements in both directions.

Batting is also available by the yard, but only 48 inches wide. This is great for baby quilts or wall-hangings, but not very convenient for anything larger.

Tools and Space

It is wonderful to have a separate sewing room or area, but I always recommend that even if your space is limited to the kitchen table, you call it the studio. Somehow, "working in the studio" just sounds so impressive and elevates your efforts.

Most of the tools you need are probably already in your sewing supplies, but wander through a quilt shop or frequent a quilt show, and you will discover there are people lying awake nights thinking up tools that we want and that will make our quiltmaking efforts easier, more accurate, more fun, and probably more rewarding. The basics you'll need include good scissors, a seam ripper, a thimble, pins, needles, thread, marking tools, and a ruler. Beyond that, it's up to you.

The Sewing Machine

My favorite, and nearly indispensable, tool is a sewing machine—or two! While a few of the projects in this book will feature hand sewing, most work, including the quilting, is done on the machine. Keep your machine in good working order; it should be well oiled and dust free at all times. Spend some time really getting to know it; it may have features you're not aware of or stitches you've never tried.

When piecing, set the machine for 10 to 12 stitches per inch. Generally, I use cotton or cotton-wrapped polyester thread, but always use good thread. Never, never go for junk bargain thread.

With machine quilting, the very fine nylon monofilament thread (usually called invisible thread) is often used, but so are the high-luster rayon threads and the metallics. I'm finding the decorative threads to be more important with nearly every quilt.

A Good Iron

While it is not uncommon in this day and age for a home to be without an iron and ironing board, pressing is not optional when it comes to patchwork. Don't worry, though; just as making quilts does not singularly qualify you to sew on buttons, pressing patchwork is not sufficient training for white shirts! Adequate pressing is a must to create flat, accurate pieces.

I prefer a good steam iron and a cotton ironing board cover. I've eliminated the reflective type of ironing board covers because I seem more likely to burn my fingers with them and had a bad experience with fabric distortion.

An iron is indispensable when working with fusible materials. A fusible material is basically an adhesive that can be heat activated. More and more, quiltmakers and fabric crafters are finding the fusible products on the market to be helpful tools.

Rotary Cutter Systems

The rotary cutter and its accompanying protective mat have revolutionized the way most quilters cut. The cutter itself looks like a glorified pizza cutter. Because it is very sharp, the rotary cutter must be used with a self-healing protective mat. As the cutter rolls along over the mat's surface, it does make a small slit, but the self-healing capability of the mat generally maintains its usefulness for years.

A thick (approximately 1/8 inch), transparent acrylic ruler is the third tool that completes the set by providing a rigid edge to cut against. In recent years in the quilting industry, these rulers have become available in many shapes and sizes, including rectangles, squares, and triangles.

Of course, the fabrics can be cut with scissors. But rotary cutter systems offer several significant advantages: They are extremely effective with multiple layers, increasing the number of pieces you can cut at one time. In addition, the fabric remains flat while being cut, increasing the accuracy of the cut; the rotary cutters are much faster than scissors; and there is less stress on your hand and fingers when doing large amounts of cutting in a short time period.

There are a few important things to keep in mind when using a rotary cutter. First, the blade is extremely sharp. Keep the cutter away from children, and always slide the blade guard into place as soon as you stop cutting. Always cut away from yourself, never toward yourself.

Straighten the edge of the fabric before measuring and cutting strips. Fold the fabric as shown in **Diagram 2**. Line up the fold in the fabric with a horizontal line on a see-through ruler. Trim the uneven edges with the cutter. To cut strips, rotate the fabric as shown in **Diagram 3**, align the ruler with the trimmed edge of the fabric, and cut. Check the strips periodically to make sure they are straight, not angled. If your strips are angled, refold the fabric, trim the edge again, and begin cutting.

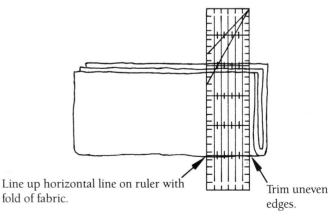

Line up horizontal line on ruler with fold of fabric.

Trim uneven edges.

Diagram 2

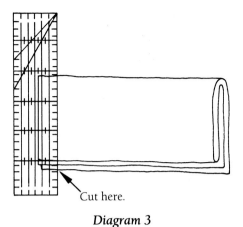

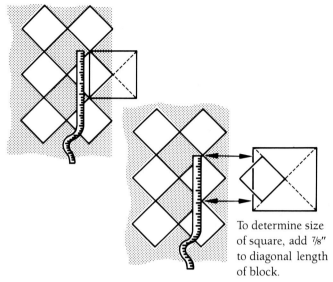

Cut here.

Diagram 3

Diagonal-Set Quilts

In a quilt with a diagonal set, the blocks are set on point rather than parallel to the sides of the quilt. The rows of blocks go diagonally across the quilt, creating the need for half squares, or setting triangles, at each end. The Cardinals in the Pines Quilt on page 59 is an example of a diagonal-set quilt.

Cutting the setting triangles can be tricky, unless you know the secret. Of course, two right-angle triangles can be made by cutting a square in half diagonally. However, when you are working in fabric and have cut the square on the straight grain, the hypotenuse, or longest side, of each new triangle would be a perfect bias and very stretchy. That stretchy edge would end up on the outside of the quilt, an arrangement that is difficult at best.

To make setting triangles with the hypotenuse on the straight grain, make a larger square and cut it on both diagonals, making four smaller triangles. See **Diagram 4**.

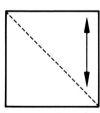

Hypotenuse is on bias.

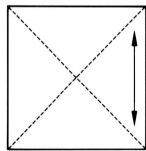

Hypotenuse is on straight of grain.

Diagram 4

To determine the size of the larger square needed, measure the diagonal of the finished block, as shown in **Diagram 5**, and add 1¼ inches. That is the size of square to quarter for a perfect, no-mistakes fit.

To determine size of square, add ⅞″ to diagonal length of block.

Diagram 5

Although the quilts in this book don't feature a "floating" set as shown in **Diagram 6**, I recommend cutting larger setting triangles that allow the design to float inside the borders. This is a good way to avoid nipping off the corners of the quilt blocks when adding the borders, which happens when the setting triangles don't fit perfectly. Add 1½ to 2½ inches to the length of the block diagonal to determine the size of square needed. The more you add, the larger the float.

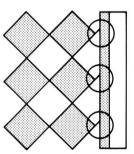

Diagram 6

Corner triangles can be cut from squares that are the same size as the block. Cut each square in half diagonally to make triangles with the legs on the straight grain. The triangles will be oversized enough to match larger floating setting triangles, and the excess can be trimmed later.

Quilting by Hand

Although I generally prefer machine quilting, and the projects in this book are machine quilted, hand quilting is always an option. Many quiltmakers enjoy the relaxed pace of handwork and don't mind the extra time involved.

The quilting stitch is simply a running stitch. Make the stitches small and even, paying as much attention to consistency as to size. Quilting needles, called "betweens," come in sizes 8 to 12, with 12 being the smallest. The smaller the needle, the smaller the stitch you'll be able to make.

Layer the backing, batting, and quilt top, keeping the layers smooth. Thread baste in lines about 3 inches apart, starting from the center of the quilt and working outward. When the quilt is basted, use a hoop or frame to keep the layers smooth and taut during quilting.

To start quilting, thread a needle with a length of quilting thread about 18 inches long, and knot one end. Insert the needle through the top and batting about an inch away from where you will begin quilting. Pull the thread up through the fabric, and gently pop the knot through the fabric so that it is buried in the batting layer. See **Diagram 7**. Repeat this step when ending a line of stitching.

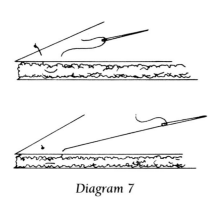

Diagram 7

Quilting by Machine

The layering and basting process for machine quilting is similar to the method used for hand quilting, except that the basting is done with safety pins rather than thread. The pins hold the layers securely, and there's no worry about quilting over basting threads that would later have to be removed.

Getting Ready to Quilt

1. Cut and piece the backing fabric to at least 2 inches larger in all directions than the quilt top. Cut the batting the same size.

2. Use a long, narrow table for the layering process. Center the backing wrong side up on the table. Layer the batting next, centered and carefully smoothed. Finally, center and layer the quilt top, right side up.

3. Using safety pins, start in the middle and work outward, pinning through all the layers. Keep the fabrics taut while pinning to avoids lumps between layers. You'll need a lot of pins; a queen-size quilt can take as many as 1,000 pins! Start with more pins than you think are necessary until you become experienced. To keep the quilt manageable when machine quilting, it is necessary to roll and fold it into a smaller package.

Folding the Quilt

1. It's generally best to start quilting in the center of the quilt. For example, if you are quilting in the ditch, your starting point is the center seam. Determine your starting point, and roll the right edge of the quilt up to within 4 or 5 inches of that point. See **Diagram 8**.

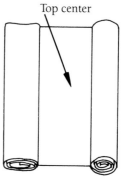

Top center

Diagram 8

2. Fold the left edge of the quilt in several 9 or 10-inch folds until it, too, is 4 or 5 inches from the starting point, as shown in the diagram.

3. Rolling your quilt like a sleeping bag seems to work best for machine quilting. Beginning at the end opposite where you will start sewing, roll up your long, thin quilt as shown in **Diagram 9**.

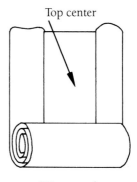

Top center

Diagram 9

At the Machine

1. Sitting at the machine, position the end of the line or seam you are quilting under the needle, and place the remainder of the rolled quilt in your lap. If you prefer not to hold the bulk of the quilt in your lap, a chair with a relatively high back, placed right beside you and with its back to the sewing machine table, makes a great support. It is still necessary to roll the quilt as described.

2. Begin quilting. To avoid having to backstitch, begin and end the lines of quilting with a few very short stitches. Use both hands to pull the fabric layers taut. Carefully hold the quilt so that its weight doesn't pull against the needle. Placing a table in front of your sewing machine will help keep the quilted section from falling down and pulling.

3. When you have finished the first line of quilting, reroll the quilt and prepare to quilt the first perpendicular line. After that, I usually continue to work outward from the center of the quilt, sewing two lines one way, one on each side of the center, then switching back to the other direction, and so on.

To maintain control of the quilt, you must reroll it for every line of quilting. As you reroll, check the quilt back for newly sewn pleats. Little puckers are often found at intersections, and my personal decision is not to take those out. Large tucks must be corrected, but anything in between is up to you.

For most machine quilting, I use invisible nylon thread in the top of the machine and match the bobbin thread to the quilt backing. Frequently the tension for nylon thread must be loosened to avoid stretching and puckering. I use eight to ten stitches per inch for machine quilting.

Continuous Stitching Technique

Machine quilting is easier and more attractive if it can be done with a continuous line of stitching. The technique is also useful when finishing the edges of fused patchwork with stitching. It means you must begin stitching in a position that allows you to move through the block without starting and stopping and clipping threads.

A good way to decide on your stitching route is to lay tracing paper over the design and use a pencil to trace the path. If you use invisible thread, there are no restrictions on the route. If you are using colored

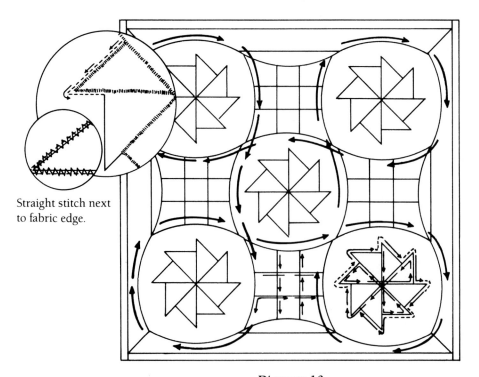

Straight stitch next to fabric edge.

Diagram 10

thread and want to stitch all of one color at a time, your route will probably have some restrictions. Once you start tracing, don't lift the pencil until you finish. If you do lift the pencil and don't put it down in the same place, the stitching is not continuous. That is a place in the block where you will have to stop and start again. If you begin and end your stitching with very small stitches, you can clip the threads close to the fabric and they will probably not pull out.

In some cases, the best route may take you over the same sections more than once. If you are using a straight stitch, try to keep the second line of stitching very close to the first. The example shown in **Diagram 10**, which is from the Christmas Pinwheels Doll Bed Quilt on page 166, shows a different situation. There, a zigzag stitch is being used both to finish the edges of the fused patchwork and to quilt the piece. For the section that must be stitched twice, switch the machine from a zigzag to a straight stitch for the length of the duplication.

Sometimes continuous stitching isn't possible to do efficiently. In the "Sew or No-Sew Miniatures" chapter on page 151, there is a discussion about looking for the less obvious way to approach something. That principle also applies here. The Circle of Hearts pattern from that chapter is a good example. Instead of stitching around each heart, a less obvious but more efficient method is to stitch around the outside of the design and then around the inside, as shown in **Diagram 11**.

Diagram 11

Free-Motion Machine Quilting

Free-motion machine quilting is, in many ways, a cross between machine embroidery and quilting. The quilting is usually done with a darning foot attachment and with the feed dogs either down or covered, depending on your machine. The real advantage is that you can quilt in any direction. That is, it is not necessary to turn an entire quilt around and continue quilting forward, as you must do when the feed dogs control the movement of the fabric.

The machine provides the power for the needle going up and down, but you determine the speed of the needle and the direction, and you provide the power that moves the fabric. A stitch is made wherever the fabric is when the needle goes down. It is the combination of the speed of the needle and the direction and speed with which you are moving the fabric that determines the size of the stitch and the consistency of size. It may sound complicated, but it really isn't. Just layer some pieces of fabric with batting, and give it a try. Work with pieces at least 10 inches square. I hold the fabric edges and pull to keep the fabric fairly taut, almost as if it were in a hoop.

The hardest thing for most people to do is stitch fast enough. The natural tendency is to think that if you stitch very slowly, you can control the stitch better, but the reality is that you can't move the fabric slowly enough to accomplish that. In the beginning, just practice moving the fabric any direction and see how the stitches develop.

The quilt is layered and pin basted in the same manner as for straight-line machine quilting. As with straight-line quilting, I often use invisible nylon thread in the top of the machine and thread to match the backing in the bobbin. Some of the projects in this book use special threads with free-motion quilting. For example, look at the Elegant Trapunto Stocking on page 240; there, gold metallic thread adds a special touch. No matter what thread is used on the top, however, it's best to have the bobbin thread match the backing fabric.

Machine Stipple Quilting

Close, meandering lines of quilting that fill a background area are called stipple quilting. Stipple quilting can be done by hand, of course, but it is extremely time-consuming. Stipple quilting can be done quickly and easily by machine using free-motion quilting techniques. The quilting lines are not marked; rather, the pattern is created by eye. It is almost like "doodling" on the machine! As you stitch, try to keep the lines from crossing each other. For an example of machine stipple quilting, see My Ladies' Vest on page 87.

Adding a French-Fold Binding

There are several methods for binding a quilt, but my favorite style is the French-fold, a double-thick binding. While there is no standard width, probably the most common finished binding width for a full-size quilt is ½ inch. Smaller quilts often have smaller bindings, but the deciding factor is what looks right to you. The desired finished size determines the width that the binding will be cut.

In general, cut the binding strips four times as wide as the desired finished width *plus* ½ inch for seam allowances *plus* ⅛ to ¼ inch of ease to go around the thickness of the quilt. The fatter the batt is, the more it is necessary to allow this ease.

1. Measure the quilt to determine the length of binding strips needed. Measure, cut, and sew the side bindings first. My preference is to cut binding strips on the lengthwise grain of the fabric. Cutting on the bias is only necessary if the binding is going around curved edges or for decorative purposes.

2. Fold the binding strips in half lengthwise, with wrong sides together and raw edges even. Press.

3. Prepare the quilt by hand or machine basting ¼ inch from the raw edge of the quilt top. Please don't trim the excess batting or backing now; wait until the bindings are stitched onto the front of the quilt.

4. Place a binding strip along one side of the quilt top with the raw edges of the binding even with the edge of the quilt top. Machine stitch with a ¼-inch seam. Allow the batting and backing to extend beyond the quilt top almost twice as wide as the finished width of the binding, as shown in **Diagram 12**. Trim the excess, but trim as little as possible so that the binding will be nice and full.

5. Fold the binding to the back of the quilt so that the batting and backing are folded double to make a nice full binding. Slip stitch the binding down with a hidden hand stitch, using the row of machine stitching as a guide. In the blind hem stitch I use, the needle comes out of the quilt, takes a bite of the binding and reenters the quilt directly behind the

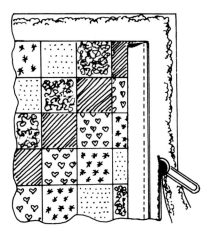

Diagram 12

bite. The thread is carried in the layers of the quilt, not on the outside. Add the binding strip for the opposite side of the quilt in the same manner.

6. Measure the quilt ends for binding strips, and add ½ inch to each binding end. Turn under the ends of the strips before sewing to eliminate the raw edges. At the corners, carefully trim the batting and seam allowances to make the binding thickness uniform. Stitch the ends shut. See **Diagram 13**.

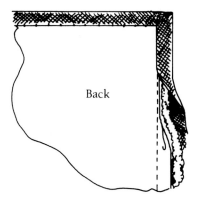

Back

Diagram 13

ALL SNUG IN THEIR BEDS

If there is anything that a quilter's house should have for Christmas, it is a Christmas quilt for every bed. Over the years, I had casually talked about Christmas quilts, but I had not really been committed until I started this book. Now, of course, I'm feeling compulsive about it.

Since I began to think seriously about having quilts just for Christmas, I have been driven. How can I get a Christmas quilt for every bed this year? If you don't have any Christmas quilts now, it may sound like a lot to take on before next Christmas. But once you realize there are several ways of looking at Christmas quilts, you'll see that it is possible to have one on every bed.

First, obviously enough, Christmas quilts are those done in the colors we normally associate with the season—the warm reds and bright greens, and the burgundies and deep spruce and forest greens. In a similar vein, obvious Christmas quilts are the ones that have some design element—for example, a wreath or a tree—that ties in with the symbols we associate with the holiday. The quilts in this chapter include several in definite Christmas colors and patterns and others that would be appropriate at Christmas or year-round.

Quilts that are so special you bring them out only at the holidays can also be considered Christmas quilts. For example, my husband and I collect antique quilts. Since many of them could be called Christmas quilts (due to their colors and designs), I already have a head start on my goal of a Christmas quilt for every bed. We could use antique quilts for starters and gradually replace them as new ones are finished, perhaps one a year, until everyone in my family has a new Christmas quilt. Or maybe we will use antique quilts at our house and new ones at the kids' houses. Some antique-quilt collectors believe that an antique quilt has to be slept under to be personalized by its current caretaker. If you own antique quilts, Christmas is a nice reason to sleep under them without having to worry about the wear and tear that would come from using them year-round. The same is true for a treasured family quilt or a special quilt you spent months stitching; bringing such a quilt out for the holidays each year could become a new tradition. And there's no rule that says that a quilt you reserve for the holidays has to look Christmassy!

A third way to approach this idea of Christmas quilts is to focus on the gift-giving aspect. A Christmas quilt can be any quilt you give to someone on Christmas!

If you are as taken with the idea of covering everyone's bed with a quilt for Christmas as I am, this is the point where you need to pause and take a deep breath. It really isn't necessary to be compulsive about getting a quilt made for everyone *this* year. It's fine just to get started. Maybe this Christmas only the oldest generation gets a quilt, or better yet, the youngest member of the family, and every year thereafter someone else gets one. What about drawing names? That could become part of the tradition. You might choose the lucky recipient this year and, on next Christmas Day, have that person draw the name of the one who gets a quilt the following year.

I hope that these ideas have inspired you and you're ready to start sewing your own Christmas quilts. This chapter contains a number of different projects, most of which include some sort of time-saving approach. For those quilters who like to savor the process, I've also included several quilts based on traditional piecing and appliqué.

◀ *Shown in the photo is the Cardinals in the Pines Quilt (page 59).*

USER-FRIENDLY QUILTS

User-friendly is a descriptive term that is often used in connection with computer technology and electronic gadgets but that I believe can be applied equally to fabrics. The concept for fabrics is not new, just the name. Over the years, fabric designers have been inspired to print fabrics that look like quilts, thereby eliminating the need to piece or appliqué. It was most likely the proficient piecers who turned up their noses and nicknamed the fabrics "cheater quilts."

Personally, I've always found that "C" word offensive. I believe it should be added to the list of politically incorrect expressions and replaced with the phrase "user-friendly fabrics." There are plenty of times when you want a great effect without a great effort. That might be the case with Christmas quilts, and if so, user-friendly fabrics are a great solution. The User-Friendly Carolina Lily Quilt on page 15 is a good example: It's made from a beautiful printed fabric that results in a traditional-looking quilt with less time and effort than traditional methods would require.

Great Ideas

Printed Christmas squares, such as the deer print used in the Double Irish Chain wallhanging and pil-low shown in the photo on page 46, are readily available every year and are a great way to create beautiful Christmas quilts. Most of the printed squares are approximately the size of a quilt block. If you don't want to figure out a quilt layout for yourself, just substitute a printed block of the correct size into another layout.

There are so many wonderful Christmas fabrics every year, the hardest part is selecting just one. In fact, I know someone who collected the panels and then, with every block a different pattern, put them together like a sampler quilt.

Another possibility for Christmas quilts is to use the 36 × 60-inch fabric door panels that have become available in recent years. Some are very suitable as the center for a twin-size quilt. Any arrangement of borders that equals 15 inches in width would turn this into a quilt top ready for tying or quilting. The Christmas Tree Quilt on page 22 has three borders added to the door panel fabric. The finished quilt is 66 × 90 inches, perfect for a twin bed. It was machine quilted using both the meandering and straight stitch techniques with assorted metallic and rayon threads. The quilting took an experienced machine quilter five hours.

USER-FRIENDLY CAROLINA LILY QUILT

The tricky part of showing projects based on specific user-friendly fabrics is that the availability of a specific printed design may change, and what you decide to make is dependent upon being able to get that same design. Here, I've shown a diagonal-set, red and green Carolina Lily on a tan background that's designed to resemble tea-dyed fabric. The quilt in the photo was made using continuous-print fabric. But the directions for the quilt are written two ways: the user-friendly way, using preprinted fabric; and the traditional way, in case you can't find the fabric but love the quilt.

Make sure block is complete before trimming fabric.

Make sure block is complete before trimming fabric.

Diagram 1

Approximate Size

82 × 98 inches

Materials Required

- 5 yards of continuous-print fabric* for quilt top
- 5½ yards of coordinating fabric for backing
- Queen-size batting

The Carolina Lily pattern is available from Fabric Traditions. See "Resources" on page 256 for details.

Making the Quilt

1. Divide the fabric in half crosswise into two 2½-yard pieces. Pay attention to the block design at each cut end; the design should be complete on every other vertical row. The rows in between will have only partial blocks visible. If necessary, trim the ends.

2. Cut the printed border off the right side of one of the pieces and off the left side of the other piece. These will become the top and bottom borders.

3. Sew the two pieces together at the center seam, carefully aligning the design blocks. See **Diagram 1**.

4. Sew the trimmed borders to the top and bottom edges of the quilt.

5. Cut the backing fabric in half crosswise into two 2¾-yard pieces. Trim the selvages, and sew the pieces together along the long edge. Layer the backing, batting, and quilt top, and baste. Quilt as desired. See page 1 for detailed directions on quilting.

6. To bind the edges, bring the backing fabric around to the front, fold the raw edges under ¼ inch, and stitch them in place. As an alternative, you could add a separate French-fold binding as described on page 10.

TRADITIONAL CAROLINA LILY QUILT

To duplicate exactly the User-Friendly Carolina Lily Quilt on page 15 would require 40 pieced Carolina Lily blocks and a very intricate border. Instead, the directions below will result in a quilt using only 20 Carolina Lily blocks and a simple border, as shown in the **Quilt Diagram**.

Quilt Diagram

Approximate Size

74 × 91 inches

Materials Required

- 3 yards of fabric for background of lily blocks, alternate blocks, side setting triangles, and corner setting triangles
- 2¼ yards of fabric for border and binding
- 1½ yards of fabric for sashing
- ¾ yard of dark green print fabric for lily blocks
- ⅜ yard of dark red print fabric for lily blocks
- ¼ yard of light green fabric for lily blocks
- ¼ yard of light red plaid fabric for lily blocks
- ¼ yard of contrasting fabric for corner squares in sashing
- 5¾ yards of fabric for backing
- Batting, larger than 74 × 91 inches

Block Diagram

Making the Blocks

1. Make a template for the diamond using pattern piece A on page 21. Using a large needle, make a small hole in the template at each of the four dots. Mark four diamonds on dark red print fabric, two on red plaid fabric, and two on dark green print fabric. Use a pencil to mark the dots on the pattern pieces through the holes in the template. (These dots will serve as guides for the starting and stopping lines of stitching.)

2. Cut out the eight diamonds. Arrange the diamonds into an eight-pointed star as shown in the **Block Diagram**, paying attention to the color placement. Join the diamonds into pairs, then the pairs into halves, and then the two halves into the star. For this step and those that follow, start and stop stitching seams at the marked dots; do not stitch through the seam allowances. Stitching dot-to-dot in this manner helps to create perfect angled seams. When sewing the halves together, stitch from the center out in each direction, rather than straight across. Press all the seam allowances in one direction.

3. Using the patterns on page 21, cut four B squares and four C triangles from background fabric. Add the B squares to the unfilled outer edges of the star, as shown in **Diagram 1**. Place a square right sides together with one side of a diamond edge. Match

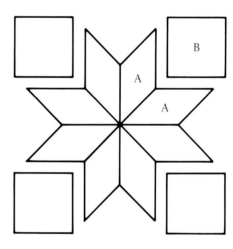

Diagram 1

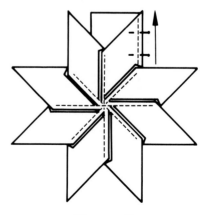

Diagram 2

corners and pin, as shown in **Diagram 2**. Stitching dot-to-dot, sew the seam from the inner corner to the outside edge. Press this seam away from the diamond.

4. Reposition the pieces so that the adjacent side of the square and the other diamond edge line up, right sides together. In the same manner, sew the second seam from the inside corner to the outside edge, starting a stitch or two away from the inside corner. See **Diagram 3**. (Although this leaves a very small hole in the corner between the diamonds and the square, the hole is not visible when the seams are pressed, and it allows the seams to lie much more smoothly.) Press this seam away from the diamond.

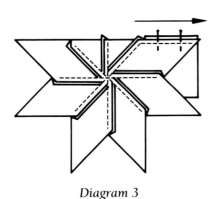

Diagram 3

5. Using the same technique as for the squares, set the triangles into the remaining openings, as shown in **Diagram 4**. Complete three of these lily sections for each lily block.

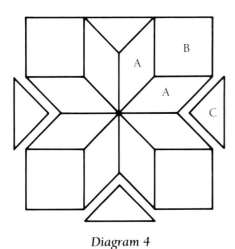

Diagram 4

6. Cut a 5¾-inch square from background fabric. Referring to the **Block Diagram**, join the square with the three completed lily sections to make one block.

The completed block should measure approximately 11 inches square, including seam allowances.

7. Cut 1-inch bias strips for stems. Turn the edges under ¼ inch before applying. For the leaves, cut a light green leaf using the small leaf pattern and a dark green print leaf using the large leaf pattern, both on page 21. Referring to the **Block Diagram** for correct placement, use your favorite appliqué technique to add the stem and the leaves to the block. See page 70 for details on appliqué. Complete a total of 20 blocks in this manner.

Adding the Sashing

1. Cut twelve 11-inch squares for the alternate blocks.

2. The sashing strips, which include corner squares, are 1¼ inches wide finished. In the user-friendly quilt, they match the background fabric. In this quilt, they would probably be more attractive done in a contrasting fabric. Use one fabric for the sashing strips and a different contrasting fabric for the corner squares. To make the sashing with corner squares, cut a 1¾-inch-wide strip across the width of the corner square fabric. Cut a 12-inch-wide strip across the width of the sashing fabric. Sew the strips together along the long side. Make two of these strip sets. Cut 1¾-inch-wide strips across the strip set, as shown in **Diagram 5**, for a total of 44 sashing strips with corner squares. Cut thirty-six 1¾ × 12-inch sashing strips without corner squares at the end.

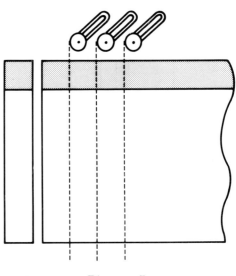

Diagram 5

3. For the side setting triangles, cut four 20-inch squares of background fabric, and cut each square diagonally in both directions. You will use 14 of the 16 triangles. For the corner setting triangles, cut two 10-inch squares from background fabric, and cut each square in half diagonally.

4. Sew one sashing strip without a corner square to the upper left side of each lily block and alternate block, as shown in **Diagram 6**. Sew one sashing strip without a corner square to the right side of four of the side setting triangles, as shown in **Diagram 7**. Refer also to the **Quilt Assembly Diagram** for guidance while adding the sashing.

5. Referring to **Diagram 8**, sew a sashing strip with a corner square to the lower left side of each lily block and alternate block. For one lily block, which appears in the upper right corner of the **Quilt Assembly Diagram**, you will also need to sew a sashing strip with a corner square to the upper right side.

6. Sew a sashing strip with a corner square to four of the seven side setting triangles that already have sashing as shown in **Diagram 9**.

7. The three side setting triangles and the right-side corner setting triangle at the bottom of the quilt have sashing on the left side, with a corner square at the bottom instead of the top. The three side setting triangles at the top of the quilt have sashing on the

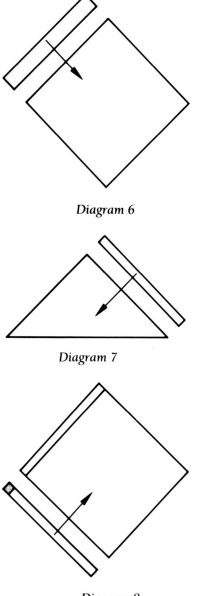

Diagram 6

Diagram 7

Diagram 8

Quilt Assembly Diagram

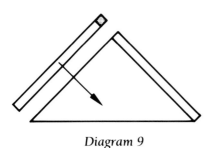

Diagram 9

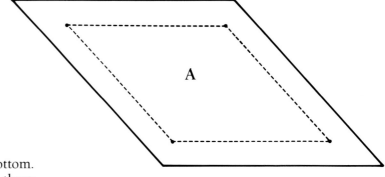

A

right side, with the corner square at the bottom. Referring to the **Quilt Assembly Diagram**, add these last four sashing strips.

Assembling the Quilt

1. Lay out the blocks and setting triangles in diagonal rows as shown in the **Quilt Assembly Diagram**. Sew the blocks together, pressing the seams in opposite directions from row to row.

2. Sew the rows together, carefully matching seams. Press the seam allowances in one direction.

3. The border shown in the **Quilt Diagram** is 3 inches wide finished. Measure the length of the quilt top, and cut two 3½-inch-wide strips of border fabric to the correct length. Use a long ruler to mark straight edges along the outside of the quilt. Sew the strips to the sides of the quilt top, then trim off any excess fabric along the edge. Press the seam allowances toward the border.

4. Measure the width of the quilt top, including the borders, and cut two 3½-inch-wide strips for the top and bottom of the quilt. Add the borders to the quilt, trim any excess fabric, and press the seam allowances toward the border.

5. Layer the quilt top with batting and backing, baste, and quilt as desired. Add a French-fold binding. See page 10 for complete directions.

B

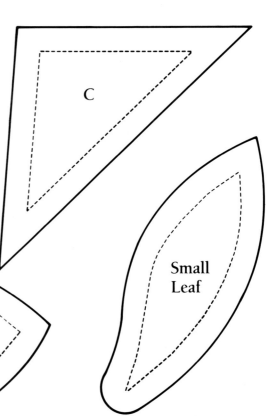

C

Small Leaf

Large Leaf

CHRISTMAS TREE QUILT

Approximate Size

66 × 90 inches

Materials Required

- 1¾ yards of red print fabric for border
- 36 × 60-inch fabric door panel for interior of quilt top
- 1⅛ yards of red striped fabric for border and binding
- 1⅛ yards of green print fabric for border and corner squares
- 5 yards of fabric for backing
- Twin-size batting

Adding the First Two Borders

The red border is part of the door panel. The first added border is a red striped border with mitered corners.

1. To determine the correct length to cut border strips for mitering, add the length of the quilt top plus twice the finished width of the border plus ½ inch. The striped border is 3 inches finished, so the border strips are cut 3½ × 42½ inches and 3½ × 66½ inches.

2. Place the border strips right sides together with the quilt top. Match the middle of the strips to the middle of the quilt edge so there are equal amounts left on both ends to make the miter. Stitch, stopping ¼ inch from the end of the quilt. Press the seam allowances toward the quilt top.

3. To make the miter, work from the top of the quilt on an ironing board or other flat surface. Extend one border strip flat. Fold the adjacent border strip to make a 45 degree angle, lay it on top of the flat border strip, and match the stripes. See **Diagram 1**. Pin the strips together.

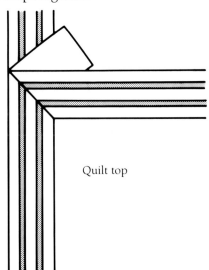

Quilt top

Diagram 1

4. Carefully stitch along the fold by hand with a hidden stitch. Trim the excess strips on the back side.

5. To add the green print border, measure the length of the quilt top. Cut two 5-inch-wide strips to the required length. Add the strips to the sides of the quilt top, and press. Measure the width of the quilt top, including the borders, and cut two 5-inch-wide strips to the required length. Add the strips to the top and bottom of the quilt top.

Adding Borders with Corner Squares

Corner squares, sometimes called cornerstones, add interest to a border. Here, the red print border has corner squares cut from the green print fabric.

Before adding the border strips to the quilt, make sure that the corners are all 90 degree angles. Measure the sides and ends of the finished quilt top, and make sure that opposite sides match in length. When cutting the strips, add 2 inches to the measured length.

1. Measure the length of the quilt top, and cut two 8-inch-wide border strips to the required length. Measure the width of the quilt top, and cut two 8-inch-wide border strips to that length.

2. The corner squares are cut the same width as the border. Cut four 8-inch squares from green print fabric.

3. With right sides together, sew one corner square to one end of each border strip. Press the seam allowance toward the square.

4. Add the first border strip to one side of the quilt. With right sides together, match the seam line of the square with the sewing line at the top end of the quilt. See **Diagram 2**. Begin sewing approximately 5 inches from the top end of the quilt. Open the border, and press the seam allowance toward the border.

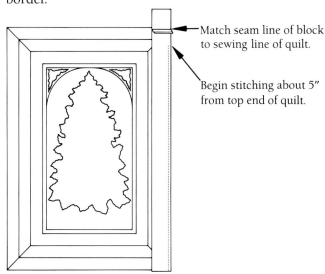

Match seam line of block to sewing line of quilt.

Begin stitching about 5″ from top end of quilt.

Diagram 2

When sewing border strips to the quilt top, excess length of strips may be trimmed after stitching. If you have less than 1 inch of excess length to trim, check the tension or the pressure of the presser foot on your sewing machine. If too much fabric is eased in as the border strips are added, the borders will tend to ruffle.

5. When adding borders with corner squares, work in a clockwise fashion. Add the border strip to the bottom end of the quilt next, matching the seam lines of the corner square and the first border strip, as shown in **Diagram 3**. Open the border, and press the seam allowance toward the border. Continue around the quilt. As subsequent borders are added, it is easy to perfectly match the seam lines. On the second, third, and fourth border strips, the entire seam is sewn.

6. When adding the final border strip to the top end of the quilt, fold the loose end of the first border strip out of the way. After sewing the final border strip to the quilt top, fold the first border strip right sides together with the quilt top. Match the seam lines of the final strip and the corner square of the first strip, and finish sewing the end of the first strip.

Finishing the Quilt

1. Layer the quilt with batting and backing fabric, and baste. Quilt as desired. If you plan to machine quilt, see the detailed directions on page 7 for help on folding the quilt.

2. The edges are finished with a separate ⅜-inch French-fold binding made from the red striped fabric. See "Adding a French-Fold Binding" on page 10.

Diagram 3

STRIP TECHNIQUE QUILTS

If you're the kind of quilter who loves the satisfaction of piecing bits of fabric together but still wants to minimize the amount of time invested in a project, look to quilts made with strip techniques. Sunshine and Shadows and my favorite variation of it, Trip around the World, are great quilts that lend themselves to strip piecing, so I've used them here to demonstrate the techniques. Timesaving shortcuts are perfectly suited to quilts you want to finish in time to meet an important deadline—like Christmas!

Introduction to Strip Piecing Techniques

These strip techniques can be applied to many quilts—lots more than you probably realize. Going through the learning process is definitely worth the effort. Not only can you make more quilts in the same amount of time, but you can make them more easily and more accurately.

The number one reason for learning strip techniques is to reduce the amount of cutting and handling of individual little pieces. You may never cut and handle an individual square again! You certainly won't need to for the quilts in this section. Strip techniques are easiest to understand in quilts in which most of the pieces are strips or squares and in which the same combination of fabrics appears repeatedly. A Sunshine and Shadows quilt offers a perfect opportunity to sample the method because all of the pieces are squares of the same size and the fabrics always appear in the same order.

Another advantage of strip techniques is that your work is basically pattern free. Look at either **Diagram 1** on page 26 or **Diagram 2** on page 27 and you will see a grid pattern just like graph paper. **Diagram 1** shows a five-fabric Sunshine and Shadows layout, and **Diagram 2** shows the same layout with eight fabrics used. It's easy to see from these diagrams that the same Sunshine and Shadows quilt can be made any size simply by changing the size of the squares. For example, to make a full-size quilt, every square would equal 4¼ inches finished. The wonderful Homespun Sunshine and Shadows Throw on page 29 was made using an eight-fabric rotation and 3-inch squares. Use a 2-inch finished square to make a wonderful crib quilt. Or see page 32 for a small wallhanging interpreted in a typical Amish color palette. In it, each square finishes to 1¼ inches, further emphasizing the validity of the grid system.

You can make these quilts with any number of fabrics, but the technique is most efficient when the number of squares in one direction or the other divides equally by the number of fabrics selected. With the quilts in this section, it is the number of squares in the horizontal rows that is divisible by the number of fabrics.

My favorite descriptive name for this particular strip technique is Sew-Before-You-Cut. You are, in fact, going to cut long strips of fabric as wide as one of the squares, sew those strips together in the proper order, and then make a second cut across those sewn strips, as shown in **Diagram 3** on page 27. With the second cut, you really do cut squares, but they are already sewn together! Truly, it is easier to do than to read about.

In case you have not used a rotary cutter before, this is a perfect opportunity to learn. While you can use scissors, the rotary cutter system increases the efficiency of strip techniques. Please review "Rotary Cutter Systems" on page 5 before beginning.

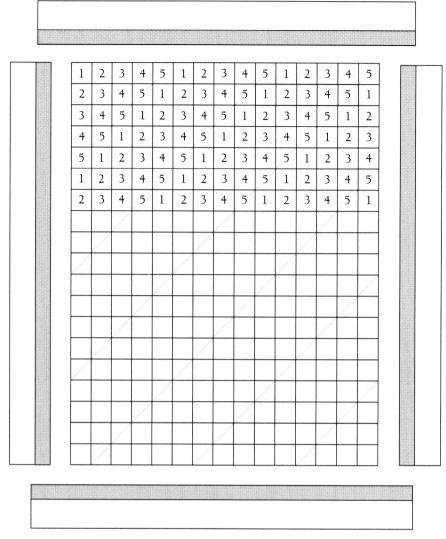

1	2	3	4	5	1	2	3	4	5	1	2	3	4	5
2	3	4	5	1	2	3	4	5	1	2	3	4	5	1
3	4	5	1	2	3	4	5	1	2	3	4	5	1	2
4	5	1	2	3	4	5	1	2	3	4	5	1	2	3
5	1	2	3	4	5	1	2	3	4	5	1	2	3	4
1	2	3	4	5	1	2	3	4	5	1	2	3	4	5
2	3	4	5	1	2	3	4	5	1	2	3	4	5	1

Diagram 1

Cylinder Method of Assembly

In addition to strip piecing techniques, this section introduces a special procedure for keeping those squares in order when assembling the quilt top. I call it the Cylinder Method.

In looking at **Diagram 2** on the opposite page, you can easily see that Row 1 is made up of two strip sets, each with Fabrics 1 through 8, joined together. To create Row 2, you could sew together two more sets, then take the first piece off one end and sew it to the other end. Then, for each row, you would need to

take an additional square off the end and add it to the other end. With this method, it becomes easy to make a mistake and sew the wrong block to the opposite end.

That is why I love the Cylinder Method. It involves no extra work; the work is just in reverse order. The original way, you would take a block off one end and sew it to the other. With the Cylinder Method, you actually sew the correct block to the other end first.

1. For Row 1, sew two sets together into one long strip, as shown in **Diagram 4**. Make sure all the seam allowances are pressed in the same direction. To make Row 2, sew two sets together at *both* ends to make a cylinder, or circle. Rotate the cylinder until the Fabric 2 square is in line with the Fabric 1 square

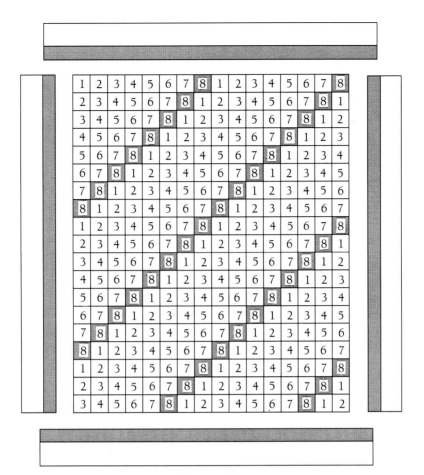

Diagram 2

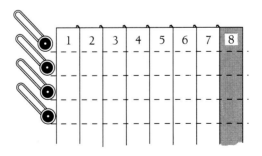

Diagram 3

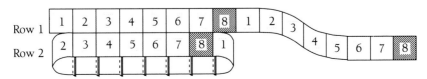

Diagram 4

in Row 1, as shown in the diagram. If necessary, flip the cylinder so that the seam allowances are facing in the opposite direction from the seam allowances in Row 1. Now, remove the short row of stitching to the left of the Fabric 2 square so that the cylinder can become a flat row again.

2. Put the new long rows right sides together. Sew the rows together, making sure that you are sewing the bottom of Row 1 to the top of Row 2. See **Diagram 5**. This seems pretty obvious, but the first time you sew the bottom of Row 2 to the top of Row 1, you'll understand how easy it is to make that mistake when you are working with only two rows.

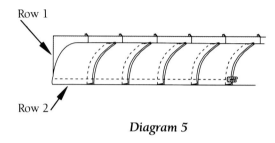

Diagram 5

3. Continue with the additional rows. It seems silly at first to sew all the sets of strips together at both ends, but it really works, and you can't mistakenly reverse a small group of blocks. Oh yes, every row that starts with Fabric 1 will be in the correct position automatically; no cylinder is necessary.

Fast Finishing

Once the quilt top is stitched together, you're ready to layer it with batting and backing. To keep time to a minimum, you can either machine quilt in the ditch or tie the quilt like a comforter. If you are going to tie, you will probably want to use a higher-loft batting than you would if you were to machine quilt. Please review the information in "Batting Selection" on page 3.

Use a 5- to 7-inch sharp-pointed dollmaker needle with a large eye, and use baby-weight yarn that is no heavier, and preferably lighter, than typical afghan yarn.

1. Thread the needle with the yarn. It's hard to say how long a piece of yarn to use. The best answer is to experiment with the specific yarn and batting combination you are using, but at least 2 yards of yarn should work.

2. Stitch continuously from square to square without cutting the yarn. Beginning on the top side of a corner square, take a ¼-inch stitch down and back up through the center of the square, leaving a 6-inch tail of yarn. Move to an adjacent square, and take another ¼-inch stitch. Do not cut the yarn yet or pull it tight, but leave comfortable ease between the squares. Continue to stitch from square to square, as shown in **Diagram 6**, until all squares are completed. Try to make all the stitches in the same direction; the finished ties will look more attractive if you do.

Diagram 6

3. Cut the yarn between each square, leaving yarn tails for tying.

4. Take a yarn end in each hand, pull the yarn taut, and give it a little back and forth motion to confirm that there are no knots or loops on the back side of the quilt. Tie the yarn tails in a square knot (left over right, right over left) in each square, pulling firmly but not too tightly.

5. Go back and clip the yarn tails to an even and consistent length.

HOMESPUN SUNSHINE AND SHADOWS THROW

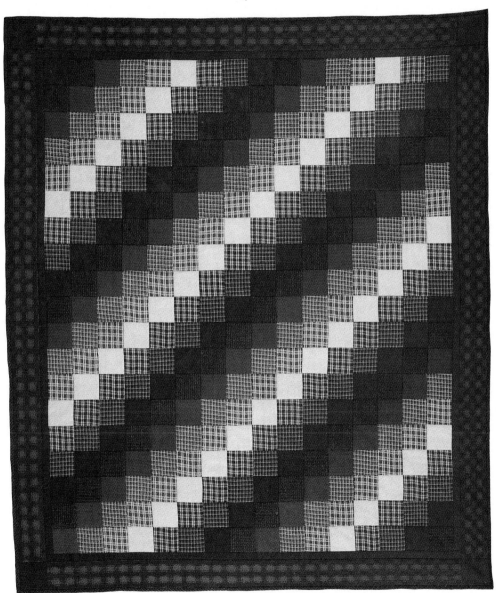

Eight homespun fabrics were selected for the interior of this quilt, and an additional homespun was used in the outside border. The combination of burgundy, hunter green, and tea-dyed muslin is very rich and comfortable and could easily be used year-round. Use **Diagram 2** on page 27 as the guide for the interior of this quilt. The borders are relatively smaller than those represented in the diagram. This quilt contains Thermore batting, a very lightweight polyester batting with a soft drape that's perfect for a throw.

Approximate Size

57 × 66 inches

Materials Required

- 1¾ yards of fabric for wide border
- ½ yard *each* of 8 fabrics for interior of quilt top
- ⅜ yard of fabric for narrow border and corner squares
- 3½ yards of fabric for backing
- ½ yard of fabric for binding
- Twin-size Thermore batting

Cutting the Fabrics

1. Decide on the order of fabrics, and number them from 1 to 8. It is a good idea to make a chart with a scrap of each fabric and its assigned number to keep at the sewing machine.

2. Neatly stack the eight fabrics. A rotary cutter should be able to cut all eight layers at one time. Cut 3½-inch-wide strips on the lengthwise grain—that is, along the 18-inch edge. You should be able to get 12 strips from each piece of fabric, each one 3½ inches wide and 18 inches long. The lengthwise fibers are firmer, and cutting on the lengthwise grain makes every subsequent step more accurate. You may have noticed that the homespun fabrics were not straightened before cutting. This was a conscious decision. The homespun fabrics were chosen because of their association with antique quilts, and since very often the homespun in antique quilts is crooked, it was decided not to straighten these fabrics.

Sewing Strip Sets and Making the Second Cut

1. Keeping the strips in numerical order, sew them into sets of eight as shown in **Diagram 3** on page 27. You will have a total of 12 sets. Because I use the Cylinder Method, I make all the sets identical. There are other ways of organizing, such as sewing the strips into sets in which each set starts with a different fabric. I prefer the Cylinder Method because I believe that it is less restrictive and more adaptable to other projects and that errors are less likely to

> ### SELECTING FABRICS FOR CHRISTMAS QUILTS
>
> *The quilts in this section provide some interesting examples of fabric selection. If you are making a Christmas quilt, your fabric choices will be influenced by your idea of Christmas decorating. The eight fabrics in the Holiday Trip around the World Quilt on page 35 are the most typical Christmas colors. They are also a good example of contrasts: The combinations of light and dark colors, large- and small-scale prints, and dense and open designs really make this quilt interesting. In the Homespun Sunshine and Shadows Throw on page 29, the burgundy and hunter green homespun fabrics are certainly appropriate for Christmas but would also be suitable year-round in many family-room decorating schemes. The throw is also an example of picking four shades each of two complementary colors and repeating them in a light-to-dark order.*
>
> *The five fabrics in the Miniature Sunshine and Shadows Wallhanging on page 32 were selected because they came from the same general palette and looked good together. Most people would be hard-pressed to call this wallhanging a Christmas quilt, but if you look at some of the more contemporary wrapping papers, these colors are frequently used.*
>
>

occur in the placement of the fabrics. This is especially important if you do not finish all of the piecing in one sitting.

Be aware that selecting a fabric with a definite directional pattern requires more thought during the construction process. If you've cut your strips on the lengthwise grain, then all you have to do is make sure that when you sew the strips together, the one-way design is going in the correct direction in relationship to the rotation.

2. Press all the seams in one direction on six of the strip sets and in the other direction on the other six.

3. The eight-fabric strip sets are now 24½ inches wide and 18 inches long. Cut each strip set into 3½-inch strips, cutting across the 24½-inch width. When this second cut is completed, you have actually cut squares, but they are already sewn together!

4. Referring to **Diagram 2** on page 27 and using the Cylinder Method described on page 26, sew the rows together to complete the interior of the quilt top. The throw shown was made up of 19 rows; you may have more strips than you need to make a throw that size. The choice is yours: You can add more rows to this throw, or devise a multiple border treatment and make a second, smaller throw.

Cutting the Borders

In my experience, deciding on the number of borders, their width, and the fabrics used to make them is something best done after a quilt interior is completed. Only then will you have a true sense of the effect created by the colors and pattern and know what contribution the borders should make to the overall effect. I believe the borders should not be predetermined for a quilt. That philosophy, however, doesn't fit with what most people who read how-to books expect, so we authors routinely include measurements for the quilts as shown.

But this Homespun Sunshine and Shadows Throw is a perfect example of why I don't want you to feel bound by the border measurements as given. For this quilt, the first border is cut 1½ inches wide and finishes to 1 inch. The second border, however, was specifically cut 3⅞ inches wide to take advantage of the burgundy stripes; I wanted the wide stripes to fall

---

> ## MANAGING
> ## THE STRIP SETS
>
> *The 24½-inch strip set is a little wider than some rotary cutter mats. If that becomes a problem and you find it difficult to make the second cut, just fold the strip set in half carefully so that all the seams are parallel to each other.*
>
>

evenly on both sides of the border. For another fabric, it would be so much easier and would make much more sense to cut the strips 4 inches wide. The point is, do what works best for the fabrics you are using.

Corner squares, sometimes called cornerstones, were used here to add interest to the border. They also solve a problem of directional borders with an uneven plaid that wouldn't look nice mitered. Cut the corner squares the same width as the border strips. For complete directions, see "Adding Borders with Corner Squares" on page 23.

Finishing the Quilt

The throw was layered with lightweight polyester batting and the backing fabric and machine quilted in the ditch with smoky invisible thread on the top and cotton-covered polyester to match the back in the bobbin. The French-fold binding was cut on the bias purely for decorative purposes. See page 10 for complete directions on making and adding a French-fold binding.

MINIATURE SUNSHINE AND SHADOWS WALLHANGING

This beautiful miniature quilt was made using the five-fabric rotation shown in **Diagram 1** on page 26. Here, each square is 1¼ inches finished. The colors were selected from a typical Amish color palette. In planning this book, I felt it was important to show that many of the designs could be interpreted in non-Christmas colors for year-round use. Then my daughter said of this quilt, "But I used those colors to decorate for the holidays last year." Maybe it would be better to say Christmas isn't just red and green anymore!

Approximate Size

25 × 30 inches

Materials Required

- 1 yard of fabric for wide border, binding, and backing
- 12 × 18-inch piece *each* of 5 fabrics for interior of quilt top
- 4 × 27-inch piece *each* of 2 fabrics for narrow borders
- Crib-size batting or ¾ yard of roll batting

Making the Quilt

Before beginning, read through the general directions for Strip Technique Quilts on page 25. This quilt is constructed in exactly the same way as the Homespun Sunshine and Shadows Throw on page 29, except that five fabrics are used for the interior instead of eight.

1. Cut 1¾-inch-wide strips from the five fabrics. Cut the strips lengthwise; you should get six strips from each piece of fabric.

2. Sew the strips together into strip sets. Cut the strip sets crosswise into 1¾-inch-wide strips. You should get ten strips from each set. Being careful to keep the fabrics in the correct order, sew the strips into rows.

3. Following the directions for the Cylinder Method on page 26, sew the rows together to complete the interior of the quilt top.

4. Cut four 1-inch-wide border strips from the first narrow-border fabric. Add a border strip to each of two opposite sides of the quilt top, and press. Trim the excess fabric. Add the remaining strips to the two ends of the quilt top, press, and trim the excess. In the same manner, cut 1-inch-wide border strips from the second narrow-border fabric, and add them to the quilt top.

MARKING QUILTING DESIGNS

Practice marking quilting designs on newsprint until you are confident about marking corners and adjusting the length of the design. For a wallhanging, cut and piece the newsprint to match the size of your quilt, then practice on that real-life replica to see where the cables might need adjusting.

5. Measure the length of the quilt top. Cut two 3-inch-wide outer border strips to the needed length, and add them to the quilt top. Measure the width of the quilt top. Cut two 3-inch-wide strips, and add them to the two ends of the quilt top.

6. Layer the quilt top with batting and backing, and baste. The quilt shown was machine quilted with a cable design in the wide border. The cable is a very nice continuous line design; the pattern is provided on page 34. Using an art knife on template plastic or cardboard, cut the design exactly as shown. Don't forget, the "bridges" are necessary to hold the holes together.

Test your marking tool to make sure that the mark is easily removable from the border fabric. At each corner and working in the same direction around the quilt, mark the corner using the entire template. Reverse direction, and overlapping to get the correct repeat, mark the cable the other direction from each corner. As you get toward the middle of each side, do a little calculating to see if it will be necessary to stretch or squeeze any of the cables.

7. Add a French-fold binding. See page 10 for complete directions.

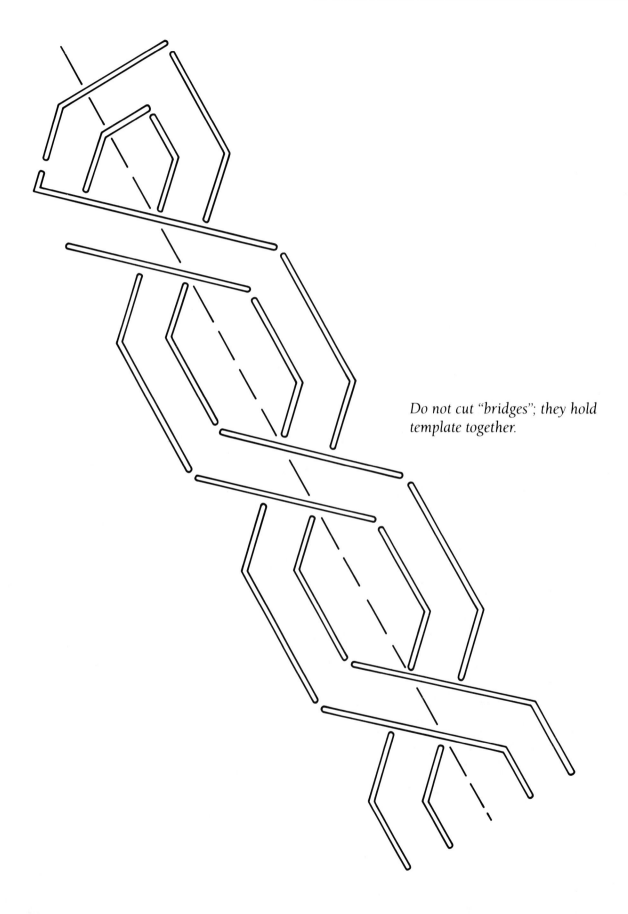

Do not cut "bridges"; they hold template together.

HOLIDAY TRIP AROUND THE WORLD QUILT

All of the prints selected for this quilt were designed especially for holiday use. The sparkle of the light background fabrics helped to balance the strong red and green prints. The black background print, however, was probably the most important in making these fabrics work together. To me, the introduction of black as a background color in traditional Christmas prints is long overdue and most welcome. Please read through the general directions for Strip Technique Quilts on page 25 before beginning this quilt. It is important to understand how the Cylinder Method works.

Approximate Size

83¾ × 100¾ inches

Materials Required

- 1¾ yards of fabric for wide border
- ¾ yard *each* of 8 fabrics for interior of quilt top
- ¾ yard of fabric for narrow border and large corner squares
- 6 yards of fabric for backing
- ¾ yard of fabric for binding
- Queen-size batting

Making the Trip around the World

1. Cut 4¾-inch-wide strips along the lengthwise grain from each of the eight fabrics. Sew the strips together into strip sets. Cut the strip sets crosswise into 4¾-inch-wide strips.

2. The technique for joining the rows is essentially the same as for the Sunshine and Shadows quilt on page 29, except that a different pattern is created in the fabrics. Study **Diagram 1** carefully to understand the order of the fabrics. Instead of sewing two strips together to get a long strip across the width of the quilt, the pattern for the Trip around the World is created by working in two halves. The order of the fabrics on the right half is the reverse of the order on the left half.

1	2	3	4	5	6	7	8
2	3	4	5	6	7	8	1
3	4	5	6	7	8	1	2
4	5	6	7	8	1	2	3
5	6	7	8	1	2	3	4
6	7	8	1	2	3	4	5
7	8	1	2	3	4	5	6
8	1	2	3	4	5	6	7
1	2	3	4	5	6	7	8
2	3	4	5	6	7	8	1
1	2	3	4	5	6	7	8
8	1	2	3	4	5	6	7
7	8	1	2	3	4	5	6
6	7	8	1	2	3	4	5
5	6	7	8	1	2	3	4
4	5	6	7	8	1	2	3
3	4	5	6	7	8	1	2
2	3	4	5	6	7	8	1
1	2	3	4	5	6	7	8

7	6	5	4	3	2	1
8	7	6	5	4	3	2
1	8	7	6	5	4	3
2	1	8	7	6	5	4
3	2	1	8	7	6	5
4	3	2	1	8	7	6
5	4	3	2	1	8	7
6	5	4	3	2	1	8
7	6	5	4	3	2	1
8	7	6	5	4	3	2
7	6	5	4	3	2	1
6	5	4	3	2	1	8
5	4	3	2	1	8	7
4	3	2	1	8	7	6
3	2	1	8	7	6	5
2	1	8	7	6	5	4
1	8	7	6	5	4	3
8	7	6	5	4	3	2
7	6	5	4	3	2	1

Diagram 1

Begin with the left half. Using the Cylinder Method and carefully following **Diagram 1**, sew the rows together for the left half of the quilt top.

3. The rows on the right half of the quilt top contain seven squares instead of eight. One square is removed from each row when the cylinder is opened. If you have not selected any fabrics with a one-way design, you can simply turn the strips around to get the correct sequence for the right side.

Again using the Cylinder Method and closely following the diagram, sew the rows together for the right side, and remove one square each time.

Adding the Borders

There are two borders, each with corner squares. While the borders on the quilt shown were cut 3¼ inches (2¾ inches finished) and 7¼ inches (6¾ inches finished), any combination of borders totaling approximately 10 inches would work. Cut corner squares the same width as the border strips. See "Adding Borders with Corner Squares" on page 23 for complete directions on adding the borders. For the quilt shown, the wide border was cut on the crosswise grain and pieced because of directional printing of the animals in the fabric.

Quilting

This quilt was machine quilted in the ditch as well as free-motion machine quilted around the shapes in the fabric on the outside border. The quilting was done with invisible nylon thread in the top of the machine, with a bobbin thread to match the backing fabric.

Cut and piece the backing fabric to at least 2 inches larger in all directions than the quilt top. Cut the batting the same size. Layer the backing, batting, and quilt top, and baste with safety pins. See page 7 for complete directions on machine quilting.

Add a French-fold binding. See page 10 for complete directions.

DOUBLE IRISH CHAIN QUILT

The strong diagonal pattern of the Double Irish Chain makes it an easily recognized design. It may be the same thing that makes it a very popular quilt design. What I love most about the Double Irish Chain is that it looks complex, yet it is quite simple. What looks like an allover pattern is made from two basic blocks that alternate across the quilt. Using strip techniques, this quilt could be easily varied by simply changing the size of the squares as I did here. The directions for the Double Irish Chain Wallhanging, shown on the headboard, begin on page 43.

Approximate Size

84 × 104 inches

Materials Required

- 4 yards of ecru print fabric for blocks
- 3¼ yards of red print fabric for blocks
- 1⅝ yards of green print fabric for blocks
- 1⅜ yards of light red print fabric for border and binding
- 1⅛ yards of dark red print fabric for border
- ⅜ yard of cream fabric for border
- 2½ yards of fabric for quilt backing
- 2⅜ yards of fabric for border backing
- King-size batting

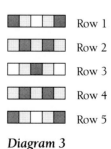

START WITH A SAMPLE

To start, cut just enough strips to make some sample blocks. Even the most experienced quilter can be surprised at the way selected fabrics look when they are cut and sewn together. If you do want to make a change, you haven't wasted time cutting something you don't want, and your fabric is still in big pieces. If you like the way it looks when a few blocks are together, strip techniques allow you to proceed full steam ahead.

Making Block A

Finding the two basic blocks is the first step in making this quilt. Block A is made up of twenty-five 2-inch squares, and Block B is made up of a 10-inch square with a 2-inch square in each corner, as shown in **Diagram 1**.

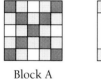

Block A   Block B

Diagram 1

1. Cut 2½-inch-wide strips from the red, green, and ecru print fabrics. I prefer to cut a 27-inch length of fabric and then cut strips from that along the lengthwise grain. Choose the length of strip and method that work best for you. There are three different strip sets that make up Block A; you'll need to cut a strip for each square in the row, as shown in **Diagram 2**.

Rows 1 & 5   Rows 2 & 4   Row 3

Diagram 2

2. Using **Diagram 2** as a guide, sew the strips together into sets. Row 4 is the same as Row 2, and Row 5 is the same as Row 1. Press the seams toward the darker fabrics. The finished strip sets should be 10½ inches wide.

3. Cut these strip sets into 2½-inch-long segments. For each Block A, cut five segments: one each for Rows 1 and 5; one each for Rows 2 and 4; and one for Row 3.

4. To make Block A, sew the segments for Rows 1 through 5 together according to **Diagram 3**. Press the seam allowances toward Row 3.

Row 1
Row 2
Row 3
Row 4
Row 5

Diagram 3

5. Complete 32 Block A's in this manner. Each block should measure 10½ inches square, including ¼-inch seam allowances. If they do not measure 10½ inches, you will need to make adjustments in the sizes of the strips in Block B as described on page 40.

Making Block B

One technique for making Block B is to cut a square the size of Block A and then appliqué a 2½-inch square in each corner. However, strip piecing is recommended for making Block B, especially if you plan to machine quilt in the ditch as I did on this quilt. By piecing Block B with strip techniques, you create more ditches.

1. There are two different strip sets in Block B, as shown in **Diagram 4.** Begin with the strip set for Rows 1 and 3. Double-check the size of the completed Block A. The width of the center three squares plus two ¼-inch seam allowances should equal 6½ inches. If it does, cut 2½-inch-wide strips from red print fabric and 6½-inch-wide strips from ecru print fabric to make the strip set. If the measurement does not equal 6½ inches, adjust the width of the ecru strip accordingly.

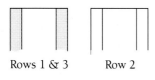

Rows 1 & 3   Row 2

Diagram 4

2. Sew the red strips onto each side of the ecru fabric. Press the seams toward the red fabric. The finished strip set should be 10½ inches wide. Cut this strip set into 2½-inch-long segments, two for each Block B.

3. For Row 2, cut ecru fabric into strips 2½ inches wide and 6½ inches wide. (If you had to adjust the width above, be sure to do so again on this strip.) Oh yes, if your friends are already wondering why you cut all that fabric up into little pieces and then sew it back together, this is something you might want to do in the dark of night. I really am telling you to cut the same fabric apart and then sew it back together! The block just looks better when it has these seam lines.

4. Again referring to **Diagram 4,** sew the narrow strips of ecru fabric onto two opposite sides of the wide strip. Press the seams toward the center. The finished strip set for Row 2 should be 10½ inches wide. Cut this strip set into 6½-inch-long segments, one for each Block B.

5. To make Block B, sew the segments together as Rows 1 through 3 according to **Diagram 5.** Press the seams away from the center.

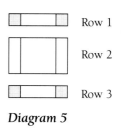

Row 1

Row 2

Row 3

Diagram 5

6. Complete 31 Block B's in this manner. Each block should measure 10½ inches square, including ¼-inch seam allowances.

Joining Blocks A and B

1. Blocks A and B alternate in a checkerboard pattern. Referring to the **Quilt Layout,** join the blocks into nine rows of seven blocks each. Press the seam allowances toward the Block B's.

2. Join the rows. The quilt top should now measure 70½ × 90½ inches, including ¼-inch seam allowances. Press the quilt top. If you are planning to quilt traditionally, you may add the borders now; alternatively, these instructions will cover adding the borders later using a Quilt-As-You-Sew technique.

Layering and Quilting

1. Cut and piece the backing fabric to about 2 inches larger in all directions than the interior section of the quilt top (74½ × 94½ inches). Cut the batting to the same size.

2. Layer the backing, batting, and quilt top, and baste the layers together with safety pins. Machine quilt in the ditch. See page 7 for complete directions on machine quilting.

Adding the First Border

The borders for this quilt are added using a Quilt-As-You-Sew technique. There are two ways to do this. One way is to layer the quilt top on an oversized batting and backing and then add the borders one at a time, stitching through all the layers. That technique is used for the Merry Chris-Moose Wallhanging on page 181. In this quilt, however, the technique differs somewhat. The interior of the quilt is machine quilted first, then strips of border fabric,

Quilt Layout

batting, and backing are added. The idea is to keep the size of the quilt top to a minimum for machine quilting; by adding the borders after the majority of the quilting is done, you have a smaller quilt to manipulate at the machine.

1. A ¾-inch-wide cream border is the first border added. The dimensions that follow are correct for this quilt, but since no two quilts are exactly alike, double-check the length and width of your quilt to be sure the borders are cut long enough. Cut 1¼-inch crosswise strips from the fabric, and join them to make two strips 1¼ × 90½ inches long for the sides

and two strips 1¼ × 72 inches long for the ends of the quilt.

2. For the side border batting and backing strips, measure the length of the quilt sides, and add 15 inches (twice the total of the border widths combined plus 1 inch for a separate binding). Cut the strips of batting and backing to this length and 7½ inches wide (the combined width of the borders plus ½ inch). Repeat for the top and bottom borders. For this quilt, there should be two strips of both batting and backing 7½ × 105½ inches long and two strips of each 7½ × 87 inches long.

3. Spread the quilt out on a large surface, right side up. With raw edges even, place the first side border strip right sides together with the quilt top. Pin it in position. Working on the same side, fold the edge of the quilt over so that the back is face up, and place the border backing strip right sides together with the quilt back. Place the border batting on top of the backing, and align the raw edges. Pin carefully through all layers. Your quilt top should look like the one shown in **Diagram 6**.

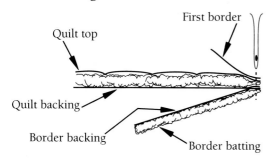

Diagram 6

4. Stitch with a ¼-inch seam allowance through all layers for the length of the quilt, as shown in **Diagram 7**. Trim the excess batting to within ⅛ inch of the seam. Press the border, batting, and backing firmly away from the quilt top.

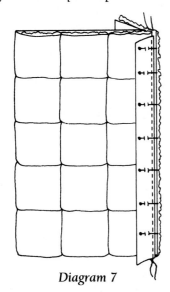

Diagram 7

5. Complete the opposite side of the quilt in the same manner. After adding both side borders, trim all four ends even with the quilt interior.

6. The end borders are added in the same manner as the side borders, except that the end borders will extend beyond the quilt interior to the outer edges of the side borders. See **Diagram 8**.

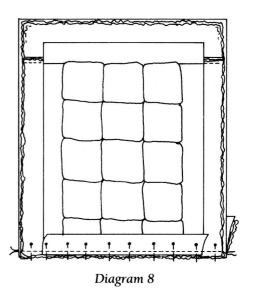

Diagram 8

Adding the Additional Borders

1. The second border is a 1¾-inch light red print border. Cut the fabric crosswise into 2¼-inch strips, and join them to make two 92-inch-long strips for the sides and two 75½-inch-long strips for the ends of the quilt.

2. Place the side border strips on top of the first border, right sides together and raw edges even. Pin them in position, and stitch through all layers. Open the borders, and press them away from the quilt top. Add the end border strips in the same manner as the side border strips.

3. The final border is 4½ inches wide finished. Cut the dark red print fabric lengthwise into 5-inch strips, and join them to make two 95½-inch-long strips for the sides and two 84½-inch-long strips for the ends of the quilt. Add this border in the same manner as the second border.

Finishing the Quilt

Add a separate French-fold binding to complete the quilt. Cut 2½-inch-wide strips from binding fabric, and piece them together to achieve the needed length. You will need approximately 380 inches of binding. Fold the long strip in half lengthwise, wrong sides together, and pin it to the front side of the quilt, even with the raw edges. Stitch the binding in place on the front, bring the folded edge around to the back side of the quilt, and hand stitch the edge in place.

DOUBLE IRISH CHAIN
ON POINT WALLHANGING

This small-scale version of the Double Irish Chain Quilt is shown on the headboard in the photo on page 38. Setting the blocks on point is an unusual variation that gives this easy wallhanging an entirely new look; the strong diagonal lines usually found in the pattern are now straight.

Approximate Size

36½ inches square

Materials Required

- ¾ yard of ecru print fabric for blocks
- ⅝ yard of red print fabric for border and binding
- ½ yard of red print fabric for blocks
- ¼ yard of green print fabric for blocks
- ⅛ yard of cream fabric for border
- 1⅛ yards of fabric for backing
- Crib-size batting or 1¼ yards of roll batting

Making Block A

Except for the size, the two basic blocks in the wallhanging are the same as in the Double Irish Chain Quilt on page 38. Read through the directions for that project, and refer to those directions and diagrams when constructing the blocks for this wallhanging.

1. Cut 2-inch-wide strips from the red, green, and ecru print fabrics. Referring to "Making Block A" on page 39, sew the strips into three different strip sets. Press the seams toward the darker fabrics. The finished strip sets should be 8 inches wide.

2. Cut the strip sets into 2-inch segments. For each Block A, cut one segment each for Rows 1 and 5; one each for Rows 2 and 4; and one for Row 3. Sew the segments together as Rows 1 through 5. Complete nine Block A's in this manner. The finished

blocks should measure 8 inches square, including ¼-inch seam allowances.

Making Block B

1. Cut 2-inch-wide strips from red print fabric and 2-inch- and 5-inch-wide strips from ecru print fabric. Sew the strips together into two different strip sets as described in "Making Block B" on page 40.

2. Cut 2-inch segments from the first strip set and 5-inch segments from the second strip set. Sew the segments together to create the block, pressing the seam allowances away from the center. The finished block should measure 8 inches square, including ¼-inch seam allowances. Make nine of these blocks; four are used in the center of the wallhanging, and the remaining five are cut apart and used as side and corner setting units.

Making the Side
and Corner Setting Units

Diagonal-set quilts have triangle-shaped spaces at the ends of each row that need to be filled to finish the edge of the quilt. These filler pieces are called setting triangles or units. In this quilt, there is also the need to continue the actual Double Irish Chain pattern. Generally, these pieces are made with separate triangle pattern pieces. For this quilt, we've made extra Block B's that we can now cut apart to use as setting units.

For the eight side setting units, cut four Block B's in half diagonally. To make the four corner units, cut one Block B diagonally both ways. See **Diagram 1**. Cutting setting and corner units from Block B in this manner means they are actually a seam allowance smaller than a perfect-size setting triangle. As a result, a tiny corner of Block A will be nipped off when the borders are added. I decided I could live with that, since the alternative is to create patterns and cut individual pieces.

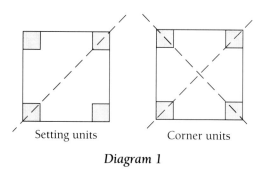

Setting units   Corner units

Diagram 1

Laying Out the Quilt Top

1. Referring to the **Quilt Layout**, lay out the quilt blocks with the side and corner setting units. Join the blocks and setting units in each diagonal row.

Quilt Layout

2. Join the rows. The quilt top should measure 32½ inches square, including ¼-inch seam allowances. Press the quilt top.

Layering and Quilting

1. Cut the batting and the backing fabric about 3 inches larger in all directions than the quilt top.

2. Center and layer the backing, batting, and quilt top, and baste. If you will be machine quilting, baste with safety pins. If you will be hand quilting, baste with thread.

3. Quilt as desired. The quilt shown was machine quilted with a poinsettia pattern in Block B, and in the ditch along all other seam lines. The poinsettia was free-motion quilted with the feed dogs down, using red metallic thread. The poinsettia quilting design is provided on page 45.

Adding the Borders

This Quilt-As-You-Sew method of adding borders is also used in the Merry Chris-Moose Wall-hanging on page 181. It does not involve cutting separate backing and batting for the border sections. Please measure your quilt before cutting your borders. If your measurements differ from those given, adjust the length of your borders accordingly.

1. The first ½-inch border is made from cream fabric. Cut 1-inch-wide strips, two 32½ inches long and two 33½ inches long.

2. With right sides together and raw edges even, pin the first short border strip to the quilt top. Stitch it in position, through all layers of the quilt top, batting, and backing. Open the border, and press it away from the quilt top. Complete the opposite side of the quilt in the same manner. Add the longer border strips to the two remaining sides using the same technique.

3. The second border is cut from red print fabric. Cut two 2 × 34-inch strips and two 2 × 37-inch strips. Add the second border strips in the same manner as for the first border.

4. Finish the quilt with a separate ⅜-inch French-fold binding. See page 10 for directions on making and attaching a French-fold binding.

DOUBLE IRISH CHAIN WALLHANGING WITH USER-FRIENDLY PANELS

One of the pretty printed panels available, as I write, features a deer in a dark green circle with holly and cardinal accents. The circle is set in a lovely red-on-red paisley-style printed square that is in turn surrounded by a dark green print. Most people will make pillows with these, much like the one shown in the photo. But then I wanted to see what else I could do with it.

Even if you can't find this particular print, or don't want to, please keep reading. This project is really about understanding the process of using printed panels, whether or not you make this specific project.

Approximate Size

49 inches square

Materials Required

- 1 yard of user-friendly fabric (4 pillow panels)
- ⅝ yard of light green print fabric for blocks
- ½ yard of fabric for wide border
- ½ yard of fabric for narrow border, corner squares, and binding
- ⅜ yard of dark green print fabric for blocks
- Scraps of red print fabric for blocks
- 1½ yards of fabric for backing
- 55-inch square of batting

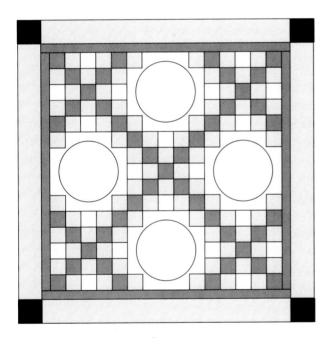

Quilt Layout

One of the fun things about quiltmaking is problem solving, and the best thing about that is there are virtually no rights or wrongs. Of course, before a problem can be solved, you have to know what it is. In this case, the problem was twofold: figuring out how to make the printed panel work in the Double Irish Chain pattern and what size to make the squares that complete the diagonal chains.

First, I made a copy of the **Quilt Layout** on page 41, in the Double Irish Chain Quilt project. (If you don't have a copy machine readily available, tracing paper laid over the book page also provides a good way to design on paper.) I decided to work with a three-block by three-block section in one corner of the quilt. There were five Block A's and four Block B's in the section. In each Block B, I sketched a circle that almost filled the open space. So far, the idea looked as if it would work, but what size would the small squares in the Irish Chain be?

The printed circle is 11 inches, but that wouldn't look right if it extended to the edge of the Block B. Therefore, the blocks must be larger than 12 inches. There are five rows in each Block A; if each row was 2½ inches finished, the block would be 12½ inches. That would work, but it seemed that not enough of the pretty red print would show. Since 3-inch squares seemed too big, the obvious thing was to try something in between. I settled on 2¾-inch squares, which seems an odd size but results in a 13¾-inch block, which is just right for this panel.

Another problem that had to be solved in this wallhanging was caused by the fact that the pretty red print that surrounds the panel was not available separately, so the squares that appear in Block A would have to be cut from the printed panel fabric. I could see I wouldn't be able to get the 20 squares I needed from that fabric, but it looked as if I could probably get 12 squares, enough to fill every position where they touch the red background, and I could substitute a similar red print from my scrap bag for the other 8 positions.

Once I figured out the sizes of the squares, the rest of the quilt was easy. The block construction for Block A is the same as for the Double Irish Chain Quilt on page 39. Block B must be made a little differently, however, to avoid cutting apart the printed panel. To make Block B for this wallhanging, I cut 3¼-inch squares from the light green print fabric and appliquéd them to the corners of the printed panel squares. To do this, simply press under ¼-inch seam allowances on two adjacent sides of the square. Position the square on the printed block so that the two raw edges of the corner square line up with the edges of the background block. Hand appliqué the square in place.

Putting this all together meant lots of cutting of squares and special cutting of pieces to take advantage of the printed panel. I believe if you look back at the introduction to strip techniques, you will see that I said, "You may never cut a single square again." Well, that theory didn't last long, did it? The point is, of course, that this printed fabric was worth making exceptions for.

To finish it, I added a 1-inch border, a 3½-inch border with corner squares, and a separate French-fold binding. The wallhanging is machine quilted.

PIECED QUILTS FEATURING TRIANGLES

Triangles, and squares made from triangles, appear in many traditional quilt patterns. In the Temperance Tree Quilt below and the Cardinals in the Pines Quilt on page 59, triangles of various sizes are the main elements in the block. The Sew-Before-You-Cut technique makes putting the blocks together faster and easier.

TEMPERANCE TREE QUILT

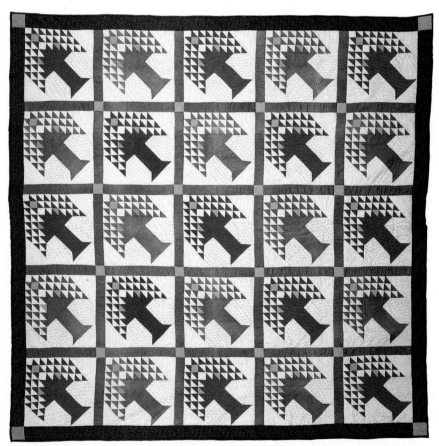

I once read about a quiltmaker who would buy an antique quilt and then make a duplicate of it to use. She called the new quilts second-generation quilts. In this book, I am going to share a couple of antique quilts that make nice second-generation Christmas quilts. The first one is this Temperance Tree.

Approximate Size

94 inches square

Materials Required

- 5 yards of white fabric for blocks
- 3⅛ yards of green fabric for blocks and sashing
- 2 yards of red fabric for blocks
- 1 yard of dark green print fabric for border
- ¾ yard of gold fabric for blocks, sashing corner squares, and border corner squares
- 8 yards of fabric for backing and binding
- King-size batting

I purchased this antique as a quilt top. At the time, I noted that it should be quilted and used as a Christmas wallhanging. At 88 inches square, it would be a very large wallhanging. If you were reproducing it specifically to use on a wall, 9 blocks, as shown in the **Wallhanging Layout**, instead of 25 blocks, as in the quilt, would make a wallhanging approximately 54 inches square.

In the bed-size version of this quilt, 13 red and white tree blocks alternate with 12 green and white tree blocks. Each block is highlighted with small gold accents, adding a bit of "sparkle" to the red and green. Additional gold accents appear in the sashing separating the blocks. As a final touch, I added a border with gold corner squares. If you isolated the gold fabric, your observation might well be that it is really quite garish. In fact, it is the color that antique-quilt authorities call chrome yellow or chrome orange. These dyes were available commercially before 1850 and are frequently found in old quilts, but it probably isn't necessary for me to mention that this color is not in favor in many decorating guidebooks. Clever antique dealers who want to put a positive spin on this color never refer to it as chrome orange, but instead call it "cheddar." An antique quilt with "lots of cheddar" will sell much sooner than a chrome orange quilt, don't you think?

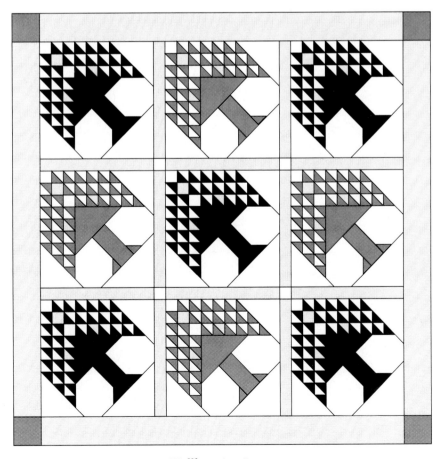

Wallhanging Layout

Because all the blocks are made in the same manner, the red or green fabric is referred to in the directions as the colored fabric. Also, the background fabric that appears white and is called white in the instructions is really a fine chicken-wire-like black design on a white background.

Cutting the Fabrics

The pieced squares for the blocks are made using the Sew-Before-You-Cut method, described in "Making Pieced Squares" below. In addition to the pieced squares, you will need to cut the pieces listed here. Use the pattern pieces beginning on page 55.

From the white fabric, cut:
50 A pieces
25 C triangles
50 E triangles
50 F squares

From the green fabric, cut:
12 B rectangles
12 D triangles
96 G triangles
Forty 2⅝ × 16⅜-inch sashing strips

From the red fabric, cut:
13 B rectangles
13 D triangles
104 G triangles

From the gold fabric, cut:
25 F squares
Sixteen 2⅝-inch squares
Four 3½-inch squares

From the dark green print fabric, cut:
Four 3½ × 90-inch border strips

Making Pieced Squares

With the Sew-Before-You-Cut method, you create bicolor "pieced squares" without cutting or handling any triangular pieces. This method is accurate and quick, and it dramatically reduces the number of small triangles, with their easily stretched bias edges, with which you must deal.

The technique is simple: First, you draw a grid of appropriate-size squares on the wrong side of the

JUDGING FABRICS

Squint at a print fabric to help decide if it has the right characteristics to look like a solid color fabric without requiring all the fancy quilting that a plain color demands. A solid color fabric without any pattern will show off extensive quilting. A print background fabric will create an interesting surface design itself, and won't necessarily need as much quilting to make it look nice.

lighter fabric. (Note that the squares in this grid are not the size of the pieced square itself, nor is the number of squares in the grid equal to the number of pieced squares in the quilt. See "Calculating the Grid" below.) Draw diagonal lines on the grid. You may also want to draw stitching guidelines ¼ inch away on each side of the diagonal lines. Layer the two fabrics, right sides together, and stitch them together with ¼-inch seam allowances on both sides of the diagonal guidelines. Cut on the drawn lines, open the two layers, and you have pieced squares! This technique can be used on any project in which you have pieced squares.

Calculating the Grid

1. Calculate the size of the grid square. The size of the grid square is the size of the pieced square plus ⅞ inch. The pieced squares in this quilt are 1⅝ inches; therefore, the grid squares should be 2½ inches.

The amount added is always ⅞ inch, regardless of the size of the pieced square. This guarantees that you will still have ¼-inch seam allowances after the square has been cut diagonally.

2. Determine the number of pieced squares needed. In this quilt, there are 28 pieced squares in each block, and there are 25 blocks total, 13 red and 12 green. This comes out to 364 red and white and 336 green and white pieced squares. In addition, you'll need 26 red and gold and 24 green and gold pieced squares.

3. Calculate the number of squares in the grid. To determine the number of squares in the grid, divide the number of pieced squares needed by two. In this quilt, you would need a total of 182 squares for the red trees and 168 for the green trees, plus 13 red and gold squares and 12 green and gold squares.

4. Determine the amount of fabric needed. I find that fabric pieces 18 × 22½ inches (half a yard, cut in half) are about as large as can be comfortably marked and sewn. First, determine how many grid squares can be drawn on a piece of fabric about that size. For this quilt, approximately 7 rows of 8 squares each (or 56 squares) fit on an 18 × 22½-inch piece of fabric. This just happens to be exactly enough for four trees.

Now, divide the total number of grid squares needed (182 and 168) by that number (56) to determine how much fabric to mark. If you cut seven pieces (18 × 22½ inches each) of background and four of red and three of green, there should be a few extra pieced squares of red when you are done and just enough green. Obviously, the red and gold and the green and gold accent squares can be cut from much smaller pieces of fabric. A 10½-inch square of each color should be large enough.

Marking and Sewing the Squares

1. Begin by marking 2½-inch squares on the wrong side of the lighter fabric. Use a ruler and marker to make horizontal lines. Draw vertical lines perpendicular to the first lines until you have enough squares. See **Diagram 1**.

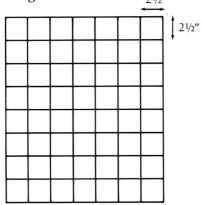

Diagram 1

2. Referring to **Diagram 2**, draw diagonal lines through every other row of squares. Then, starting

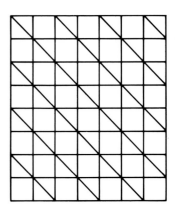

Diagram 2

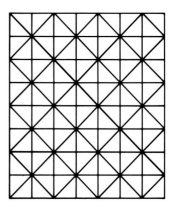

Diagram 3

with the first empty square, draw diagonal rows in the opposite direction, as shown in **Diagram 3**.

3. Lay the marked fabric piece atop the unmarked fabric piece, right sides together, and pin. Referring to **Diagram 4**, sew the layers together, stitching along both sides of the diagonal drawn lines with an accurate ¼-inch seam allowance. It is important that these seam allowances be accurate. You may want to draw stitching guidelines to make sure the seam allowances are accurate.

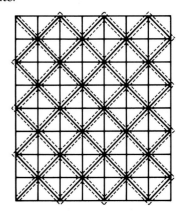

Diagram 4

4. Cut the fabric apart on *every drawn line*. Press the resulting triangles open to form pieced squares. You may have to tug on the corners of a few squares to get them open; just pull gently and the stitches will come out. Press the seam allowances to the darker side.

Piecing the Units

Be very careful to keep the proper orientation of all triangles when assembling the following units. Study all the diagrams carefully.

1. Create two basic nine-patch units, as shown in **Diagram 5**, by combining one accent pieced square with eight other pieced squares for each unit. The units will be mirror images of each other.

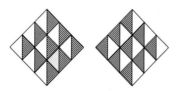

Diagram 5

2. Make the alternate nine-patch unit shown in **Diagram 6** by combining one gold and two white F squares with six pieced squares.

Diagram 6

3. For each of the two half-nine-patch units shown in **Diagram 7**, combine three pieced squares with three colored G triangles.

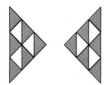

Diagram 7

Piecing the Block

Be very careful to keep the proper orientation of all triangles and to match all seam allowances when assembling the block. Study the assembly diagrams carefully.

1. Referring to **Diagram 8**, begin by sewing the two small G triangles to the A background pieces. Sew these two units to the B tree trunk. Sew the D triangle to the top and the C triangle to the bottom, as shown.

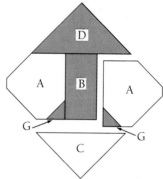

Diagram 8

2. Combine one half-nine-patch unit and one basic nine-patch unit as illustrated in **Diagram 9**.

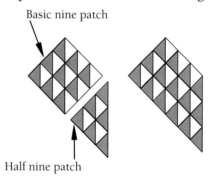

Diagram 9

3. Sew the completed section from Step 2 to the right side of the Step 1 section, as shown in **Diagram 10**.

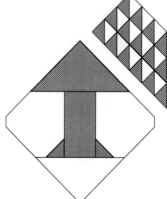

Diagram 10

4. Sew together the remaining basic nine-patch, alternate nine-patch, and half-nine-patch units as shown in **Diagram 11**.

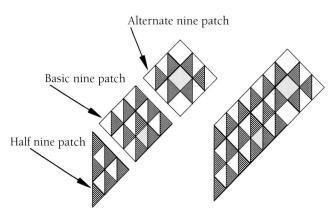

Diagram 11

5. Join the completed Step 4 section with the Step 3 section as shown in **Diagram 12**. Referring to **Diagram 13**, add an E triangle to each side.

Diagram 12

Diagram 13

6. In this manner, complete 13 blocks using red triangles and 12 blocks using green triangles. Each block should measure 16⅜ inches square, including ¼-inch seam allowances. If your block finishes larger or smaller than 16⅜ inches, adjust the cut length of the sashing strips in the following steps.

Adding the Sashing

Green sashing with gold corner squares separates and highlights the blocks. Be sure to maintain the correct orientation of blocks and sashing strips in the following steps.

1. With right sides together and raw edges even, sew a green sashing strip to the right side of ten green and ten red blocks. See **Diagram 14**. Press the seam allowance toward the sashing strip.

Diagram 14

2. Sew a gold square to the end of 16 sashing strips. Sew these strips to the bottom edge of eight of the green and eight of the red blocks from Step 1. See **Diagram 15**. Press the seam allowance toward the

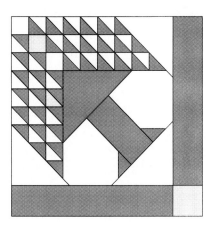

Diagram 15

sashing strip. Two blocks of each color will be left with sashing strips on the right side only.

3. Sew the remaining four sashing strips to the bottom edge of two red and two green blocks. These four blocks will have sashing on the bottom edge only. One red block will be left with no sashing strips.

Assembling the Quilt Top

1. Referring to the **Quilt Layout**, lay the blocks out in five rows of five blocks each. Alternate the blocks in checkerboard fashion, with a red block in each of the four corners. Blocks along the right side of the quilt have only bottom sashing strips, and

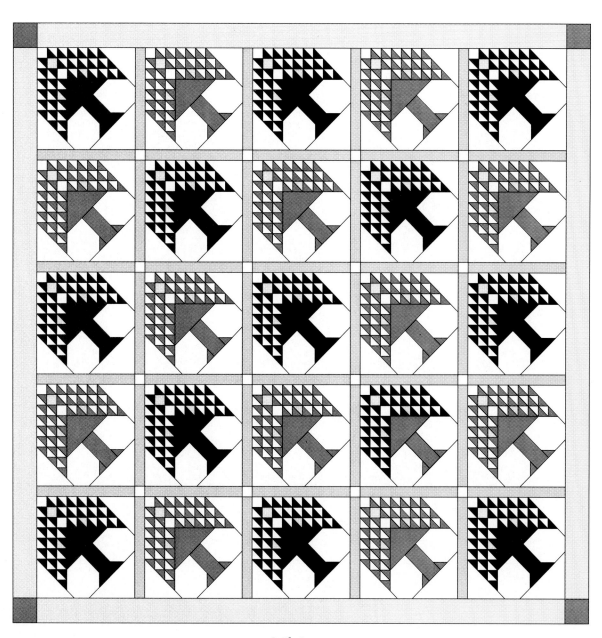

Quilt Layout

blocks along the bottom row of the quilt have only side sashing strips. The red block in the bottom right corner of the quilt has no sashing strips.

2. Sew the blocks together in each row, and press the seam allowances toward the sashing.

3. Sew the rows together, and press the seam allowances toward the sashing.

Adding the Border

Read "Adding Borders with Corner Squares" on page 23 before beginning.

1. Measure the completed quilt top, and make any necessary adjustments to the borders.

2. Sew an accent square to one end of each of the border strips.

3. Working in a clockwise direction, add the four border strips to the quilt top.

Finishing the Quilt

1. Piece the backing fabric. Layer the backing, batting, and quilt top, and baste.

2. Hand or machine quilt as desired. Finish with a French-fold binding. Refer to page 10 for complete directions on making and adding a French-fold binding.

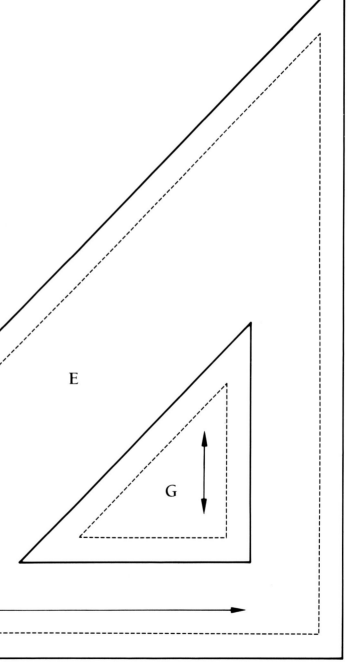

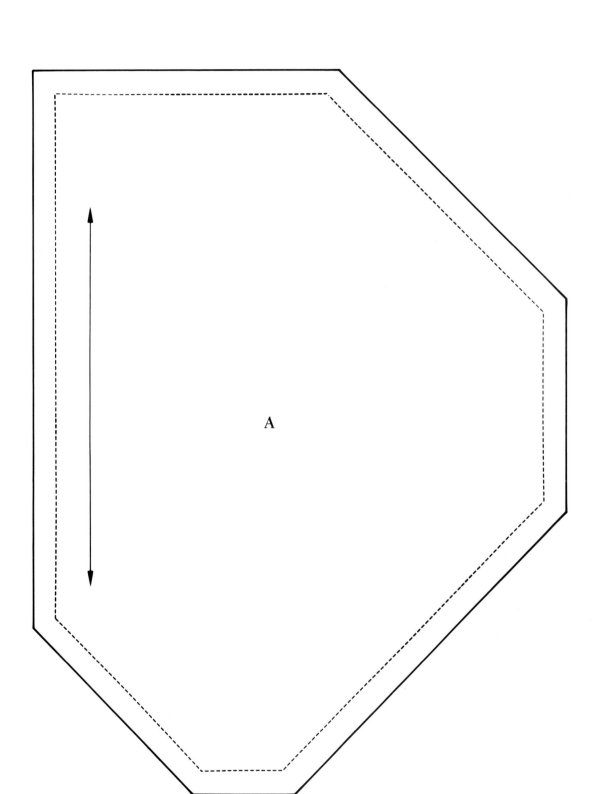

A

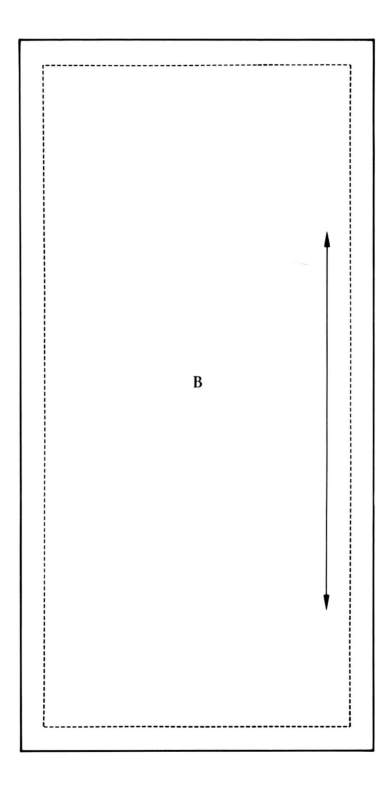

B

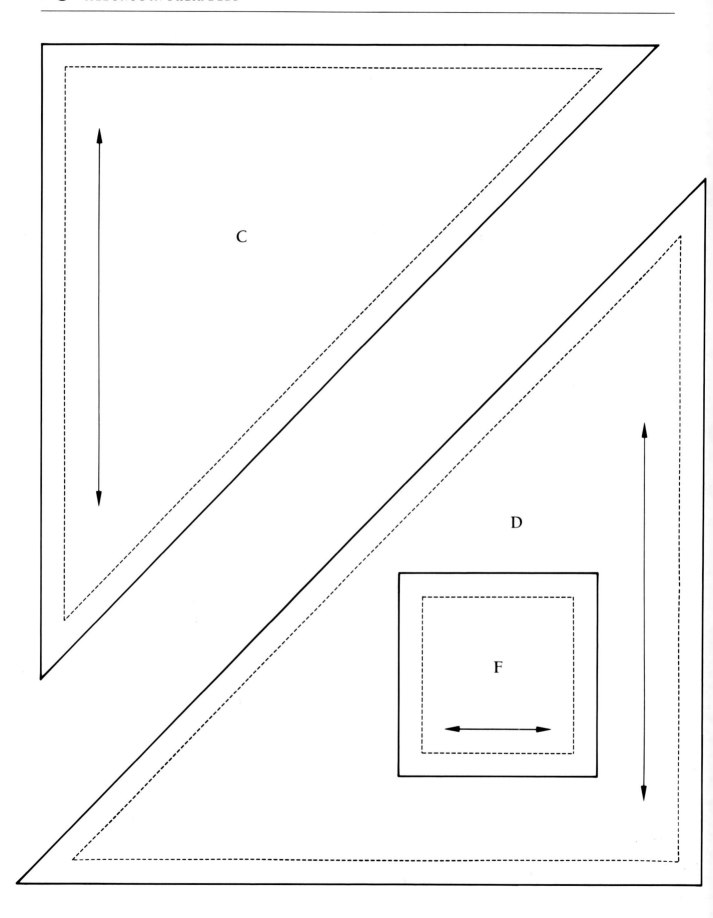

CARDINALS IN THE PINES QUILT

Not long after starting this book, I spotted this quilt at a show. I was already planning to include the antique Temperance Tree Quilt on page 48, and I thought that this quilt, which uses the same block pattern, would be a perfect complement to it. In the Temperance Tree Quilt, the blocks were arranged in a straight set, creating a somewhat primitive, but very strong, graphic look. This quilt, made by Kathryn Jones with help from the Boone Slick Quilters, is much more refined and incorporates the sophistication of the diagonal set, random fabric placement, and a border designed specifically for the quilt. It is mostly green pieced pine trees, with a light print background and touches of red. Hence the name, Cardinals in the Pines.

When I asked Kathryn if I could feature her quilt, she said she would be delighted. She also said that while the tree pattern is certainly a traditional pattern, she had seen the idea for the random red triangles in a quilt made by Jane VanDenburg and featured in the magazine *Traditional Quilts*. When she was lucky enough to have her name drawn for the Friendship Quilt in her guild, the Boone Slick Quilters, Kathryn gave everyone the background fabric and pattern. They added the red and green fabrics of their choice and pieced the trees. Then Kathryn put the blocks together and designed the border and the quilting design.

Approximate Size

90 × 108 inches

Materials Required

- 7½ yards of white fabric for blocks, setting triangles, and border
- 4¼ yards total of assorted green fabrics for blocks and border
- ⅝ yard of red fabric for blocks and border
- 7¾ yards of fabric for backing
- ¾ yard of fabric for binding
- King-size batting

Cutting the Fabrics

This quilt uses the same Sew-Before-You-Cut method of creating bicolor pieced squares as used for the Temperance Tree Quilt. In addition to the pieced squares, you will need to cut the pieces listed here. Use the pattern pieces beginning on page 64.

From the white fabric, cut:
Seven 18⅝-inch squares. Cut five of these diagonally both ways, for border setting triangles. Cut the remaining two in half diagonally, for corner setting triangles.
Four 18¼-inch squares, cut diagonally both ways, for side setting triangles
Two 12¼-inch squares, cut in half diagonally, for corner setting triangles
Twelve 12¾-inch squares
40 A pieces
60 C triangles
60 F squares
14 H triangles
28 J squares

From the green fabrics, cut:
Nine 9¾-inch squares, cut diagonally both ways, for border setting triangles
20 B rectangles
20 D triangles
40 E triangles
120 G triangles
14 H triangles
14 I rectangles

From the red fabric, cut:
Two 1½ × 74-inch border strips
Two 1½ × 91-inch border strips

Making Pieced Squares

Review the directions for making Sew-Before-You-Cut pieced squares beginning on page 50 in the Temperance Tree Quilt project.

Each block in the interior of this quilt requires twenty-nine 1⅜-inch green and white pieced squares, for a total of 580 squares. In addition, there are 20 green and red pieced squares, one for each block. In the Temperance Tree Quilt, one green and one red fabric were used, and these were cut to 18 × 22½-inch pieces, the largest practical size to handle for this technique. In this quilt, however, many different green fabrics are used, so each fabric piece need not be so large.

To obtain the 580 green and white squares needed, a total of 290 grid squares, each 2¼ inches, must be drawn. To determine the number of grid squares to draw on each piece of fabric, divide the total number of grid squares by the number of fabrics you've chosen to use. For example, if you have 15 different green fabrics, draw 20 grid squares on each. Of course, there is no reason that the same number of grid squares must be drawn on each fabric piece; just be sure to create a total of 290 grid squares. Cut a piece

Quilt Layout

of background fabric of matching size for each piece of green fabric.

Draw the grids, layer the fabrics, stitch, cut, and press the resulting pieced squares. Don't drive yourself crazy counting squares as you go. Piece as many squares as you think you need, then start making trees. If you run out of pieced squares, make some more!

Making the Blocks

The Pine Tree block is the same as the Temperance Tree block, except for the change in colors. **Diagram 1** shows the individual units of the block as well as the completed block. The red and green pieced square, which represents the cardinal, is randomly placed; use it in place of one of the green and white pieced squares in either a nine-patch unit or a half-nine-patch unit in each block.

To make the blocks, follow the directions in "Piecing the Units" and "Piecing the Block" on page 52. The completed Pine Tree blocks should measure 12¾ inches square, including ¼-inch seam allowances.

Assembling the Quilt Top

1. Referring to **Diagram 2**, lay out the blocks in diagonal rows.

2. Join the blocks in each diagonal row, pressing the seam allowances in opposite directions from row to row.

3. Add the setting triangles on the ends of each row. Line up the right angle of the setting triangle with a corner of the block so that the hypotenuse (the longest edge) will become the outside edge of

Diagram 2

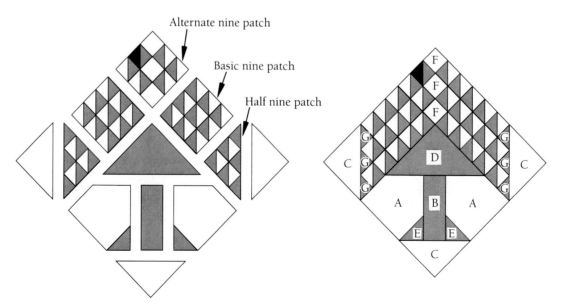

Diagram 1

the quilt. See **Diagram 3**. The tips of the triangles will extend beyond the quilt blocks, as shown in **Diagram 4**. Stitch, and press the seams toward the triangles.

Diagram 3

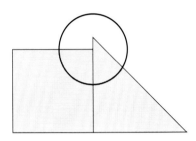

Diagram 4

4. With right sides together, and matching seams carefully, join the diagonal rows to each other. See **Diagram 5**.

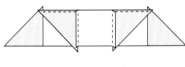

Diagram 5

5. With right sides together, sew the four corner triangles to the quilt top as shown in **Diagram 6**. Trim the quilt top as necessary. The quilt top should measure approximately $70 \times 87\frac{3}{8}$ inches.

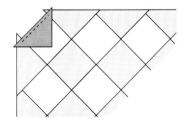

Diagram 6

6. Add the red border strips to the two sides of the quilt, trimming the length as necessary. Press. Add the red border strips to the top and bottom of the quilt, and press.

Making the Border Units

The elaborate border on this quilt contains 14 small Pine Tree blocks. Each block contains 14 green and white pieced squares and 1 green and red pieced square. For the 196 green and white pieced squares, a total of 98 grid squares must be drawn. For the 14 green and red pieced squares, you'll need 7 grid squares. Since the squares in the small border blocks are 1¼ inches, the grid must consist of 2⅛-inch squares. As with the large tree blocks, the size of fabric pieces depends on the number of green fabrics used. Cut a piece of white fabric of matching size for each green fabric.

1. Refer to the **Block Assembly Diagram** throughout the next steps. First, create two basic units of six pieced squares each. The units should be mirror images of each other. Make 14 pairs of units, one for each border block. In 10 of them, randomly replace one green and white pieced square with one green and red "cardinal" pieced square.

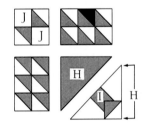

Block Assembly Diagram

2. Make 14 four-patch units by combining two J squares with two pieced squares. In 4 of the units, randomly replace one green and white pieced square with one green and red pieced square.

3. For each block, center the green I rectangle on the white H triangle, and pin it in place. Place the remaining green and white pieced square on the same H triangle, aligning the outside raw edges. Appliqué the tree trunk and the pieced square in place on the H triangle. Carefully trim the excess fabric from behind the completed appliqué. Then, sew this unit to the green H triangle.

4. Being careful to keep the triangles oriented correctly, add one six-patch unit to the left side of the Step 3 unit.

5. Sew the second six-patch unit to the four-patch unit, and sew the completed section to the top of the Step 4 section, carefully matching seams. Be sure that each block includes a single "cardinal" pieced square.

Assembling the Border

1. Sew a green triangle to the top sides of each tree block to form 14 larger triangles, as shown in **Diagram 7**.

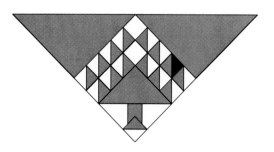

Diagram 7

2. Join the pieced triangles and the large white triangles as shown in **Diagram 8** to form the top, bottom, and two side borders. As shown in the **Quilt Layout**, the top and bottom borders are each made up of seven large triangles plus two small green triangles. The side borders are each made up of nine large triangles plus two small green triangles.

3. Sew the side border strips to the quilt top. Sew the top and bottom border strips to the quilt top.

4. Add the four large corner triangles. After the corners are sewn in place, trim the excess white triangle fabric from the back side.

5. Straighten all edges, trimming as necessary.

Finishing the Quilt

Layer the quilt top, batting, and backing, and quilt as desired. The alternate blocks and the setting triangles in the quilt shown were hand quilted with a lovely wreath pattern. Keep in mind that where and how much to quilt are personal choices; don't feel that you must duplicate the sample quilt. Finish the edges with a ½-inch French-fold binding. See page 10 for complete directions on making and adding a French-fold binding.

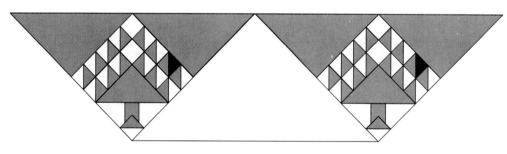

Diagram 8

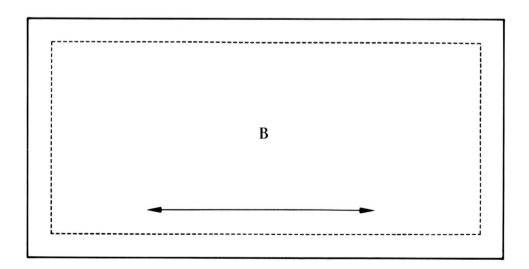

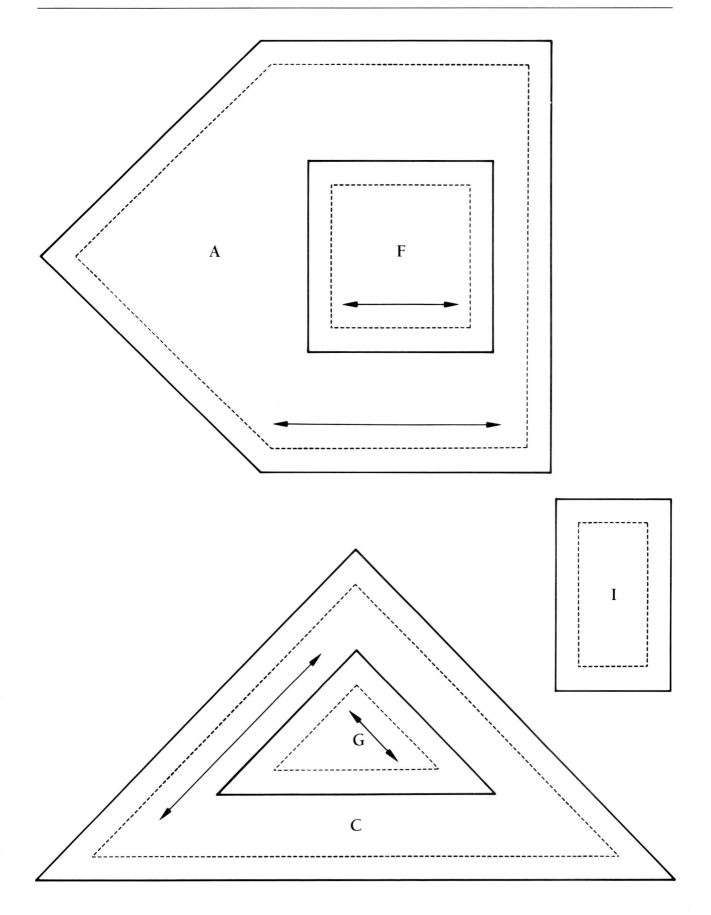

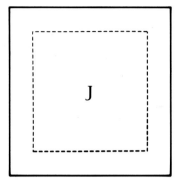

J

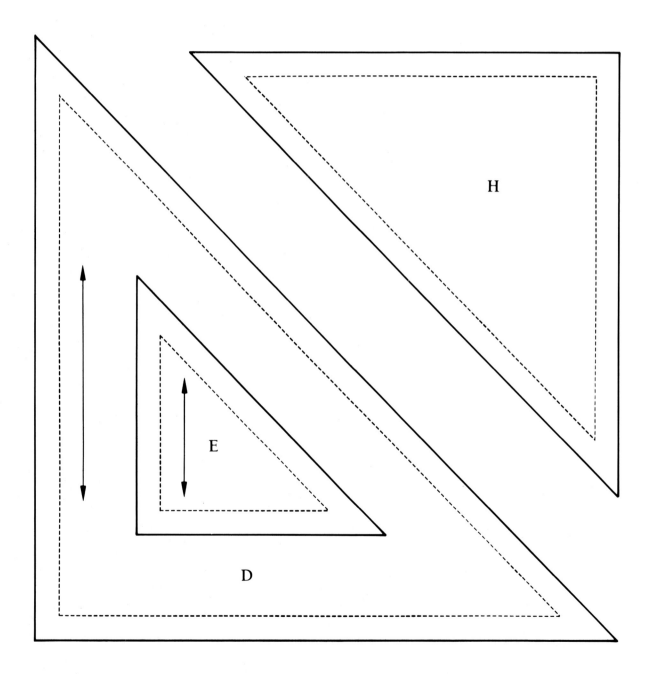

H

E

D

APPLIQUÉ QUILTS

The lovely antique Rose Wreath quilt shown in the photo on page 73 would make a great second-generation quilt. It appears to have red flowers with camel-colored leaves. However, antique-textile specialists would most likely say this fabric started out green, but was an unstable green, and either oxidation or sunlight caused the dye to change. Wreaths are certainly a Christmas symbol, and to me, this quilt qualifies as a beautiful Christmas quilt.

The instructions for reproducing the quilt are provided beginning on page 74. Granted, it's not as fast as buying an antique, but then, you may not be driven to have a quilt for everyone in one year. You can start this now and plan to finish it for a future Christmas.

To reproduce the quilt, the first thing you have to decide is which appliqué technique to use.

Hand Appliqué versus Machine Appliqué

Appliquéing by hand can be distinctly advantageous for people who frequently find themselves away from their sewing machines with spare time on their hands. Some find handwork very relaxing. The stitches are certainly more invisible, and the density of stitches can be easily adjusted (as needed for leaf points) when working by hand. The ease of manipulating folded-under seam allowances when hand appliquéing is also an attractive feature.

Appliquéing by machine is a great alternative when arthritis or other conditions make handwork difficult. Speed is also a consideration. As nearly as I can tell, it is 2 to 2½ times faster to work by machine. That is, if it takes me 5 minutes to appliqué a leaf by

hand, it only takes me 2 to 2½ minutes by machine. Your ratio may be different from mine. On a pillow, the difference might not represent much more than 1 or 1½ hours. On 20 quilt squares, however, that extra time becomes 20 or 30 hours. My personal incentive to machine appliqué is much greater.

Preparing Your Machine

If you are planning to use the machine for this project, you will probably need to experiment a little, maybe even get out your instruction book. The Rose Wreath Pillow on page 68 was made with a decorative buttonhole stitch. To make the stitch bite so tiny, the machine was put in the double-needle position, even though it was being stitched with a single needle. Not every machine will be able to do quite as beautiful a stitch as this, but any machine that has instructions for blind hemming can do almost as nicely. The blind hem stitch will make a V instead of a straight perpendicular stitch. See the example in **Diagram 1**.

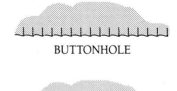

BUTTONHOLE

BLIND HEM

Diagram 1

An easy way to practice the appliqué techniques and decide on the final method and fabrics is to make a pillow.

ROSE WREATH PILLOW

The Rose Wreath pattern provided here is slightly refined
compared with the one in the antique quilt on page 73. In the
original, which has a more primitive look, there are large leaves on
the inside as well as the outside of the wreath, the leaves are more
perpendicular to the wreath band, and there are no flower centers.
The **Block Diagram** illustrates both designs; you may want to
experiment to determine which effect you like best.

Block Diagram

Approximate Size

21 inches square

Materials Required

- ½ yard of beige print fabric for pillow background and mock double ruffle
- ½ yard of cream print fabric for ruffle
- ½ yard of green print fabric for mock double ruffle
- ⅛ yard of green print fabric for leaves and wreath band
- 12 × 18-inch piece of red print fabric for flowers and border
- 14-inch square of fabric for lining
- 14-inch square of coordinating fabric for backing
- 8-inch square of gold fabric for flower centers
- 14-inch square of batting
- Polyester fiberfill for stuffing
- Freezer paper

Preparing the Leaves

The pillow features almost invisible machine appliqué using freezer paper. The freezer-paper technique is also perfect for hand appliqué, if you prefer.

1. Using the pattern on page 72, make a template for each of the two leaf shapes. With the shiny side of the paper down, trace the leaves onto the freezer paper. Cut the paper pieces the exact finished size of the leaves. Because the leaves are so similar, there will be less confusion if you cut, press, and appliqué all of the inside leaves before starting on the outside leaves.

2. Loosely cut rectangles of leaf fabric slightly larger than the paper pieces. Center a paper leaf,

shiny side up, on the wrong side of the leaf fabric, and pin it securely. Trim the excess fabric for approximately one-fourth of the leaf, leaving about 3/16 inch of fabric extending beyond the paper.

3. Press that section of fabric over the freezer paper with the tip of your iron. See **Diagram 1**.

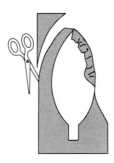

Diagram 1

4. Trim the second quarter of the leaf, fold the seam allowance over, and press it in place. Proceed all around the leaf. At the point, use a touch of glue to hold the layers of fabric in place. It is not necessary to press under the small section at the end of the stem, since it will be covered with the band later. Prepare all the leaves at one time, and set them aside.

Cutting the Wreath Band

1. Cut four ⅞ × 4-inch bias strips of fabric for the wreath band. Cut strips of freezer paper to the actual shape of the band using the pattern on page 72.

2. Using the same technique used for the leaves, wrap and press fabric strips around the freezer-paper strips to make the band sections.

Cutting the Flowers

1. Make a template for the large flower using the pattern on page 72. Using the same method as for the leaves, cut the flower pieces from freezer paper and from fabric, except allow a ¼-inch seam allowance.

2. To make the flower centers, cut two pieces of fabric for each center, allowing a ¼-inch seam allowance. Place the fabric pieces right sides together, and stitch around the circle on the traced line, leaving a small opening for turning. Trim the seam allowances slightly, turn the flower center right side out through the opening, and hand stitch the opening closed. Press.

Preparing the Background Square

1. Cut a 15-inch square from beige print fabric to be used as the background for the appliqué pieces. This is larger than the finished size because the edges get roughed up during the appliquéing process. After the block is completed, you will trim it to 14 inches square.

2. Fold the square in half, then fold it in half again to find the center point.

3. Very lightly trace the outline of the pattern onto the background fabric. Each quarter of the wreath is identical from the center of one flower to the center of the next. As you trace each quadrant of the block, use the registration marks and the outside edge to align the sections and create a perfect circle.

Trace as much or as little of the design as you feel you need to be comfortable positioning the appliqué pieces. If you trace *just inside* the lines, you shouldn't have to remove the marks.

4. Cut a small slit in the background fabric in every leaf section now. It doesn't change the stability of the background, and it does make removing the paper and trimming the excess background fabric easier.

Selecting the Thread

For hand appliqué, I recommend a cotton or cotton-wrapped polyester thread that matches a solid or blends with a print appliqué fabric. When in doubt, go to a slightly lighter shade rather than darker; go to a duller shade rather than brighter.

For very intricate hand appliqué, many teachers recommend a single-filament silk thread. It is definitely a luxury to use, but if you have it and want to use it, great!

For machine appliqué, my preference is still the cotton or cotton-wrapped polyester thread, but because the stitch completely surrounds the appliqué piece and "lies" on the surface of the background, color decision is more difficult.

Usually there is considerable contrast between the two fabrics in question. Most often my decision is still to thread both the top and the bobbin with the closest match and be very careful to stitch *right beside* the appliqué.

Sometimes invisible nylon thread is the best choice for the top thread, especially if you are switching rapidly from one color of appliqué to another. Use a neutral cotton or cotton-wrapped polyester thread in the bobbin.

Appliquéing the Block

One good method is to appliqué the inside leaves first, then the outside leaves, then the bands to cover the ends of the leaves, and finally, the flowers with the centers already appliquéd in place. If your machine has the feature that allows it to stop with the needle in the fabric, make sure you take advantage of it when doing machine appliqué.

1. Position the leaves, and press them in place. There is enough waxy surface on the freezer paper to hold them without pins.

2. Starting at the stem, stitch all the way around, paying special attention to the points.

3. Trim the excess background fabric from behind the leaves, leaving about a ¼-inch seam allowance. This is most important if you will be hand quilting in this area; trimming the excess means you'll have one less layer to quilt through.

Whichever quilting technique you use, it is necessary to remove the freezer paper. Run a finger under the appliqué seam allowance to release the paper from the fabric. Try to grasp an edge of the paper. Tug against the stitches to tear away the paper. (This is easier with hand appliqué than machine.) Sometimes tweezers are helpful in retrieving a torn-off section of freezer paper.

4. Continue with additional pieces, making sure that you remove all paper from a section before stitching over it with another piece.

5. Press the completed appliqué lightly from the back side. Trim the block to 14 inches square, which includes a ¼-inch seam allowance.

Quilting the Pillow Top

Layer the pillow top with the batting and the lining fabric, and baste. Quilt as desired. The pillow shown was free-motion machine quilted with invisible thread on the background fabric, with no quilting at all on the appliqué pieces.

Finishing the Pillow

1. Add the red print border first. Cut two 1½ × 14-inch strips and two 1½ × 16-inch strips of red fabric for the border. With right sides together and raw edges even, pin the first short strip to the pillow top. Stitch it in position, open the border, and press it away from the pillow top. Add the second short border to the opposite side of the pillow top. Add the longer strips in the same manner.

2. A very full 1½-inch-wide cream print ruffle is added next. Cut 3½-inch-wide strips of fabric, and piece them as necessary to obtain 192 inches for triple fullness. Fold the fabric strip in half, wrong sides together and raw edges even, and press. Gather along the raw edges to make a ruffle approximately 64 inches long. Matching all raw edges with the pillow top, baste the ruffle in place. Where the ruffle ends meet, turn under the raw edge on both ends, overlap the ends, and baste them in place.

3. A mock double ruffle gives the appearance of two separate ruffles, but is actually two different fabrics sewn together and gathered as one ruffle. This method saves fabric and eliminates bulk. A green and beige mock double ruffle completes this pillow top. Cut 3¾-inch-wide strips of green print fabric, and piece them as necessary to obtain 160 inches for 2½ times fullness. Cut 2¾-inch-wide strips of beige print fabric, and piece them as necessary to obtain 160 inches. Sew the green and beige strips together to make one long strip 6 inches wide. Fold this strip in half, wrong sides together, and press. Gather the raw edges to make a ruffle approximately 64 inches long. Baste the ruffle to the pillow top in the same manner as for the cream print ruffle.

4. For the pillow back, cut a 14-inch square of backing fabric. Layer the pillow top and back right sides together, with ruffles turned to the inside away from the stitching line. Sew around the outside edge with a ¼-inch seam, leaving a few inches open along one side. Trim the corners and clip the seams if necessary. Turn the pillow right side out through the opening. Stuff the pillow. Slip stitch the opening closed.

One-quarter of Rose Wreath design

ROSE WREATH APPLIQUÉ QUILT

This quilt, a reproduction of the one shown in the photo, features nine appliqué blocks alternating with muslin blocks in a diagonal set. The muslin blocks and the muslin side setting and corner setting triangles provide lots of background to show off extensive quilting. If you plan to do only minimal quilting, use a tiny print background fabric instead of muslin. The print fabric will create an interesting surface design.

Approximate Size

73½ inches square

Materials Required

- 5 yards of muslin for blocks and border
- 1¾ yards of red fabric for flowers, border, and binding
- 1¼ yards of green fabric for leaves and wreath bands
- ¾ yard of gold fabric for flower centers
- 4¼ yards of fabric for backing
- Queen/double-size batting

Preparing the Appliqué

The quilt blocks are exactly the same as the blocks made for the Rose Wreath Pillow project. Following the directions beginning on page 70, make nine appliqué blocks.

Cutting the Muslin Setting Pieces

1. Cut four 14-inch muslin squares for the alternate blocks.

2. For the side setting triangles, cut two 20⅝-inch squares. Cut each square diagonally both ways to get eight triangles.

3. For the corner setting triangles, cut two 13½-inch squares, and cut each square in half diagonally.

Assembling the Quilt Top

1. Arrange the blocks in diagonal rows as shown in **Diagram 1**.

2. Join the blocks in each diagonal row, pressing the seam allowances in alternate directions from row to row.

Quilt Diagram

Diagram 1

3. Referring to **Diagram 2**, add the side setting triangles on the ends of each row. Line up the right angle of the setting triangle with a corner of the appliqué block so that the hypotenuse (longest edge) will become the outside edge of the quilt. The tips of the triangles will extend beyond the quilt blocks in both directions, as shown in **Diagram 3**. Stitch, and press the seam allowances toward the triangles.

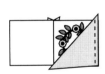

Diagram 2

Diagram 3

4. Referring to **Diagram 4**, join the diagonal rows together.

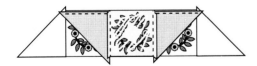

Diagram 4

5. With right sides together, sew the four corner setting triangles to the quilt top as shown in **Diagram 5**. The hypotenuse is on the bias on these triangles and will be inside. The lengthwise and crosswise grains will be on the outside edge. Square off the quilt top by trimming any excess.

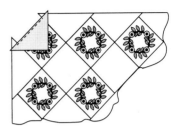

Diagram 5

Adding the Borders and Finishing the Quilt

1. Measure the quilt top, and cut two 1¼-inch red border strips to the needed length. Add the borders to two opposite sides of the quilt top, and press. Cut the remaining two strips to the correct length, add them to the sides, and press.

2. Measure the quilt top again, and cut two 7½-inch muslin border strips to the needed length. Add these to the quilt top in the same manner as for the red border. Cut the remaining two muslin strips to length, and add them to the quilt top.

3. Layer the quilt top with batting and backing, and baste. Quilt as desired. The quilt shown in the photo has traditional feathered circles quilted in the alternate blocks. A ¼-inch French-fold binding completes the quilt. See page 10 for complete directions on making and adding a French-fold binding.

PATTERNS THAT BEAR REPEATING

Pattern pieces that can be repeated in a number of projects without ever looking the same are a real treat. The patterns in this chapter are used more than once in the book; they are presented in their simplest form here, with complete directions. One reason for doing this is to save space by eliminating unnecessary repetition of directions or pattern pieces. By saving space, we could include more projects in the book. An equally important reason is to emphasize that these items can be adapted to nearly any theme in the book. Even if we haven't shown it, you can make the adaptation, expanding the usefulness of the book.

BASIC CHRISTMAS STOCKING

There are several mantle-size Christmas stockings in the book. If you have another pattern that you would prefer to use, most of the stocking designs can be adapted. These instructions are for a quilted muslin stocking with a bright red cuff, as shown in the photo. Make one for the person who can't get home for Christmas and is unexpectedly spending the holiday with you. Use a stocking to "wrap" a hostess gift at a holiday dinner party. You could even make one to fill with greens for a door decoration.

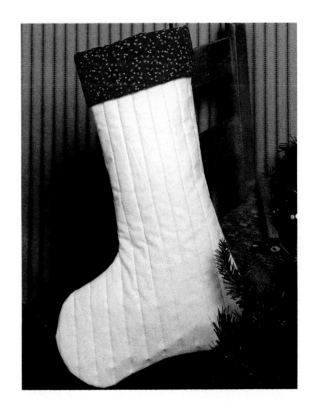

◄ *Ornaments shown are* (clockwise from top): *Quilted Diamond, page 219; Homespun Star, page 217; Basic Star, page 84; Quilted Diamond, page 219; Homespun Heart and String-Pieced Heart, page 217; and Small Stocking* (center), *page 84.*

Approximate Size

11 inches wide at the toe × 16 inches long

Materials Required

- ½ yard of muslin for stocking front, backing, and lining
- 8½ × 19-inch piece of red print fabric for cuff
- ½ yard of batting
- 3¾ × 18-inch piece of paper-backed fusible material
- 6-inch piece of ribbon or café curtain ring for hanger

Toe Pointing

Finger pointing is a definite no-no in well-mannered families, but toe pointing, as it relates to Christmas stockings, is a very important issue. My personal preference is to have the toes on the fronts of all the stockings point left, and that's the direction that all the stockings in this book point. If you are making stockings to go with existing stockings, you will probably want to determine which direction the toes in your family point, because it is definitely more attractive to have all the toes on one mantle pointing in the same direction! (Of course, in some families, individuality is more important than conformity, and if that's the case with your family, disregard this whole paragraph.)

The point is (pun intended), Christmas stockings are asymmetrical designs. If you care which way the toe points, spend a little time at each stage to make sure that the finished stocking will point in the desired direction.

Making the Stocking

1. Trace around the pattern pieces beginning on page 80, carefully joining the sections as shown in the **Stocking Layout**. For the basic stocking, you need to trace the outline only. The grid printed on the pattern is used for the Lafayette Orange Peel Stocking on page 170, and the quilting design is used for the Elegant Trapunto Stocking on page 240.

2. With the toe of the pattern facing left, cut one piece of batting and two pieces of muslin, one for the lining and one for the stocking front. Sandwich the batting between the lining and the stocking front, and baste around the outside using a ¼-inch seam

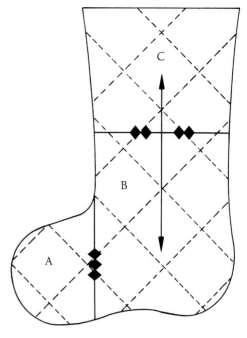

Stocking Layout

allowance. In the same manner, cut one lining, batting, and backing with the toe of the pattern facing right. Layer the pieces, and baste them together. The toes of the front and back should point in opposite directions. Quilt the sections, if desired.

3. Place the stocking pieces right sides together. Starting at the top of the seam on the toe side of the stocking, stitch all the way around to the notch on the heel side. Leave the seam open above the notch for ease in adding the cuff.

4. Trim the seam allowances, and clip the curves. Turn the stocking right side out, and press.

Adding the Cuff

1. The cuff folds to create a self-lining. Cut a piece of cuff fabric 8½ × 19 inches.

2. The batting for the cuff is approximately half the width of the cuff and does not include a seam allowance. Cut a piece of paper-backed fusible material 3¾ × 18 inches, and fuse it to the batting using a pressing cloth or a very low-temperature iron. Using the fusible material as a pattern, cut the piece of batting. Remove the paper, position the batting fusible side down on the wrong side of the cuff fabric, ½ inch in from three edges, and fuse. Press under ¼

inch on the opposite long edge of the cuff, as shown in **Diagram 1**.

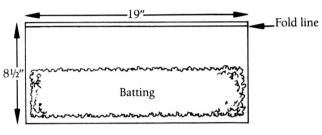

Diagram 1

3. The stocking cuff is 1 inch longer than the stocking opening. To ease the cuff, run a machine basting stitch ¼ inch from the long edge, next to the batting. Gather the cuff very slightly. Place the eased edge of the cuff right sides together with the top of the stocking, and stitch. Press the seam allowances toward the top of the stocking.

4. Turn the stocking so that the wrong side is out again, and finish the back seam. Extend the seam through the unfolded cuff, as shown in **Diagram 2**.

5. Fold the cuff down over the batting so that the pressed edge covers the seam allowances, and hand or machine stitch it in place. Turn the stocking right side out. Press the seam. Fold the cuff so that it stands up about ⅜ inch above the top of the stocking and then comes back down onto the stocking.

6. Add the necessary ribbon loop or café curtain ring to the back of the stocking for hanging.

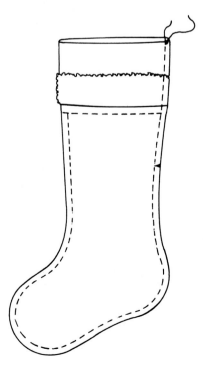

Diagram 2

Extend ¼″ seam allowance.

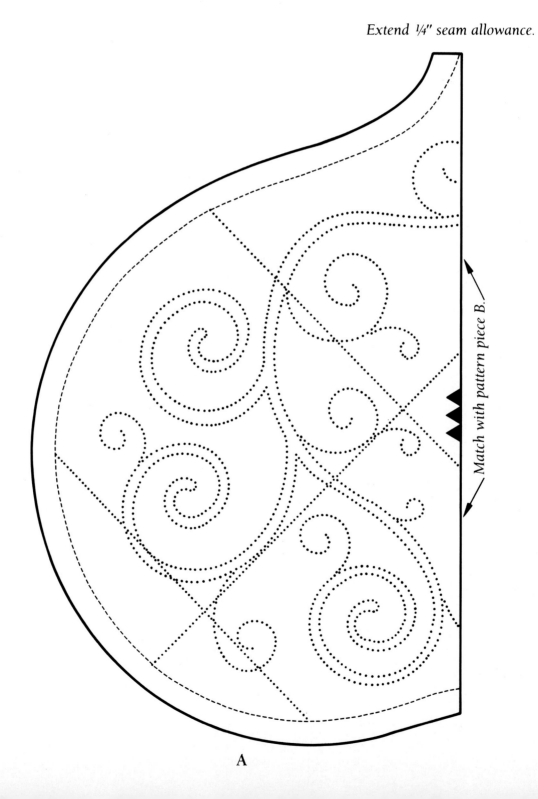

A

Match with pattern piece C.

B

Match with pattern piece B.

C

TRIO OF ORNAMENTS

These versatile ornaments are fun, easy, and a great place to experiment with colors, fabrics, techniques, or embellishments. In addition to the basic interpretation here, you'll find them string pieced in homespun fabrics on page 217 and crazy quilted and embellished on page 250. The stocking ornament has an open top just like the Basic Christmas Stocking on page 77, making it a perfect place to tuck small gifts or decorative tinsel or tissue. A heart and a jaunty little star complete the trio.

SMALL STOCKING ORNAMENT

Approximate Size

4½ inches wide at the toe × 5½ inches long

Materials Required

(for one ornament)

- ¼ yard of muslin for stocking front, backing, lining, and cuff
- 7 × 12-inch scrap of batting
- 3 × 8-inch scrap of paper-backed fusible material
- 14-inch piece of ⅛-inch-wide cream ribbon
- 10-inch piece of invisible thread for loop hanger
- ½-inch-diameter pearl button

Making the Stocking

The stocking construction is the same as for the Basic Christmas Stocking on page 77. Referring to the basic stocking directions, cut the stocking front, backing, lining, and cuff pieces using the stocking ornament pattern and the cuff pattern on pages 85 and 86, and assemble the stocking ornament. Add the ribbon and the button as desired. Use invisible thread to make a loop hanger.

HEART ORNAMENT

The heart and star ornaments are constructed in exactly the same manner, so the directions are provided just once.

Approximate Size

4½ × 4 inches

Materials Required

(for one ornament)

- 6 × 12-inch scrap of muslin for heart front and backing
- 6-inch square of batting
- Polyester fiberfill for stuffing
- 15-inch piece of ⅛-inch-diameter cream rat tail cord
- 10-inch piece of invisible thread for loop hanger
- ¾-inch-diameter pearl button

STAR ORNAMENT

Approximate Size

4½ × 5 inches

Materials Required

(for one ornament)

- 7 × 14-inch scrap of muslin for star front and backing
- 7-inch square of batting
- Polyester fiberfill for stuffing
- 12-inch piece of ⅜-inch-wide cream ribbon
- 10-inch piece of invisible thread for loop hanger
- ¾-inch-diameter pearl button

Making the Ornament

1. Prepare the fabric before cutting. Layer a piece of muslin and batting, loosely cut, approximately 6 inches square for the heart, or 7 inches square for the star, and baste the layers together. Machine stipple quilt as desired. See page 9 for directions on stipple quilting.

2. Make a template for the ornament using one of the patterns on pages 85 or 86. Trace the ornament pattern onto the quilted fabric, and cut out the ornament.

3. To make a pieced back for easy turning and finishing, fold a piece of muslin approximately 6 inches square for the heart, or 7 inches square for the star, in half. Using a ⅜-inch seam allowance, stitch in from each side along the fold, leaving a 2-inch opening in the center. Trim the seam allowance to ¼ inch, cutting off the fold. Press the seam allowance to one side.

4. Place the back and the quilted front right sides together. Stitch around the outside edge of the ornament. Trim the seam allowance, and clip the curves. Turn the ornament right side out through the center back opening. Stuff the ornament, and slip stitch the opening closed.

5. Add the rat tail cord or ribbon and the button as desired. Use invisible thread to make a loop hanger.

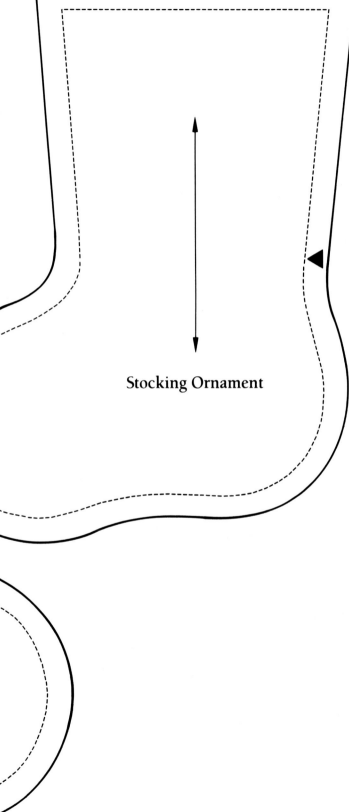

Stocking Ornament

Heart Ornament

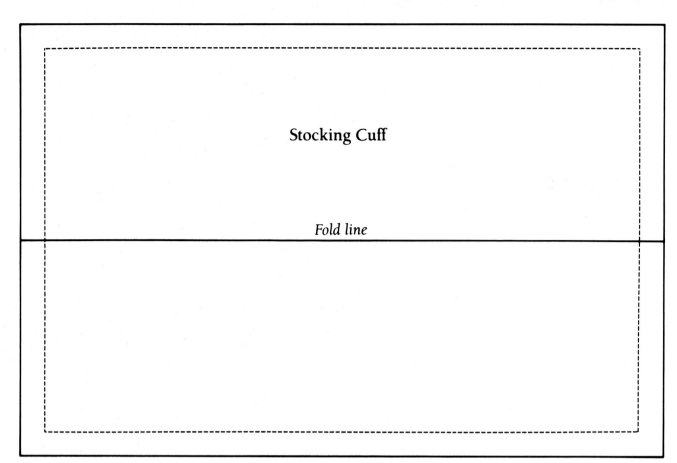

Stocking Cuff

Fold line

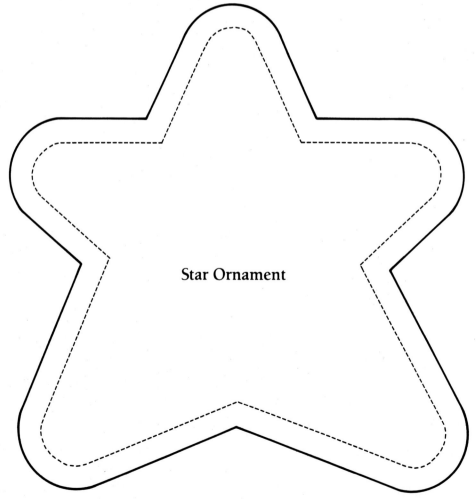

Star Ornament

MY LADIES' VEST

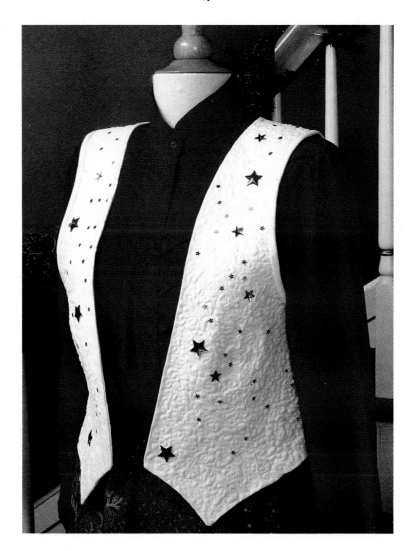

The basic vest with its flattering princess lines features beautiful front panels just waiting to be adorned. There is also an optional yoke design on the back, providing another palette for embellishment. The basic vest shown in the photo is made from muslin that has been machine stipple quilted and highlighted with stars. Some of the stars are sewn in place by hand, but most of them are attached with washable fabric glue. You could easily add other trims in the same way.

Although this vest is completely lined and layered with low-loft quilt batting, the front and the back side sections can be made without batting, which is recommended when using a heavy fabric. The armholes can be finished with or without bias binding. The optional elasticized center back can be used to create a snug waistline fit and is an easy way to make size adjustments for figures that are on the small side of small, medium, or large.

Sizes

Small (6–8), Medium (10–12), Large (14–16)

Materials Required

- 1⅛ yards of muslin for basic vest
- 1⅛ yards of fabric for lining
- 1⅛ yards of batting
- Matching machine quilting thread
- 10-inch piece of ½-inch-wide elastic for center back (optional)
- Button for center front closure (optional)
- Decorative star sequins and fabric glue (optional)

Cutting the Fabrics and Batting

1. The vest pattern pieces are all provided full size beginning on page 92. There are 11 pattern pieces; study the **Pattern Assembly Diagram** to see how the pieces fit together (including the optional yoke). Trace the pattern pieces, being careful to trace the correct size each time. Referring to the **Pattern Assembly Diagram**, join the sections carefully.

If using the optional yoke, trace the full back pattern, and cut the lining and batting before cutting apart the pattern and adding seam allowances for the yoke design. Only the surface fabric for the back is cut in two pieces. If you plan to attach the yoke, read the directions in "Adding the Optional Yoke" on the opposite page *before* sewing the vest pieces together.

2. Cut two vest fronts, two side fronts, two side backs, and one back from muslin or surface fabric, lining fabric, and batting. The pattern pieces include ⅝-inch seam allowances; use ⅝-inch seam allowances throughout the vest construction.

Sewing the Basic Vest

1. Begin with the muslin or surface fabric. With right sides together, pin the right side front to the right front at the princess seam. See **Diagram 1**. Stitch, clipping the seam as necessary, and press the seam open. Clipping into the seam allowance along the curve helps the seam to lie flat when pressed. In the same manner, sew the left side front to the left front.

2. In the same manner, pin the back to the right side back at the princess seam. Stitch, clip as necessary, and press the seam open. Repeat, sewing the left side back to the back.

3. Sew the two fronts to the back at the shoulders.

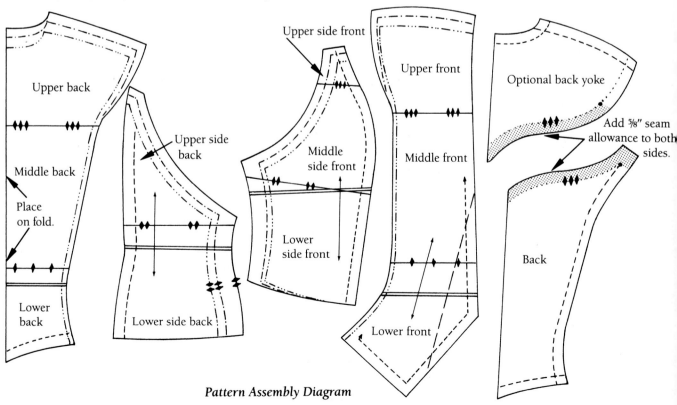

Pattern Assembly Diagram

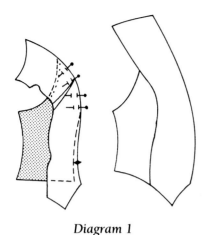

Diagram 1

Adding the Optional Yoke

There is really no reason to use the optional back yoke unless you plan to embellish the front and the yoke. The best way to attach the yoke is to topstitch it in place. Depending on the style of embellishment, you may want to have the design flow across the shoulder line. If so, attach the yoke to the front pieces, and embellish before joining the rest of the vest pieces together. When the pieces are joined at the princess and side seams, press under the seam allowance on the back yoke, and topstitch the yoke in place.

If it isn't important that the embellishment flow across the shoulder line, you can topstitch the yoke to the back piece first, then join the pieces at the shoulders.

Layering the Lining and Batting

1. Layer the matching batting piece against the wrong side of each of the seven lining pieces. Baste the layers together around the outside edges.

2. Sew the layered pieces together in the manner described in "Sewing the Basic Vest" on the opposite page. Use ⅝-inch seam allowances. To reduce bulk in the seams, trim the batting very close to the seam allowances, and trim the lining seam allowances to about ⅜ inch.

Adding the Lining to the Vest

1. To prepare the lining, fold over the ⅝-inch seam allowances at the side seams, and press.

2. Place the vest and the lining right sides together, matching seams and aligning all raw edges. Sew around the outside edges through all layers, using a ⅝-inch seam. If the vest is being made *with* bias binding on the armholes, leave the armholes and side seams open, as shown in **Diagram 2**. If the vest is being made *without* armhole binding, stitch the armholes, but leave the side seams open for turning, as shown in **Diagram 3**.

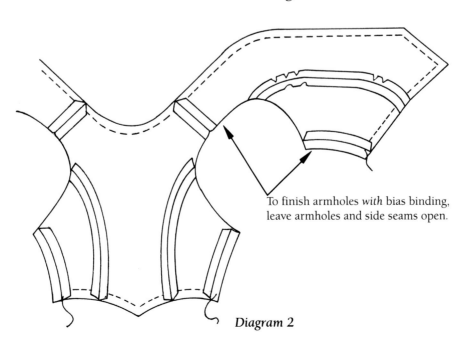

To finish armholes *with* bias binding, leave armholes and side seams open.

Diagram 2

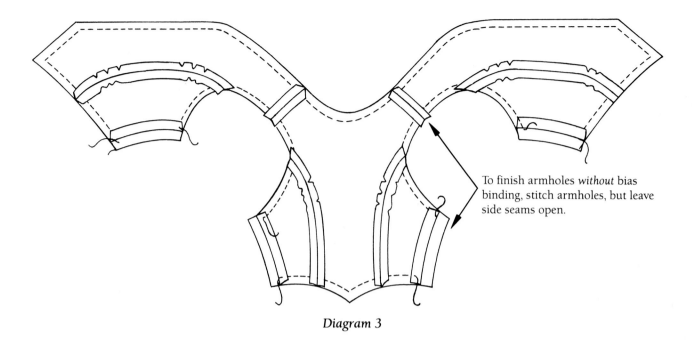

To finish armholes *without* bias binding, stitch armholes, but leave side seams open.

Diagram 3

3. Trim and clip the seams. Turn the vest right side out.

4. Stitch the underarm seams of the vest and the batting together, as shown in **Diagram 4**. Press the seam open, and tuck each side of the seam allowance behind the lining on that side. Close the underarm seam of the lining by hand.

5. If bias binding will not be added, skip to "Finishing the Vest" on the opposite page. If bias binding is to be added, stay stitch around the entire armhole a scant ⅝ inch from the raw edge.

Adding the Bias Binding

1. Use ⅜-inch double-fold bias binding to finish the raw edges of the vest armholes. Cut bias strips 2 inches wide, as shown in **Diagram 5**. Sew the strips together as shown in **Diagram 6** to obtain the length needed for each armhole. A medium-size vest requires approximately 35 inches of bias binding per armhole.

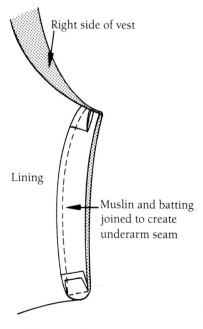

Right side of vest

Lining

Muslin and batting joined to create underarm seam

Diagram 4

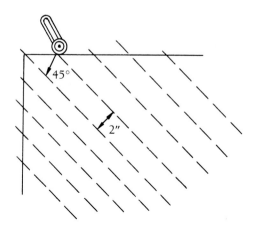

45°

2"

Diagram 5

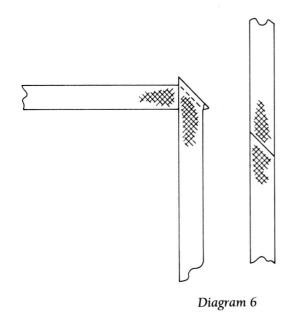

Diagram 6

2. Press the bias strip in half lengthwise, wrong sides together. Pin the strip to the right side of the vest armhole, raw edges even. Machine stitch using a ⅝-inch seam allowance.

3. Turn the folded edge of the binding to the inside of the vest armhole, enclosing the seam allowance. Slip stitch it in place.

Finishing the Vest

1. Quilt as desired. The vest shown was machine quilted in a rather tight stipple pattern.

2. If you've decided to include a button and buttonhole, add them now.

Adding Elastic to the Center Back

1. If you want a more snug fit, add elastic to the back of the vest. Cut a 2 × 5-inch rectangle of lining fabric. Fold under ¼ inch on each short end. Then fold under another ¼ inch, and stitch. Fold under ¼ inch on both long sides, and press. Pin the rectangle in place on the inside of the vest at the center back waistline.

2. Topstitch along the two long sides of the rectangle. (Yes, the stitching will show through to the right side of the vest.) Stitch down the lengthwise center of the casing.

3. Cut two 5-inch lengths of ½-inch-wide elastic. Use a safety pin in one end to run an elastic piece through each of the two tunnels you have created in the casing. Secure one end of the elastic with stitching, and adjust the length of elastic until you have created the snugness desired. Then secure the second end.

A Special Touch

As a final touch, assorted star sequins were added to the vest. These can be hand stitched or glued in place with fabric glue.

Lengthen or shorten here.

Buttonhole

Center front

Lower Front

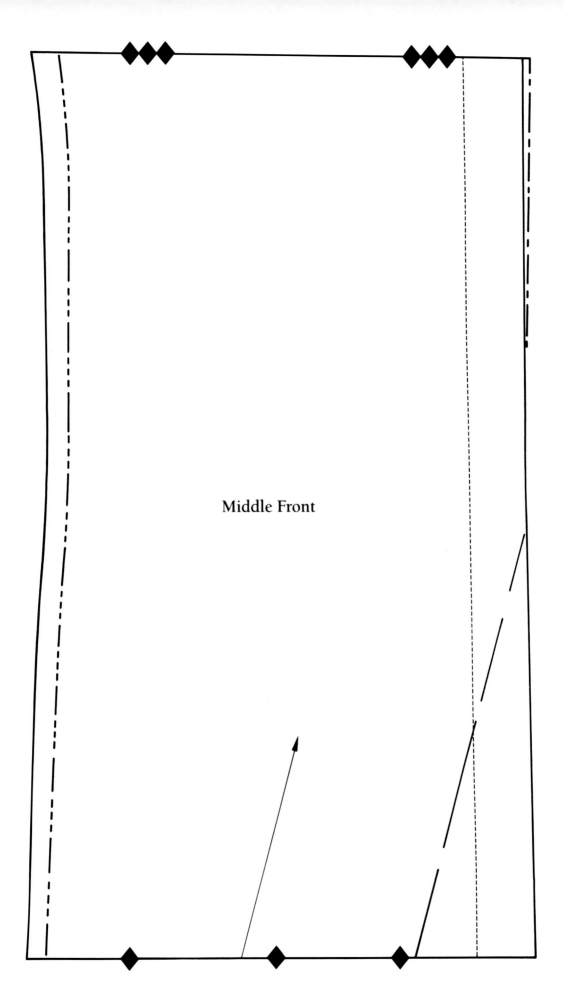

Middle Front

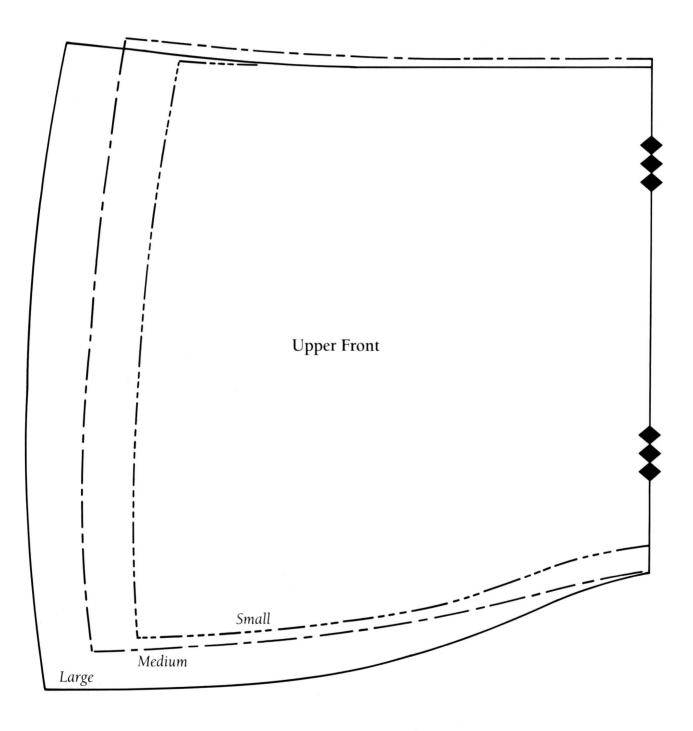

Upper Front

Small

Medium

Large

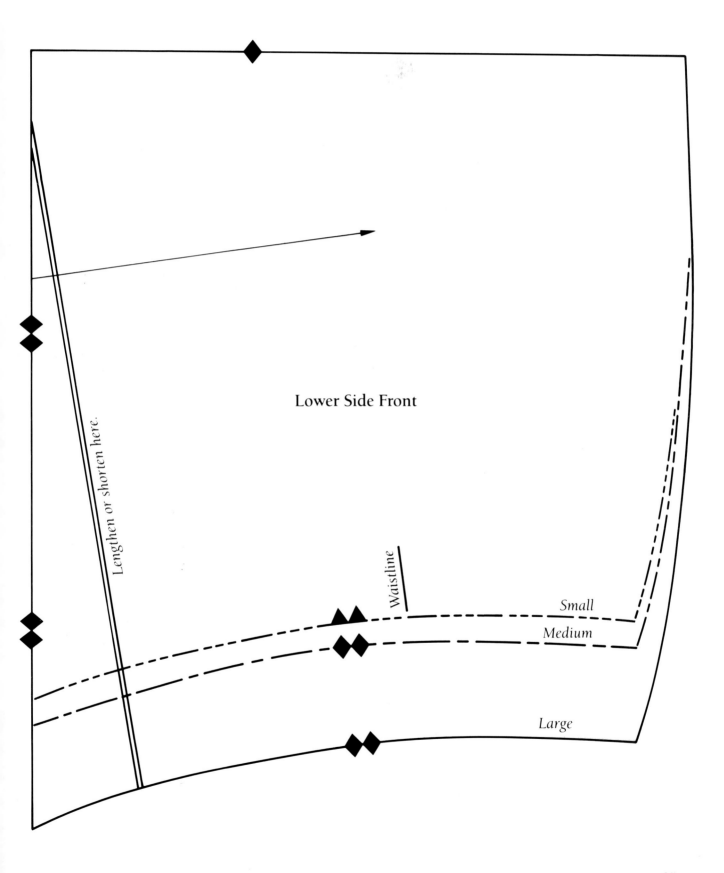

Lower Side Front

Lengthen or shorten here.

Waistline

Small

Medium

Large

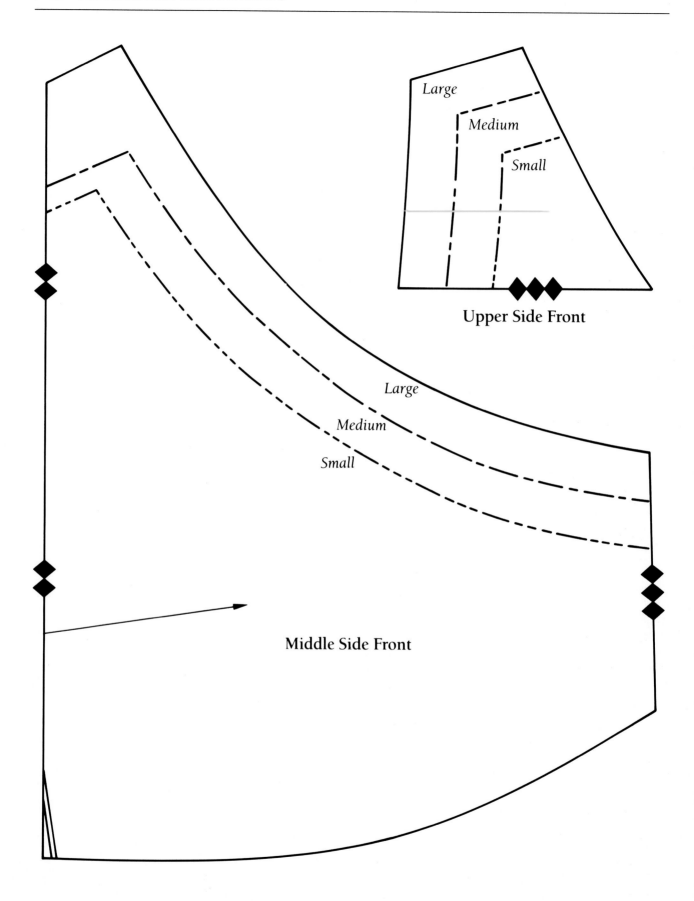

Large

Medium

Small

Upper Side Front

Large

Medium

Small

Middle Side Front

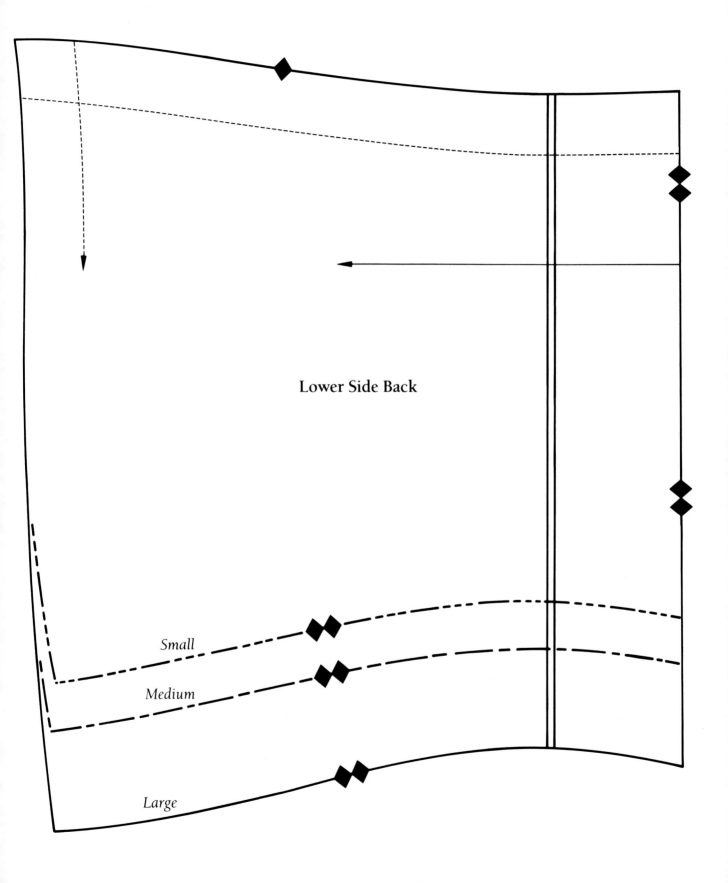

Lower Side Back

Small

Medium

Large

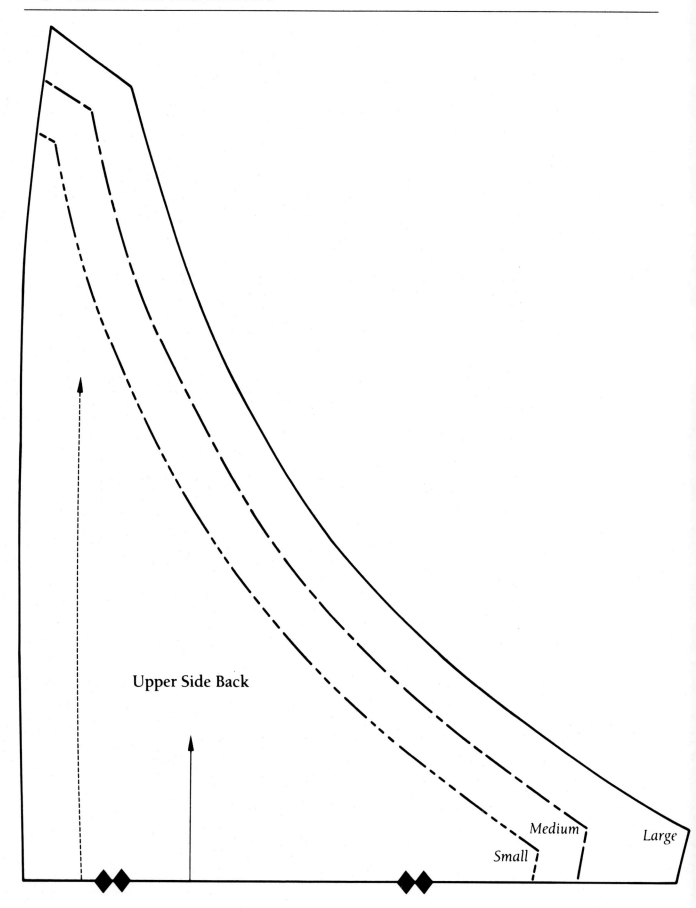

Upper Side Back

Medium

Large

Small

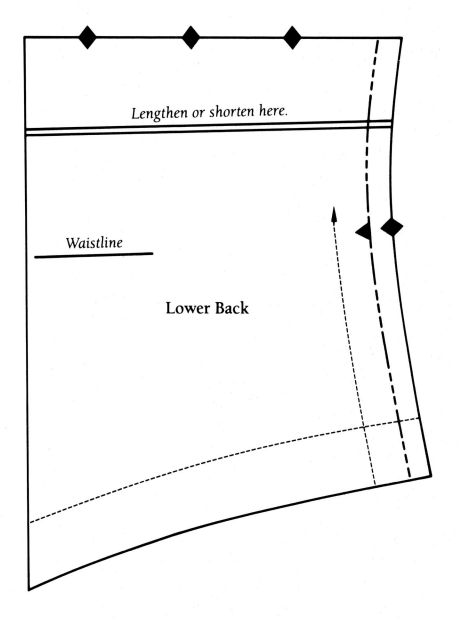

Lengthen or shorten here.

Waistline

Lower Back

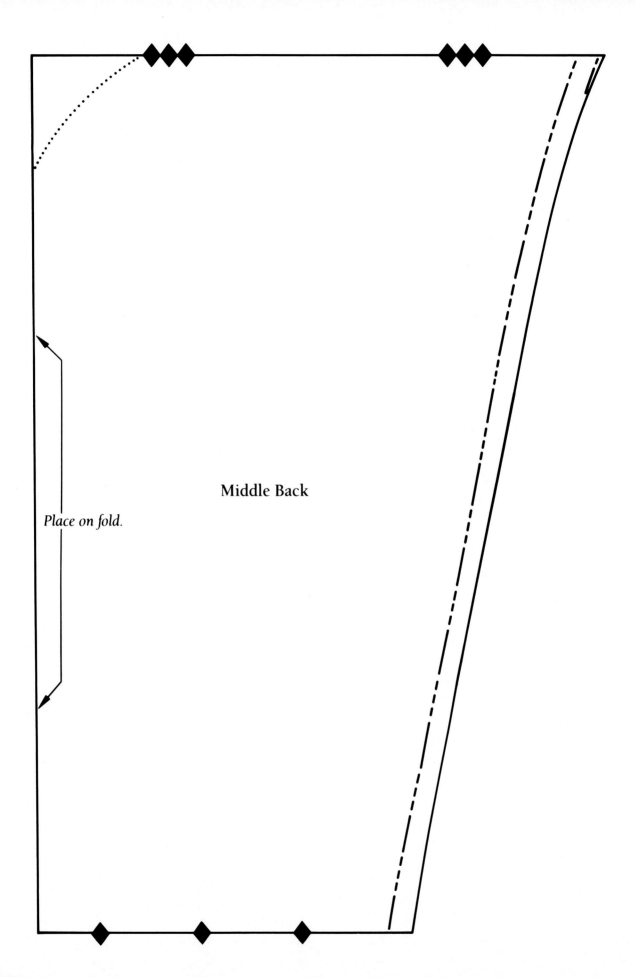

Middle Back

Place on fold.

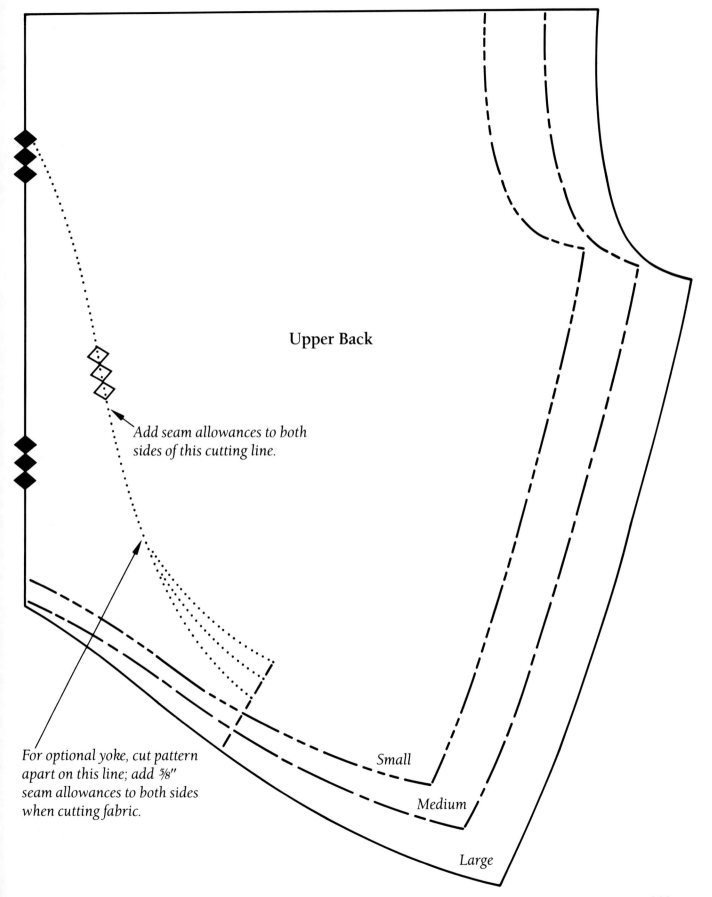

Upper Back

Add seam allowances to both
sides of this cutting line.

For optional yoke, cut pattern
apart on this line; add ⅝″
seam allowances to both sides
when cutting fabric.

Small

Medium

Large

ALL THROUGH THE HOUSE

HOLIDAY TABLECLOTH WITH STAR TOPPER

Small round tables with floor-length tablecloths have become a staple in home decorating. In my design, red piping trim and a self-fabric, shirred and corded ruffle add pizzazz to a basic round tablecloth. The Eight-Pointed Star topper is a special festive touch hinting that there is a quilter in residence.

Approximate Size

Tablecloth: 72 inches in diameter, including shirred, corded ruffle (fits a 24-inch-high table with a 24-inch-diameter top)
Star Topper: 44 inches across

Materials Required

- 5¼ yards of black print fabric for tablecloth and ruffle
- 4 yards of fabric for tablecloth lining

◄ *Projects shown are the Holly Basket Miniature Wallhanging (top left), page 160; Holiday Tablecloth with Star Topper (left), this page; and Eight-Pointed Star Pillows (right), page 111.*

- 1½ yards of fabric for star lining
- ¾ yard of red print fabric for star topper
- ¾ yard of green print fabric for star topper
- ⅜ yard of red print fabric for piping trim
- 1¼ yards of fusible fleece
- 6⅛ yards of ¾-inch jumbo piping cord
- 6⅛ yards of ¼-inch piping cord
- 8 tassles or bells to embellish star topper (optional)

Cutting the Tablecloth

The yardage requirements and cutting instructions with this project are for a floor-length tablecloth with a shirred, corded ruffle designed to fit a 24-inch-high table with a 24-inch-diameter top. However, you can easily adapt the size to fit any round table. To determine the amount of fabric needed to fit your table, see "Estimating Fabric Requirements for a Tablecloth" on page 108.

This tablecloth has a center seam. If you prefer to avoid a center seam, you can make the tablecloth with a center panel and two side panels. See "Making a Center-Panel Tablecloth" on page 105 for instructions.

1. The tablecloth is cut in two half-circle pieces, as shown in **Diagram 1**. First, trim the selvages. Then, with the fabric opened to full width, measure 35 inches in from one end of the fabric to find the center point of one-half of the tablecloth. Mark the center point.

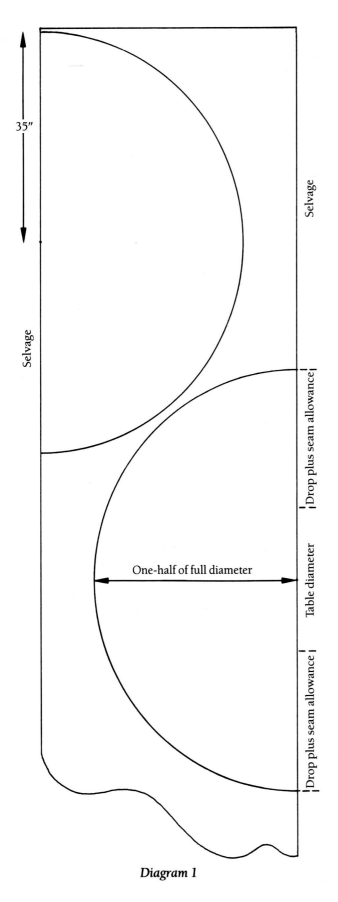

Diagram 1

2. Using a pencil and a piece of string, make a compass to mark the cutting line for the tablecloth. Tie one end of the string to the pencil, measure 34½ inches along the string, and mark the string at that point. Cut the string a few inches beyond the mark, and secure that marked spot on the loose end at the center point marked on the fabric. Referring to **Diagram 2**, pull the string taut and move the pencil in an arc to mark the outer edge of the tablecloth 34½ inches from the center point. Cut the tablecloth on the marked line. Mark and cut the second half of the tablecloth in the same manner.

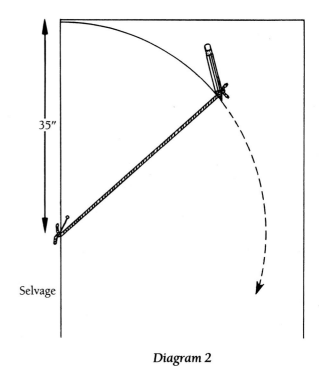

Diagram 2

3. Sew the tablecloth halves together along the center seam using a ¼-inch seam allowance.

Making the Piping Trim

Note: The zipper foot is recommended for all the steps involved in making the piping trim and the corded ruffle. Quarter-inch seam allowances are assumed in these steps, but please do a test to determine the best seam allowance for your zipper foot. The foot will run more smoothly if there is fabric

MAKING A CENTER-PANEL TABLECLOTH

The same type of tablecloth (to fit a 24-inch-diameter table) can be made without a center seam by using a full-width fabric panel for the center and half-width panels on each side. Cut the center panel 72 inches long (the total diameter of the finished tablecloth plus 4 inches extra). From the remaining piece of fabric, cut two 16 × 72-inch panels. (This assumes that the full-width center panel, minus the selvages, is 41 inches wide. If the center panel is wider or narrower than 41 inches, adjust the cut width of the side panels so that the three panels together equal 72 inches in width.) Sew the narrow fabric panels onto each side of the full-width panel with ¼-inch seam allowances, forming a square. Fold the square into fourths, and pin the layers together. Use a string-and-pencil compass to mark a circle with a 34-inch radius.

under the entire foot, so it may be necessary for you to allow slightly different seam allowances.

1. The piping trim is added to the outer edge (circumference) of the tablecloth before the corded ruffle is attached. The tablecloth is now 68 inches across, which is approximately 220 inches, or 6⅛ yards, around the circumference. You can double-check the circumference of your tablecloth by multiplying the diameter of the tablecloth, in inches, by 3.14. (Use 3.25 for easier calculations and to get a little extra fabric "just in case.") Divide by 36 inches to get the amount in yards.

2. Referring to **Diagram 3**, cut 1⅝-inch-wide bias strips from the red print fabric. (Cut the strips slightly wider if your zipper foot requires a larger

seam allowance.) Join the strips to obtain the 220 inches (6⅛ yards) needed to cover the cord.

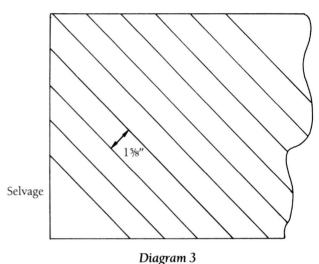

Diagram 3

3. Fold the bias strip around the ¼-inch piping cord, with wrong sides together and raw edges even. Use a zipper foot to machine baste the fabric snugly around the cord, as shown in **Diagram 4**. Stretching the fabric gently while sewing helps the finished piping trim to lie smoothly.

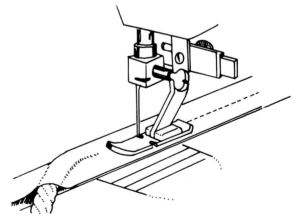

Diagram 4

4. Pin the piping trim to the right side of the tablecloth, matching raw edges. Baste it in place.

5. Where the ends meet, overlap the covered cord and bend it slightly so that the cording ends run

off the edge and are sewn into the basting. See **Diagram 5**. Trim the excess.

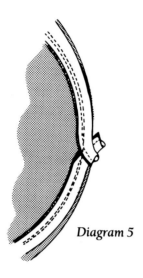

Diagram 5

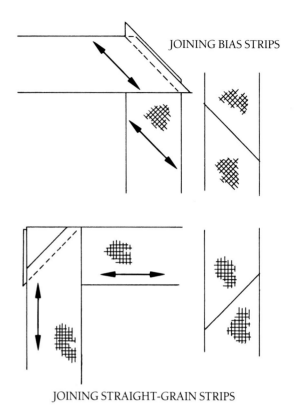

JOINING BIAS STRIPS

JOINING STRAIGHT-GRAIN STRIPS

Diagram 6

Making the Shirred, Corded Ruffle

1. Cut 6-inch-wide strips from the black print fabric. You'll need to cut a lot; the total length of fabric needed to cover the cord is twice the length of the cord. The strips can be cut either on the straight grain or on the bias; decide which type strip you prefer to work with, and cut all the strips the same way. Join the strips as necessary to obtain 440 inches (12¼ yards). Use a diagonal seam whether using bias or straight-grain strips; the seam will be much less obvious in the finished ruffle than a straight seam would be. As shown in **Diagram 6**, the finished seams will appear the same. The main differences are the direction of the grain and the excess to be trimmed when joining straight-grain fabric strips.

2. Fold the ¾-inch jumbo piping cord in half, and mark the midpoint with a pen or marker. Fold the fabric strip in half crosswise, and mark the midpoint with a pin. These marks will act as guides when you are gathering the ruffle. Add additional guidepoints if desired.

3. Fold the fabric strip around the cord, with wrong sides together and raw edges even. Pin across the end of the fabric and cord to secure the cord as the fabric is shirred. Using a zipper foot and a ¼-inch

seam allowance, stitch the fabric around the cord, creating a fabric tube. Approximately every 6 inches, stop stitching, leave the needle in the fabric, and raise the presser foot. Shirr the stitched fabric tube by gently pulling the cord toward you while pushing the fabric tube toward the secured end. See **Diagram 7**. Force the cord into the outer edge of the tube near the fold. Keep an eye on the marks you made on the fabric and the cord; keeping the guidepoints matched up will help you gauge the gathers and eliminate a lot of readjusting later.

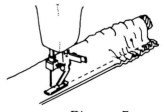

Diagram 7

Continue stitching and shirring until the entire strip of fabric is gathered. Secure the end with a pin through the fabric and cord.

4. Pin the ruffle to the right side of the tablecloth on top of the narrow piping trim, matching raw edges. Machine baste it in place, leaving both ends of the ruffle unattached.

5. Trim the ends of the cord so they butt together; there should be no overlap. Where the ends of the cord meet, sew them together using a whip stitch. Fold the raw edge of one end of the fabric tube to the inside, and enclose the remaining end with the folded edge, as shown in **Diagram 8**. Slip stitch the ends of the fabric tube together.

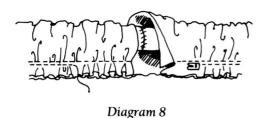

Diagram 8

Lining the Tablecloth

1. For the lining, use the same string compass to mark the fabric in the same manner as for the tablecloth. Cut out the pieces and join the panels, leaving a 12-inch opening in the seam for turning.

2. Place the tablecloth and the lining right sides together, with the piping trim and ruffle sandwiched between the two layers. Stitch around the circumference of the tablecloth with a ¼-inch seam allowance, sewing through all layers. The seam allowances for the piping trim and the ruffle will be caught in this seam as well, but check to make sure the trims themselves are not being caught. Trim the seam allowances, and clip the curves.

3. Turn the tablecloth right side out through the opening in the lining seam. Slip stitch the opening closed.

Cutting the Star Pieces

1. Trace pattern pieces A and B on pages 109 and 110. Referring to **Diagram 9**, carefully join the two pattern pieces to create one-half of the diamond

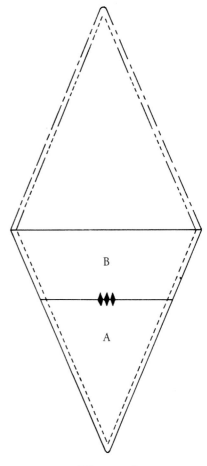

Diagram 9

shape. Use this as a pattern to create the other half of the diamond shape, and join the halves as shown.

2. Using the completed pattern, cut four diamonds from red print fabric and four from green print fabric.

3. After you have cut all the fabric diamonds you will need, trim the seam allowance from the pattern, and use the pattern to cut eight finished-size diamonds from fusible fleece.

4. Fuse the fleece to the wrong side of the fabric diamonds, making sure to stay inside the fabric seam allowances.

Piecing the Star

Arrange the diamonds to form an eight-pointed star, alternating red and green fabrics. Referring to **Diagram 10**, stitch the diamonds right sides together, taking care not to catch the fleece in the seam allowances. Join pairs of diamonds, then pairs of pairs, and then halves of the star. When stitching the halves together, stitch from the center out.

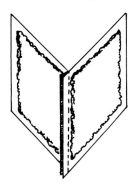

Diagram 10

Lining the Star

1. The star should just about fit on 45-inch-wide fabric. To make sure your lining is the right size, cut a 45-inch length and lay it out flat. Place the pieced star on top of the fabric, and make sure the entire star fits on the lining. If it does not, add a small strip along one edge as necessary.

2. Fold the lining fabric right sides together so that the selvages are even. Stitch along the fold with a seam allowance slightly larger than ¼ inch, leaving a 12-inch opening in the center for turning. Trim the tiniest amount at the fold to create two seam allowances. Unfold the fabric, and press the seam allowances to one side.

3. Place the pieced star right sides together with the lining, having the lining opening centered on the center seam of the star. Pin the star in position. Do not cut away the excess lining.

4. Referring to **Diagram 11**, stitch with a ¼-inch seam allowance around the star points at the edge of the fleece, beginning and ending at the center seam. Trim the excess fabric even with the star, clip at the angles, and trim at the points on seam allowances.

5. Turn the star right side out through the lining opening, and gently poke out the star points with a blunt-ended object. Slip stitch the opening closed.

Finishing the Star

Topstitch ½ inch from the edge of the star, all the way around. Add tassles to the star points. For a fun, less formal finish, attach large bells to the star points in place of the tassles.

ESTIMATING FABRIC REQUIREMENTS FOR A TABLECLOTH

*For a rough estimate of fabric requirements for a round table, first measure the height of the table and the diameter of the top. Multiply four times the desired drop (the distance from the top to the hem), and add twice the tabletop diameter, hem, and seam allowances. If working in inches, divide by 36 to find the number of yards. Cut the pieces from the fabric as shown in **Diagram 1** on page 104.*

It's easy to see that variations in table height might result in a little less fabric being required, or that cutting matching ruffles might require a little more. For plaids, stripes, or large prints, add three design-repeat lengths to the yardage requirements as a good safety measure.

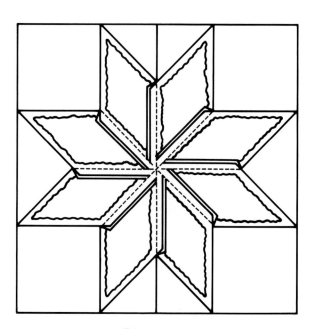

Diagram 11

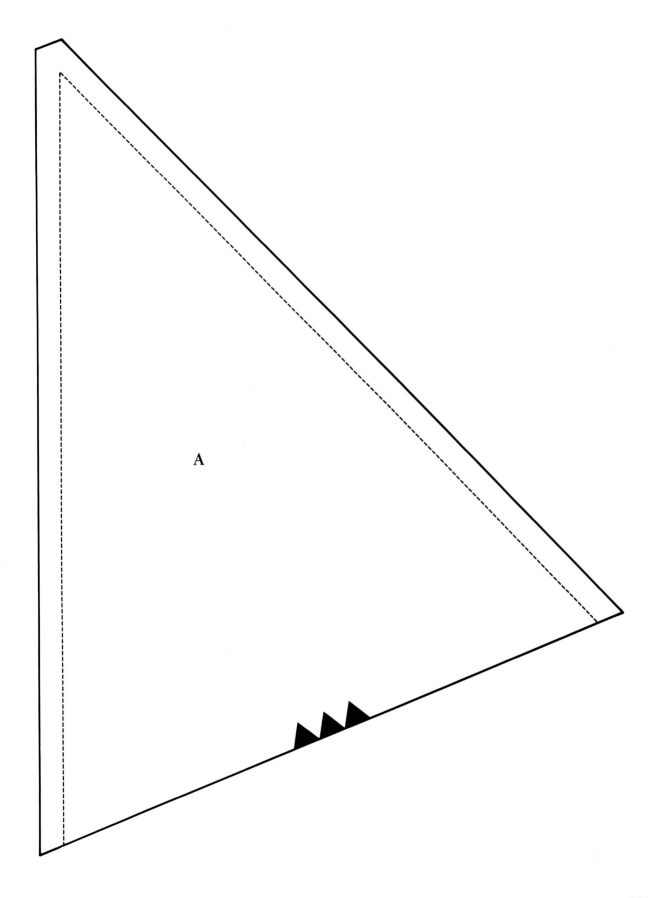

A

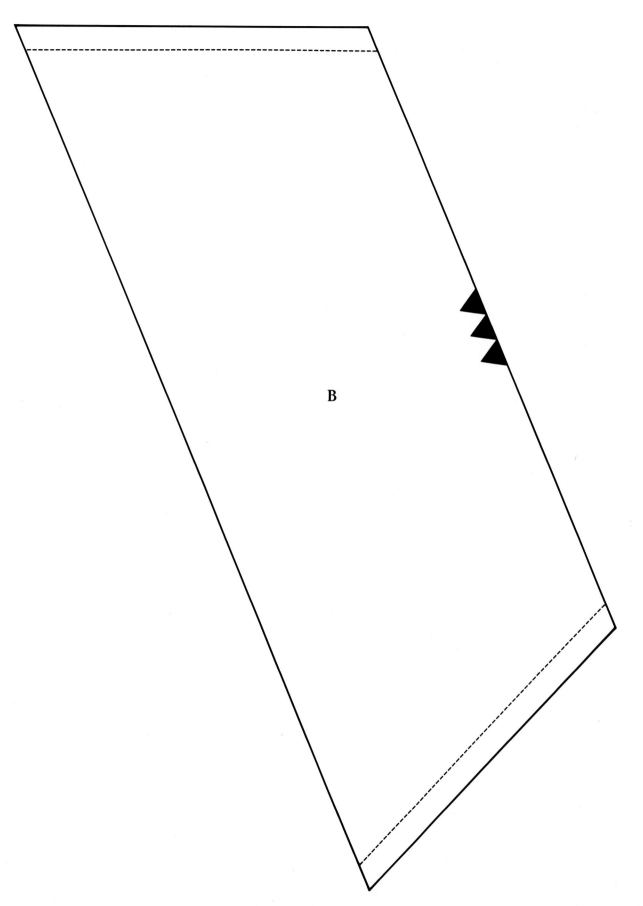

B

EIGHT-POINTED STAR PILLOWS

The first pillow (on the right in the photo) features a shirred and corded ruffle just like the one on the Holiday Tablecloth with Star Topper on page 102. The Eight-Pointed Star is set at an unusual angle and fused in position. The star could be appliquéd instead of fused, but piecing it at that angle wouldn't be much fun. On the second pillow (shown on the left in the photo), the flange with the shirred inset introduces a different kind of shirring. Here, the star is pieced in the traditional manner.

STAR PILLOW WITH SHIRRED, CORDED RUFFLE

Star Pillow with Ruffle

Approximate Size

18 inches square

Materials Required

- ¾ yard of black print fabric for ruffle
- 18-inch square of red print fabric for piping trim
- White fabric for pillow top, larger than 15 inches square
- Fabric for lining, larger than 15 inches square
- Coordinating fabric for pillow back, larger than 15 inches square
- Scraps of red and green print fabrics for star (each diamond section in the star is roughly 3 × 7 inches)
- Batting, larger than 15 inches square

111

- Polyester fiberfill for stuffing
- Paper-backed fusible material
- 2⅛ yards of ¾-inch jumbo piping cord
- 1¾ yards of ¼-inch piping cord

Cutting the Fabrics

1. Cut a 15-inch square from white fabric for the pillow top. Also cut 15-inch squares of batting, lining, and backing fabric.

2. For the Eight-Pointed Star, apply fusible material to the red and green print fabric scraps. See page 153 for directions on working with fusible material. Trace pattern piece A on the opposite page, but do not include the seam allowance. Use the pattern to cut four red and four green diamonds.

Fusing the Star to the Pillow Top

1. Find the center of the pillow top fabric by folding the fabric in half, then in half again.

2. Position the four green diamonds so that the inner tips touch at the center and the outer tips line up on the folds. Position the four red diamonds in the alternate spaces. Place all the diamonds in position before removing the paper and fusing any of them. When completely satisfied with the arrangement, fuse each diamond in place, as shown in **Diagram 1**.

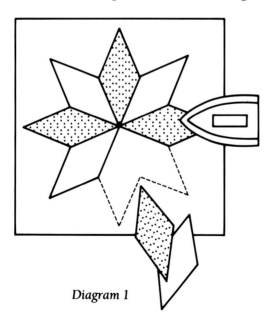

Diagram 1

Quilting the Pillow Top

1. Place the pillow top face up on the batting, then set those two layers on top of the lining fabric. Baste the layers together.

2. Quilt as desired. This pillow was free-motion quilted by machine using invisible thread in a meandering pattern all over the white background. For instructions on free-motion machine quilting, see page 9.

Making the Piping Trim

1. Make piping trim for the edge of the pillow top using the ¼-inch piping cord. Before beginning, please see the note on the zipper foot under "Making the Piping Trim" on page 104.

2. Cut 1⅝-inch-wide bias strips from the square of red print fabric, and join them with diagonal seams to achieve the needed length (approximately 62 inches).

3. Fold the long strip around the cord, wrong sides together and raw edges even. Machine baste the fabric snugly around the cord.

4. Pin the piping trim to the right side of the pillow top, matching raw edges. Baste it in place.

Making the Shirred, Corded Ruffle

1. A shirred, corded ruffle completes this pillow top. For complete directions, see "Making the Shirred, Corded Ruffle" on page 106.

2. Cut the black print fabric into 6-inch-wide strips for the ruffle. Join the strips to achieve the needed length; you will need a total of 150 inches.

3. Fold the fabric strip around the ¾-inch jumbo piping cord, wrong sides together and raw edges even. Stitch and gather the ruffle as described on pages 106 and 107.

4. Pin the ruffle to the right side of the pillow top on top of the piping trim, matching raw edges. Baste it in place, increasing the fullness of the gathers in the corners.

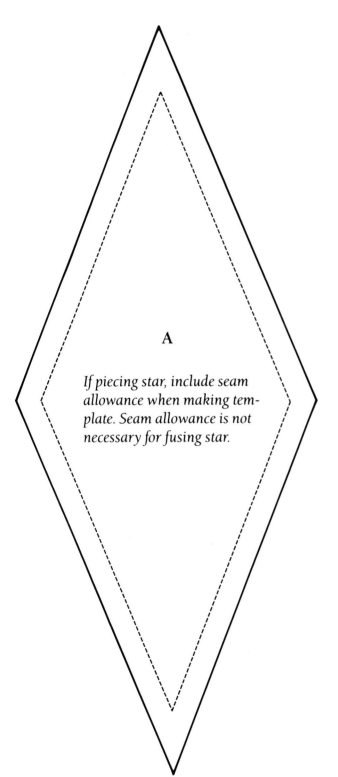

A

If piecing star, include seam allowance when making template. Seam allowance is not necessary for fusing star.

Completing the Pillow

1. Layer the pillow top and back, with right sides together and the piping trim and ruffle sandwiched between them. Sew the pillow front and back together, leaving a few inches open along one side. Check to make sure the seam allowances on the piping trim and the ruffle are caught in the seam joining the front to the back. Trim the corners, and clip if necessary. Turn the pillow right side out through the opening.

2. Stuff the pillow. Slip stitch the opening closed.

STAR PILLOW WITH FLANGE

Star Pillow with Flange

Approximate Size

18½ inches square

Materials Required

- 1⅛ yards of red print fabric for star, flange, and pillow back
- ¼ yard of black print fabric for shirred flange
- 19-inch square of fabric for lining
- Scraps of green print fabric for star (each diamond section in the star is roughly 3½ × 8 inches)
- Scraps of white fabric for background
- Two 19-inch squares of batting
- Polyester fiberfill for stuffing

Making the Pillow Top

1. Trace pattern piece A on page 113, including the seam allowance. Using a large needle, make a small hole in the template at each of the four dots. Mark four diamonds on red print fabric and four on green print fabric. Use a pencil to mark the dots on the pattern pieces through the holes in the template. Start and stop stitching seams at these dots; do not stitch through the seam allowances. Stitching dot-to-dot in this manner helps to create perfect angular seams.

2. Cut out the eight diamonds. Arrange the diamonds to form an eight-pointed star, alternating fabrics. Join the diamonds into pairs, then the pairs into halves, and then the halves of the star. When sewing the halves together, stitch from the center out in each direction, rather than straight across. Press all the seam allowances in one direction, as shown in **Diagram 1**.

Diagram 1

3. Cut four 4-inch squares and one 6½-inch square from the white background fabric. Cut the larger square in half diagonally both ways to make four triangles, as shown in **Diagram 2**. These triangles and squares are cut slightly oversized; trim any excess background fabric after the patchwork is completed.

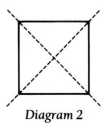

Diagram 2

4. Add the 4-inch squares to the unfilled outer edges of the star, as shown in **Diagram 3**. Place a square right sides together with one side of a diamond edge. Match the corners, and pin, as shown in **Diagram 4**. Stitching dot-to-dot, sew the seam from the inner corner of the star toward the outside edge. Press this seam away from the diamond.

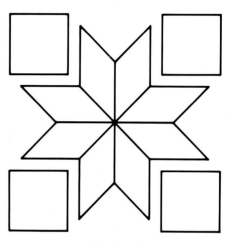

Diagram 3

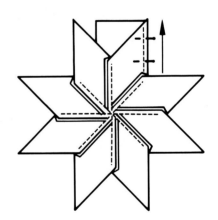

Diagram 4

5. Reposition the pieces so that the adjacent side of the square and the other diamond edge line up, right sides together. In the same manner, sew the second seam from the inside corner to the outside edge, starting a stitch or two away from the inside corner. See **Diagram 5**. (Although this leaves a very small hole in the corner between the diamonds and the square, the hole is not visible when the seams are pressed, and leaving this hole makes the seams lie much more smoothly.) Press this seam away from the diamond.

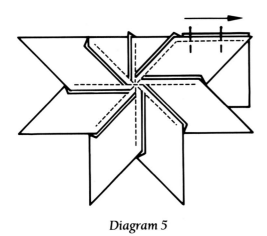

Diagram 5

6. Using the same technique as for the squares, set the triangles into the remaining openings, as shown in **Diagram 6**. The completed patchwork block should measure 12½ inches square, including ¼-inch seam allowances. This is the pillow top interior.

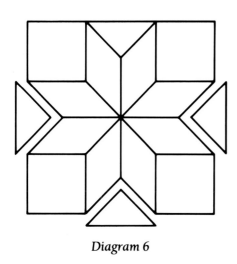

Diagram 6

Quilting the Pillow Top

1. Place one of the squares of batting on top of the lining fabric. Center the pillow top interior, right side up, on top of the batting. Pin through all layers. There will be about 3 extra inches of batting and lining extending beyond the sides of the pillow top interior.

2. Machine quilt in the ditch along all seam lines. Do not trim the excess batting and lining at this time.

Making and Adding the Flange

The pieced flange, made from three strips of fabric, is an unusual but very effective finish. The middle strip is shirred, then flat strips are sewn to each side, and then the flange is sewn as a unit to the patchwork square. The corners of the flange are mitered.

1. Cut eight 1⅝ × 20-inch strips of red print fabric. Mark the midpoint along one long edge of each strip. For the shirred inset, cut four 2 × 40-inch strips of black print fabric. Again, mark the midpoint along one long edge of each strip.

2. To shirr the four black print strips, make two rows of machine basting stitches, ⅛ inch and ⅜ inch from the fabric edge, along each long side of the strips. Gather each strip to 19 inches long, keeping the gathers parallel, as shown in **Diagram 7**.

3. Place a shirred inset strip and one red print strip right sides together, matching the midpoint marks and having the raw edges even. Using a *⅜-inch seam,* sew the strips together. Press the seam allowance away from the shirred inset. In the same manner, stitch a second red print strip to the other side of the inset strip to complete the flange. See **Diagram 8**. Make four of these flange segments.

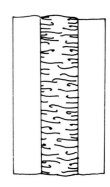

Diagram 7   *Diagram 8*

4. With right sides together, pin flange segments to two opposite sides of the pillow top interior, matching the centers and aligning the raw edges of the pillow top interior and the flange segments. Using a ¼-inch seam, stitch through all layers, including the batting and lining. So that you can miter the corners, stop sewing ¼ inch from each corner of the pillow, and backstitch. Press the segments away from the interior. In the same manner, sew flange segments to the two remaining sides of the pillow top interior. Press.

5. To miter the corners, work on the right side of the pillow top. At each corner, extend one flange end out flat, and fold the adjacent flange end under at a 45 degree angle from the inside border to the outside edge. See **Diagram 9.** Hand stitch the folded edge in place on top of the adjoining flange.

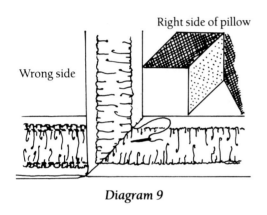

Diagram 9

6. Machine quilt in the ditch of the seam lines of the pieced flange.

Making the Pillow Back

1. This is an unusual technique that creates a center opening, with no raw edges visible, in the batting-interlined pillow back. Cut two 19-inch squares of red print backing fabric. Cut the remaining 19-inch square of batting in half.

2. Working on the wrong side of the fabric, mark a line down the center of one of the backing pieces.

3. Place the backing pieces right sides together, with the marked piece face up. Sew in 7 inches from each edge along the center line, leaving a 5-inch opening in the center of the back.

4. Place one batting half on the right-hand side of the pillow back, aligning the long edge with the center seam. See **Diagram 10.** Fold the top layer of pillow backing from the left-hand side over the batting, sandwiching the batting between two layers of backing fabric, as shown in **Diagram 11.** Only the right

side of the fabric will be facing up at this point. Pin the layers together.

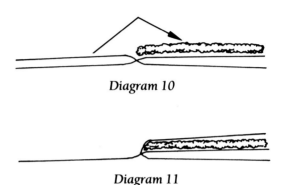

Diagram 10

Diagram 11

5. Keeping the batting on the right-hand side, flip the pillow back over so that only the wrong side of the fabric is face up. See **Diagram 12.** Place the second batting half on the left-hand side of the pillow back. Referring to **Diagram 13,** fold the remaining layer of backing from the right-hand side over the batting so that the batting is sandwiched between two layers of backing. Pin the layers together.

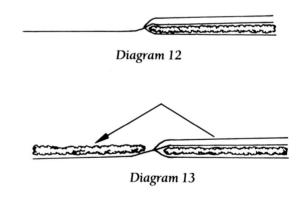

Diagram 12

Diagram 13

Your pillow back should look like the one in **Diagram 14.** Folding the fabric into layers as indicated creates a finished-edge opening in the center of the pillow back, as seen in **Diagram 15.** The batting provides a smooth surface and firmness for the flange.

Diagram 14

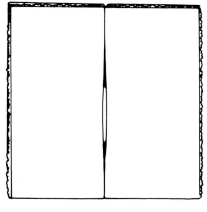

Diagram 15

Completing the Pillow

1. Layer the pillow top and back right sides together, and stitch around the outside edge. Turn the pillow right side out through the center back opening.

2. To finish the flange, stitch in the ditch along the seams that join the flange to the interior of the pillow top.

3. Stuff the pillow lightly. Too much filling distorts both the square and the flange. Slip stitch the center back opening closed.

FESTIVE TREE SKIRTS

The typical tree skirt made by a sewer is very much like a round tablecloth, except one seam is left open, a small hole is cut in the center for the tree, and usually a ruffle or gathered eyelet is added to the outside edge. The diameter, determined by the width of the fabric, is generally 45 inches plus one or two ruffle widths (or 60 inches plus one or two ruffle widths, as 60-inch-wide Christmas prints are becoming more available). Occasionally, a sewer will simply cut a really full tree skirt from 72-inch-wide felt.

Quilters, however, are usually not satisfied until they've added some kind of patchwork or appliqué. Personally, my goal is to make a tree skirt pretty enough to look good until the presents start appearing under the tree, but not so gorgeous that no one wants to put presents on top of it.

With that approach in mind, let's look at other chapters in this book for what might be called "hidden tree skirts." That means there are directions and patterns for other items that can easily be adapted to tree skirts. Repetition of a design or a fabric is an approach that ties a decorating scheme together, so looking for hidden tree skirt designs not only is an efficient way for me to include more designs in one book but also can be helpful in your decorating.

A good example can be found at the beginning of this chapter. The Holiday Tablecloth with Star Topper on page 103 is an obvious design for a two-part tree skirt. As a tablecloth, the skirt with the ruffle is 72 inches across; 54 or 60 inches across would be a nice size for the tree skirt. For instructions on cutting the center hole and back slit and on binding the edges, see "Finishing the Tree Skirt" on page 120.

Use the same diamond pattern to make an Eight-Pointed Star topper; due to the smaller dimension of the underskirt, the star points will be closer to the edge of the skirt. **Diagram 1** illustrates this idea. To keep the star topper from shifting around on the skirt, topstitch along the seams between the diamonds, and leave the points free.

6″ center

Tree Skirt Layout

TRIP AROUND THE WORLD TREE SKIRT

The tree skirt shown in the photo is a Trip around the World arrangement of the same homespun fabrics used to make the Homespun Sunshine and Shadows Throw on page 29. While the throw was made with 3-inch finished squares, the tree skirt is made with 4¼-inch finished squares. Strip techniques remain

the key for efficient construction, but the arrangement I've chosen, combined with the number of fabrics, makes the Cylinder Method used in the throw impractical for this project. Instead, I've organized the fabrics into strip sets and cut easy-to-assemble segments from those sets.

Approximate Size

62 inches in diameter

Materials Required

- 3 yards of 45-inch-wide fabric for backing and binding
- 2 yards of fabric for ruffle
- ⅝ yard *each* of Fabrics 1, 2, 3, and 4
- ⅝ yard *each* or 20 × 25-inch scraps of Fabrics 5 and 6
- ½ yard *each* or 15 × 20-inch scraps of Fabrics 7 and 8
- 60-inch square of batting

Selecting the Fabrics

To me, it was important to match the repetition of the fabrics in the homespun throw. Unfortunately, this meant I couldn't use the Cylinder Method efficiently. **Diagram 1** shows the actual layout of eight fabrics for the Trip around the World. If you also are using eight fabrics, look at **Diagram 1** and decide which fabric will go in each position. To help keep the fabrics organized, label each one with a number. If you want to use a different number of fabrics, make copies of the empty grid in **Diagram 2**, and write in the sequence of the fabrics selected.

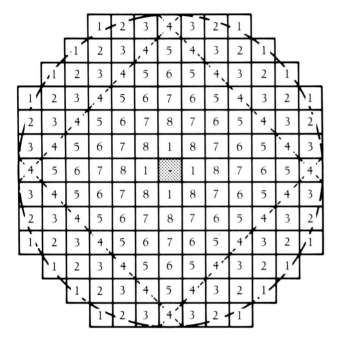

Diagram 1

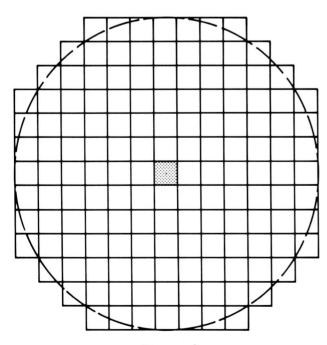

Diagram 2

Making the Patchwork

The method I have used here involves sewing fabric strips into strip sets, then cutting the strip sets into sections. By studying **Diagram 1**, you can easily see that many of the number sequences repeat themselves. The number of times a sequence is used determines the number of sets of that sequence you'll need to cut. Because there are no fabrics with a one-way design, the same strip sets for the 1, 2, 3, 4 positions can be turned 180 degrees and used in the 4, 3, 2, 1 positions. If you are using a different number of fabrics, fill in the fabric numbers on **Diagram 2**, and look for the repetitive strip sets.

I like to cut my strips on the lengthwise grain. For this project, I have found that 20-inch-long strips work best, because I can then cut four pieced sections from each strip set I have sewn. Whatever length you choose to cut the strips, you must make a strip set for each pieced section by cutting a strip for each square in that section. It's easiest to cut all the strips at one time, then sew them together into strip sets. Refer to the list to cut the correct number of sections from each strip set.

1. Referring to the table below, cut 4¾ × 20-inch strips from each of the eight fabrics.

Fabric Number	Number of 20-Inch Strips
1	6
2	6
3	7
4	7
5	5
6	4
7	3
8	2

2. Sew the strips together into sets according to the table on page 120. Then, cut each set crosswise in 4¾-inch sections to get the number of sections needed.

An easy way to keep track of which sets are done is to make a copy of **Diagram 1** and mark off the sets as they are completed. In **Diagram 3**, for example, 14

Sew Together These Strips:	Then, Cut These Sections:
1	4 squares
1,2,3	2 sections
1,2,3,4	14 sections (make four strip sets)
2,3,4	4 sections
3,4	4 sections
4	2 squares
5	4 squares
5,6	4 sections
5,6,7	4 sections
5,6,7,8	8 sections (make two strip sets)

sections of the 1,2,3,4 strip set have been completed, and the four individual number 5 blocks have been cut.

Although it may seem complicated to cut and piece strip sets in this manner, the round shape of the tree skirt makes it necessary. You could more easily piece a big 60-inch square, but there would be more waste.

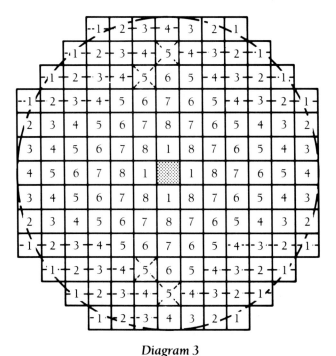

Diagram 3

3. Lay the sections out according to **Diagram 1**. Yes, there is an empty space in the center; that is where the opening for the tree will be.

4. Assemble the sections into horizontal rows. Press the seam allowances in alternate directions from row to row. Then sew the rows together. Press the seams joining the rows in one direction.

5. Use the string and pencil method described in "Cutting the Tablecloth" on page 103 to mark a circle on the patchwork. First, to determine the length of string needed, measure out from the center of the opening as far as you can without going more than 1/4 inch beyond the end of any seam. Mark the string at this length. Hold one end of the string in the center of the opening, and use the pencil at the other end to mark the circle. Do not trim the edges yet.

Finishing the Tree Skirt

1. To piece the backing, cut the 3-yard piece of backing fabric into two 54-inch pieces. Trim the selvages, and sew the pieces together along the long side.

2. Layer the tree skirt with batting and backing. Wait to trim the excess until quilting is complete.

3. Quilt as desired. The tree skirt shown was machine quilted in the ditch along all seam lines. Trim the excess along the pencil line to create the circular edge.

4. Cut the ruffle fabric into 8½-inch-wide bias strips. Stitch the strips together end to end to make one long strip. Fold the long strip in half lengthwise, wrong sides together and raw edges even. Machine baste along the raw edge, and gather the ruffle until it measures approximately 4½ yards long. Pin the ruffle in place on the right side of the tree skirt circle, with raw edges even.

5. Mark an 8-inch-diameter circle around the center opening. Since the size of opening needed can be deceiving, it is probably a good idea to double-check the size of the opening in your tree holder before cutting this circle. An artificial tree generally requires an opening smaller than 8 inches. Cut the center opening.

6. Mark a line from the center opening to the outside edge. This will become the center back opening. Carefully cut the skirt open along this line.

7. Cut 1-inch-wide bias strips from the backing fabric, and sew them together to make one long strip.

You will need a strip approximately 6½ yards long. Start on the outside edge at the center back. With right sides together and raw edges even, pin the bias strip in place on top of the ruffle, working all the way around the edge of the skirt. Without cutting the strip, work up one side of the center back opening, around the center opening, and down the other side of the center back opening to the starting point.

8. Stitch around the tree skirt center opening, center back opening, and outside edge. Press the bias strip over the seam allowance, then press under the exposed raw edge and pin it in place.

9. Topstitch ⅜ inch from the edge of the tree skirt to secure the bias and give a nice finish to the edge of the skirt.

Other Design Ideas

You could, of course, use the homespun fabrics to make a Sunshine and Shadows tree skirt instead of the Trip around the World. **Diagram 4** shows the layout of the eight fabrics. In this instance, you could use the Cylinder Method described on page 26.

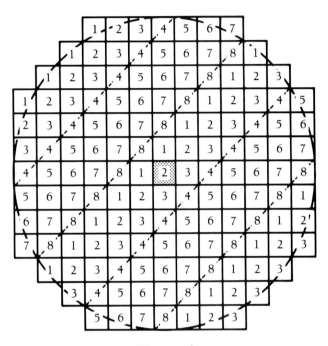

Diagram 4

SUNSHINE AND SHADOWS LAYOUT

For another option, look at the Temperance Tree Quilt on page 48. The block used there is approximately 16 inches square. Using **Diagram 5** as a guide, make four Temperance Tree blocks (two red and two green as in the quilt would be nice), and add sashing strips and borders that are at least 3 inches wide each. The finished tree skirt will measure approximately 44 inches square, which is just a little smaller than most. To create the unique octagon shape shown, simply leave off the bottom triangle in the quilt block. For the border, cut strips slightly longer than each edge of the block, and sew them to the block. Fold under the ends of the strip that is directly under the tree, and appliqué the folded edges to the adjoining strips. Finish the openings and edge as described in "Finishing the Tree Skirt" on the opposite page.

A MORE TRADITIONAL METHOD

You could also cut and piece individual squares. Cut the strips as described on page 119, then cut them into 4¾-inch squares and lay them out according to Diagram 1 on page 119. You will need the following number of squares:

Fabric Number	Number of Squares
1	20
2	20
3	24
4	24
5	20
6	16
7	12
8	8

If you are caught up in the Merry Chris-Moose theme in the "West by Southwest" chapter on page 181, think about a fun and slightly offbeat appliqué tree skirt. When enlarging the moose pattern on page 182, add a little more shoulder to fill out the circular part of the tree skirt, as shown in **Diagram 6**. Again, finish the openings and the outside edge with bias binding as described in "Finishing the Tree Skirt" on page 120.

And remember, anything that would make a good Christmas tree skirt would also make a good table-cloth. Simply eliminate the center hole and the center back opening, and you have a great table topper for a small round table.

Diagram 5

TEMPERANCE TREE
TREE SKIRT

Diagram 6

MERRY CHRIS-MOOSE TREE SKIRT

HEART APPLIQUÉ PLACE MAT

One problem with quilted place mats is that when you sew batting into a seam and turn the place mat right side out, the edge can be very thick, creating a ridge. When a glass is placed so it straddles the edge of the mat, it can tip over. The special technique used in this place mat creates as flat an edge as possible so that you'll have fewer mishaps at the table.

Approximate Size

11¾ × 17½ inches

Materials Required

(for one place mat)

- 13 × 19-inch piece of fabric for place mat backing
- 12 × 16-inch piece of fabric for heart backing
- 9½ × 13-inch piece *each* of 2 green print fabrics for place mat front
- Approx. 9 × 13-inch piece *each* of 2 red print fabrics for heart
- 13 × 19-inch piece of thin batting
- Fabric glue stick

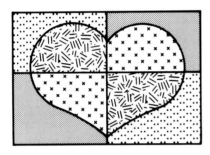

Heart Appliqué Place Mat

Cutting the Fabrics

1. Make templates for the heart sections using pattern pieces A and B on pages 126 and 127. You can make templates for the place mat front sections, too, using patterns C and D, or simply cut rectangles to the correct sizes. Section C (upper front section) measures 5¾ × 9¼ inches, including seam allowances, and Section D (lower front section) measures 7 × 9¼ inches.

2. Cut one upper and one lower place mat front section from each green print fabric.

3. Cut one upper and the opposite lower heart section from each red print fabric. Please note that the pattern is printed right side up to make the right side of the heart. Trace the templates to make the two

right sections, then flip the templates over and trace to make the two left sections.

4. The batting and backing will be cut at a later step.

Making the Heart

1. Sew the two left sections of the heart together, then sew the two right sections together. Carefully matching the seam lines, stitch the two sections together along the center seam.

2. Make a small slit in the center of the heart backing fabric. Place the completed heart and the backing right sides together, and stitch around the heart using a ¼-inch seam. Trim the seam allowances, and clip the curves. Turn the heart right side out through the slit in the backing.

Making the Place Mat

1. Stitch the two left sections of the place mat front together, then stitch the two right sections together. Again carefully matching the seam lines, join the two sections along the center seam, leaving the seam open approximately 3 inches in the center.

2. Use the pieced place mat front as a pattern to cut the batting and place mat backing fabric. Trim the batting ¼ inch smaller all around than the place mat and backing. Place the batting on the wrong side of the backing, using a fabric glue stick along the edges and on the corners to hold the batting in place. The batting will not be caught in the seam, which keeps bulk at a minimum.

3. Layer the place mat with the pieced front and the backing fabric right sides together, and stitch around the place mat. Stitch as close to the edge of the batting as possible, but not through the batting. Turn the place mat right side out through the front opening. Be careful not to pull the batting out of place in the corners.

Finishing the Place Mat

1. Topstitch ⅜ inch from the outside edge, all around the place mat.

2. Center the heart on the place mat, matching all the seam lines. Appliqué the heart in position using a blind hem stitch. Ruffles or trim could be added under the heart or around the edge of the place mat, but keep them as flat as possible.

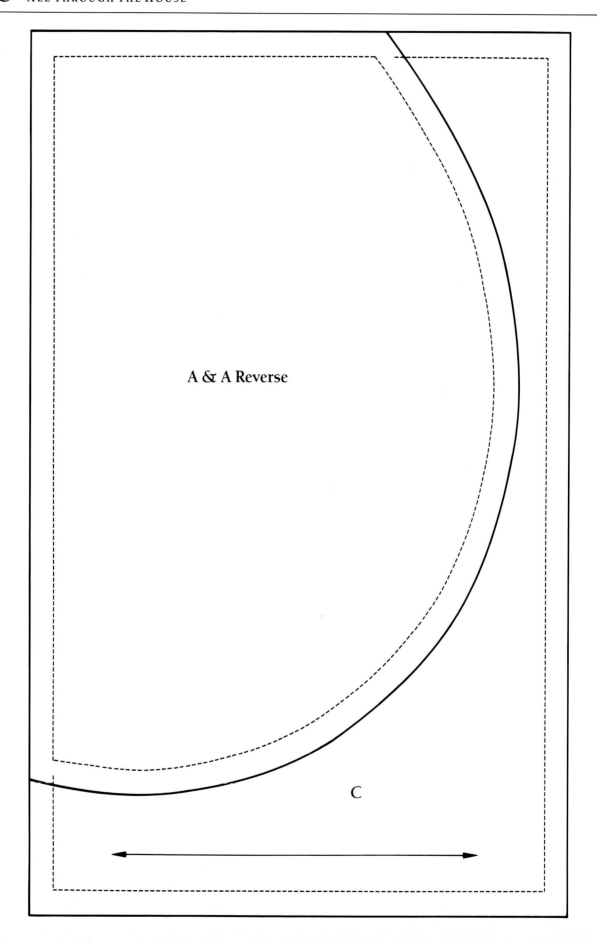

A & A Reverse

C

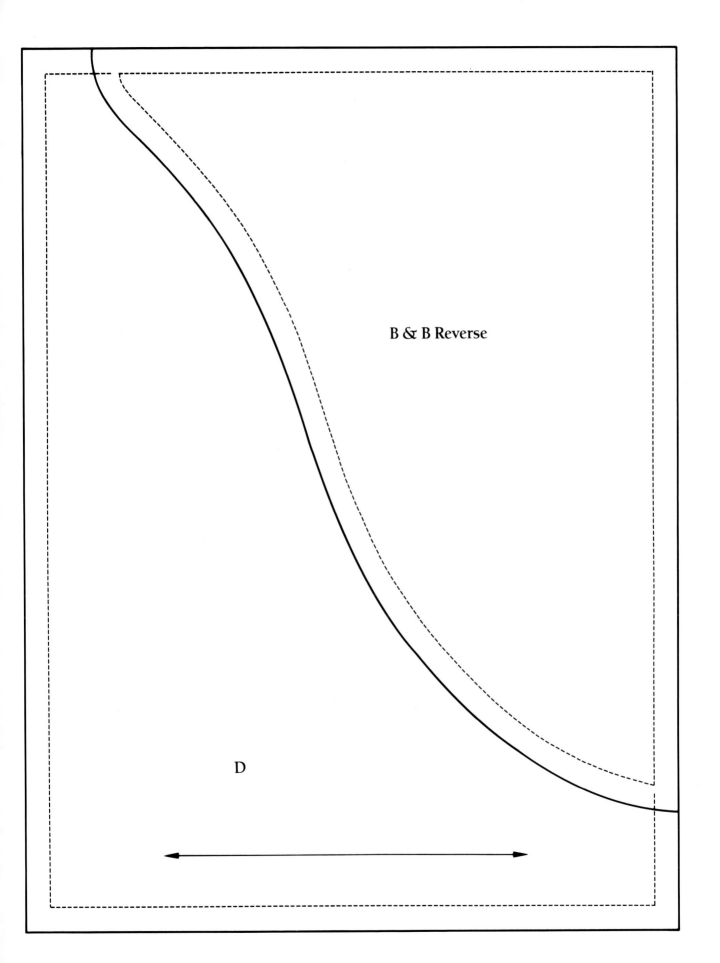

B & B Reverse

D

PINE TREE
AND HEART ADVENT CALENDAR

This tree-shaped Advent calendar features 25 pockets to hold assorted daily treats during a very special time of year. Green miniature trees with triangular pockets alternate with red heart pockets on cream background fabrics. Make the Advent calendar using scraps, as shown in the photo, or use matching fabrics for a more coordinated look. The pattern pieces are provided in two sizes to give you the option of making a large or a small calendar.

Also shown in the photo are the Santa and Mrs. Santa Ornaments, at the top left, and two Basic Tree Ornaments at the top right.

Approximate Size

Using the large patterns: 31 inches wide across the base × 31 inches long

Using the small patterns: 25 inches wide across the base × 25 inches long

Materials Required

(Yardages given are for the large calendar; you'll need slightly less fabric for the small version.)

- 1 yard of green fabric for binding and backing
- 1 yard of muslin for lining
- ⅞ yard of dark green fabric *or* 15 approx. 7 × 10-inch assorted dark green scraps
- ½ yard of light green fabric *or* 15 approx. 5 × 7-inch assorted light green scraps
- ½ yard of red fabric *or* 10 approx. 5 × 10-inch assorted red scraps
- ½ yard of cream fabric *or* 10 approx. 8-inch-square assorted cream scraps
- ⅜ yard of brown fabric *or* one 10-inch-square brown scrap and 10 approx. 5-inch-square assorted brown scraps
- 6-inch square of gold fabric
- Crib-size batting or 1 yard of 48-inch-wide batting

Selecting Scrap Fabrics

You can have a scrap look even if you don't have as many different greens as the list calls for. Make more than one tree from each of several green fabrics, and combine them with different pocket fabrics. Then place them randomly in the big tree. Notice that, while the instructions say to use dark greens for the trees and light greens for the pockets, some of the combinations shown have very little contrast, and some light pockets are actually darker than some trees. When working with scraps, there is plenty of opportunity to be creative in arrangement.

To simplify the cutting and placement process, make fabric selections in pairs: one dark and one light green for each tree, and cream and red for each heart.

Cutting the Fabrics

1. Make templates using the patterns beginning on page 132. Be sure to make the correct templates for the size calendar you have chosen. Cut the fabrics for the miniature trees and their pockets first. Working with the pairs of fabrics selected, cut one A diamond and two B triangles from each of the dark green fabrics. Keeping your fabric pairs together, cut one A diamond from each of the light green fabrics. Cut 20 C tree trunks from the brown fabrics, cutting at least two from each fabric.

2. Alternating with the trees, there are ten cream triangles highlighted with red heart pockets. Cut one cream D triangle and two red E hearts from each pair of fabrics selected.

3. To make the large trunk for the base of the tree, cut two F tree trunks from brown fabric and one from batting.

Making the Miniature Trees and Pockets

1. To make each tree pocket, fold a light green diamond in half, wrong sides together. Pin or baste it in place on top of the unfolded dark green diamond, as shown in **Diagram 1**.

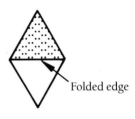

Diagram 1

2. Use the two dark green B triangles that match the dark green diamond to fill out the bottom of the miniature tree. Place one of the triangles right sides together with the light green folded pocket, and stitch with a ¼-inch seam. Repeat with the other triangle. See **Diagram 2**. Open the triangles out, and press the seam allowances away from the pocket. Complete 15 miniature trees in this manner.

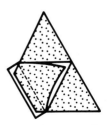

Diagram 2

3. Ten of the miniature trees will have tree trunks. The five trees used across the bottom do not have individual trunks. Use two C tree trunk pieces from the same brown fabric to make each trunk. With right sides together, sew the two trunk pieces together, leaving the top open for turning. Trim the corners, turn the trunk right side out, and press. The tree trunks will be attached when the rows of trees are assembled.

Making the Heart Pockets

1. Make each heart from two pieces of the same fabric. Place the red E hearts right sides together, and sew along the curved seam line, leaving the remaining edges open. Clip the curves, turn the heart right side out, and press.

2. Use one cream D triangle as the pocket base. Pin or baste the heart on the right side of the inverted triangle, with raw edges even. Complete ten heart pockets in this manner.

Assembling the Tree

1. Referring to the tree layout shown in **Diagram 3**, lay out the trees and hearts in five rows, beginning and ending each row with a tree. Play with the placement of the fabrics until you're satisfied with the arrangement. Sew the trees and hearts together into rows, pressing the seam allowances toward the trees.

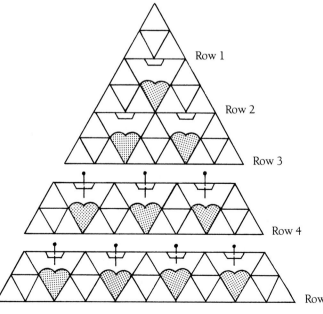

Row 1
Row 2
Row 3
Row 4
Row 5

Diagram 3

2. Before sewing the rows together, position a tree trunk at the top of each cream triangle, as shown in **Diagram 3**, and pin. Center the trunk so that it lines up with the tip of the triangle directly above it. (The five trees in Row 5 will not have trunks.) Place Rows 1 and 2 right sides together, and stitch. The tree trunks are held in place by the seam that connects the rows. It is not necessary to stitch them down on the front; instead, the little flap created adds extra interest for children. Add the remaining rows, and press all seams toward Row 1.

Quilting the Tree

The tree can be quilted and finished in either of two ways, depending on your preference for binding technique.

Traditional Quilt and Bind Method

1. Layer the pieced tree with the batting and backing, and quilt as desired.

2. To make the tree trunk, follow the directions in "Adding the Trunk and Mock Binding" on page 131. Center the trunk on the base of the tree, with right sides together and raw edges even; pin in place.

3. Make a standard French-fold binding, and stitch it to the three sides of the tree, catching the seam allowance of the tree trunk when you add the binding across the bottom. Fold the binding around to the back side, and hand stitch it in place. Press the tree trunk down. Skip to "Completing the Advent Calendar" on the opposite page for finishing instructions.

Line-and-Turn Method with Mock Binding

1. Use the completed tree as a pattern to cut muslin lining and batting at least 1 inch larger than the tree on all sides. The muslin lining helps the quilting go more smoothly. Part of the extra width is needed for the mock binding. The excess can be trimmed after quilting.

2. Place the lining on a large, flat surface. Center and layer the batting and tree right side up on top of the lining. Use pins to hold the layers in place.

3. Quilt as desired. The tree shown was machine quilted in the ditch between all large triangles.

Adding the Trunk and Mock Binding

1. Make the large tree trunk for the base of the tree. Layer the two pieces of fabric right sides together, and place the batting on top. Sew the trunk and batting pieces together around the outside edge, leaving the top open for turning. Trim the corners, and turn the trunk right side out. Quilt as desired. Center the trunk on the base of the tree, with right sides together and raw edges even. Pin or baste in place.

2. To outline the shape, the outside edge of the tree is finished with a ½-inch green mock binding. Cut three 1 × 34½-inch strips from the green backing fabric. Cut the strips lengthwise from the fabric, not crosswise. With right sides together and raw edges even, sew a binding strip to one side of the tree. Press the binding away from the tree. In the same manner, sew a binding strip to the opposite side, catching the end of the first binding strip in the second seam, as shown in **Diagram 4**. Press the binding away from the tree. Finally, sew the last binding strip to the tree bottom in the same manner, catching both side strip ends and the trunk seam allowance in the seam. Press the binding away from the tree. Press the large tree trunk down.

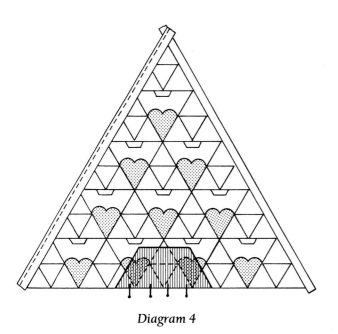

Diagram 4

3. Trim the excess lining and batting up to the unsewn edge of the mock binding.

Adding the Backing

1. To make a pieced back for easy turning and finishing, cut a 34-inch square from the green backing fabric and fold it in half (this works for both calendar sizes). Using a ⅜-inch seam allowance, sew in from both sides along the fold, leaving a 9-inch opening in the middle. Trim off the fold, as shown in **Diagram 5**, cutting very close to the fold and leaving a ¼-inch seam allowance. Press the seam allowance to one side.

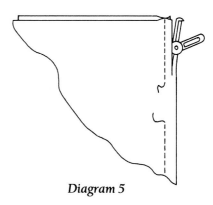

Diagram 5

2. Layer the backing and the quilted tree right sides together with the trunk folded to the inside, away from the stitching line. Stitch around the outside edge of the tree. Trim the corners, and turn the tree right side out through the center back opening. Slip stitch the opening closed.

3. Complete the mock binding by stitching in the ditch between the binding and the tree.

Completing the Advent Calendar

1. A gold star tops the tree shown in the photo. Use the pattern on page 86, and follow the instructions beginning on page 84 to complete the star.

2. Add plastic rings or fabric loops on all three corners to hang the calendar.

3. If your displayed tree's edges tend to curl, it may be necessary to stabilize the tree with a reinforcement. Cut Foamcore or cardboard slightly smaller than the completed tree, and hot glue the tree in place.

Perhaps you have a perfect spot for the tree with its trunk touching the floor, making it child height. In that case, a Foamcore backing would be especially nice.

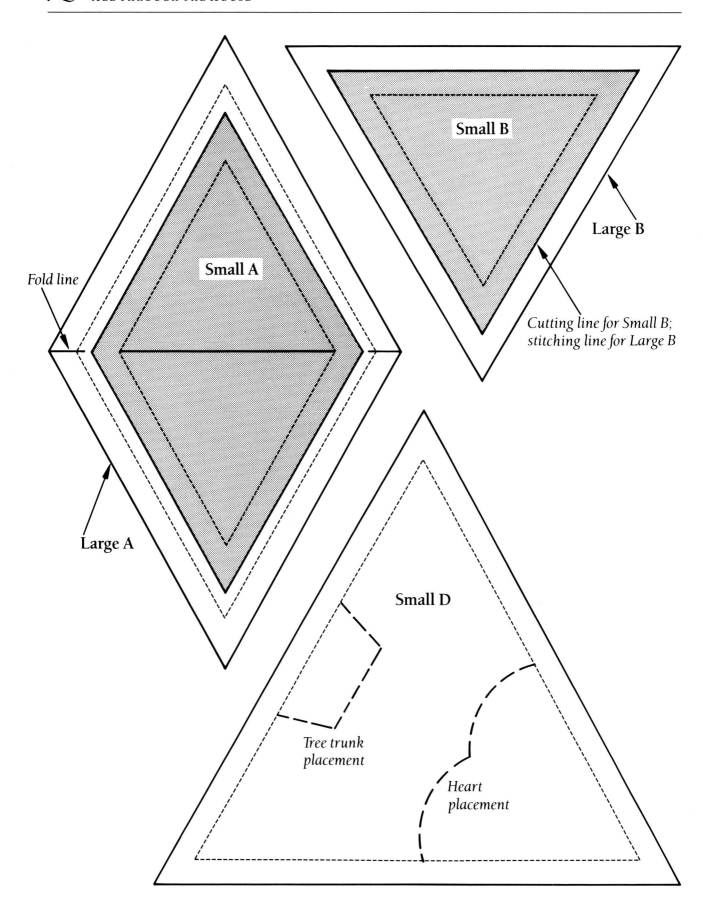

Fold line

Small A

Large A

Small B

Large B

Cutting line for Small B;
stitching line for Large B

Small D

Tree trunk
placement

Heart
placement

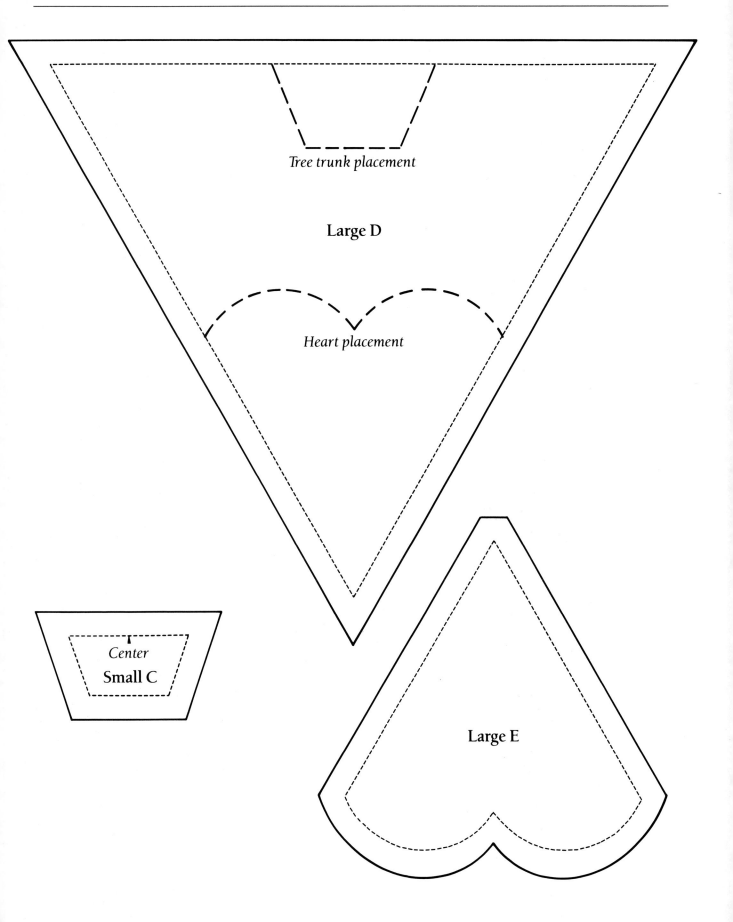

Tree trunk placement

Large D

Heart placement

Center
Small C

Large E

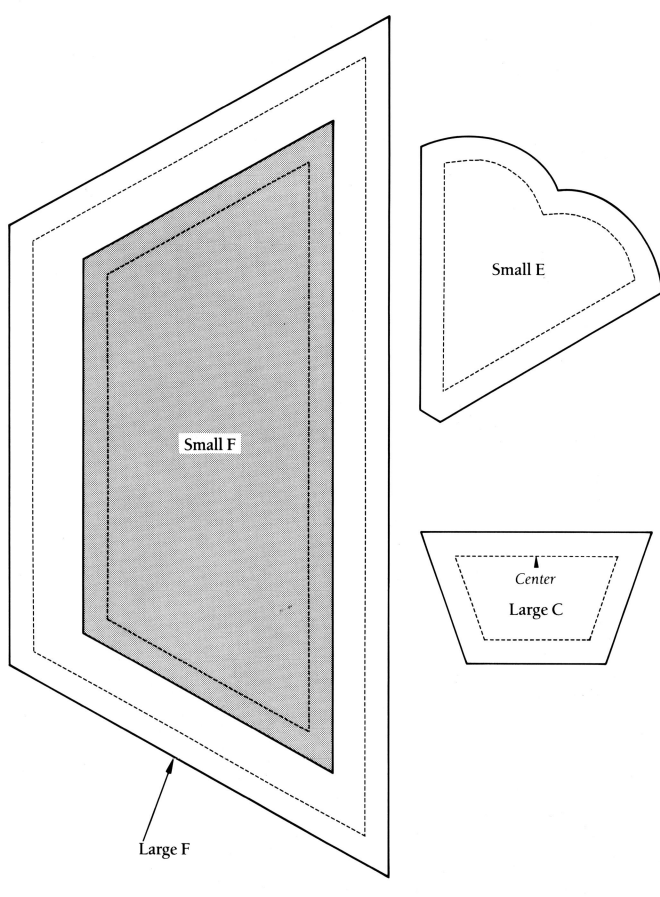

Small E

Small F

Large C

Center

Large F

COLLECTION OF ORNAMENTS

These ornaments demonstrate that the 60 degree triangle that forms the basic unit for the Pine Tree and Heart Advent Calendar on page 128 can become the basis for some fun and surprising designs. I used the pattern pieces for the small Advent calendar to make these ornaments.

BASIC TREE ORNAMENT

Approximate Size

4 × 4½ inches

Materials Required

(for one ornament)

- 6-inch square of fabric for backing
- Scraps of light green and dark green print fabrics
- 6-inch square of lightweight batting
- 8-inch piece of ribbon or invisible thread for loop hanger

Assembling the Ornament

1. This is simply the individual tree unit from the Advent Calendar made into an ornament. To include a pocket in the ornament, cut two small A diamonds and two small B triangles using the patterns on page 132. If you don't want a pocket in the ornament, cut four B triangles, three dark and one light. Sew a dark triangle to each side of the light triangle, as shown in **Diagram 1**. Using the small C pattern on page 133, complete the tree trunk as described in "Adding the Trunk and Mock Binding" on page 131.

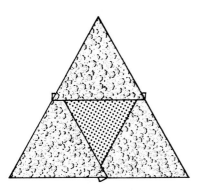

Diagram 1

2. Make ¼-inch mock binding in the same manner as for the Advent Calendar, cutting ¾ × 7-inch strips. Pin the tree trunk in place, and add the mock binding strips.

3. Using the ornament front with mock binding as a pattern, cut the ornament batting and backing fabric. Place the ornament front and back right sides together, with batting on top and raw edges even. Stitch around two sides of the ornament. Trim the corners, and turn the ornament right side out. Turn the open edge seam allowance to the inside, and slip stitch the opening closed.

4. Quilt as desired. Use ribbon or invisible thread to make a loop hanger.

SANTA ORNAMENT

Approximate Size

4 × 4½ inches

Materials Required

(for one ornament)

- 6 × 10-inch scrap of red print fabric (includes backing)
- 4 × 6-inch scrap of flesh-colored fabric
- 6-inch square of fusible fleece
- 4-inch square of paper-backed fusible material
- 8-inch piece of ribbon or invisible thread for loop hanger
- ½-inch scrap of red felt or red fabric paint for nose
- Curly craft hair
- Purchased 6 mm eyes
- Craft glue

Cutting the Fabrics

1. Using the patterns from the Advent Calendar on page 132, cut one small A diamond from flesh-colored fabric and two small B triangles from red print fabric.

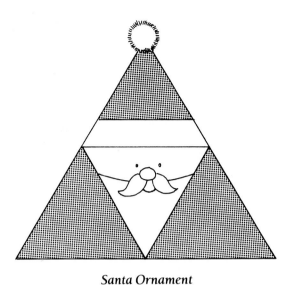

Santa Ornament

5. Machine quilt across the bottom of the hat and between the head and arms.

Finishing the Ornament

1. Give Santa a face by gluing two purchased eyes in place and adding a tiny dot of red felt or fabric paint for his nose.

2. Purchased curly craft hair is used for the beard and eyebrows. Cut hair approximately 2 inches long for the beard. Turn under the ends of the hair, and sew the hair in place below the nose. Glue two tiny curls in place for the eyebrows.

3. To give it a furrier appearance, the hat band fur is made of less curly sections of craft hair. Cut hair approximately 2½ inches long, and glue it in place across the bottom of the hat. Trim the ends at an angle to match the ornament edges. Use a twist of craft hair for the trim at the top of Santa's hat.

4. Use ribbon or invisible thread to create a loop hanger for the ornament.

2. Trace the Santa's hat pattern opposite onto the paper side of the fusible material, and cut loosely around the shape. Working with a scrap that is slightly larger than the pattern piece, apply the fusible material to the wrong side of the red print fabric. Cut out the pattern piece. See page 153 for details on working with fusible material.

Piecing and Fusing Santa

1. Sew one red B triangle to each side of the A diamond. Open out, and press the seam allowances toward the B triangles.

2. Fuse Santa's hat in place on the A diamond.

Layering and Quilting

1. Cut backing fabric using the small D triangle pattern on page 132. Use the same pattern to cut a piece of fusible fleece, but eliminate the seam allowance.

2. Fuse the fleece to the wrong side of the backing, inside the seam lines.

3. Layer the ornament top and the backing fabric right sides together. From the wrong side, sew around the ornament, leaving 3 inches open along the bottom. Be careful not to catch the fleece in the seam when sewing. Trim the corners.

4. Turn the ornament right side out. Slip stitch the opening closed.

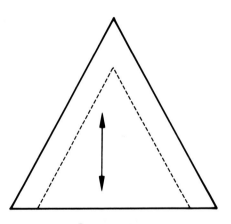

Santa's Hat

MRS. SANTA ORNAMENT

Approximate Size

4 × 4½ inches

Materials Required

(for one ornament)

- 6 × 10-inch scrap of red print fabric (includes backing)
- 4 × 5-inch scrap of flesh-colored fabric
- 3 × 6-inch scrap of white print fabric
- 2-inch square of green print fabric
- 3-inch square of Thermore batting
- 6-inch square of fusible fleece
- 2-inch square of paper-backed fusible material
- 8-inch piece of 1/16-inch-wide red ribbon
- 8-inch piece of ribbon or invisible thread for loop hanger
- 5½-inch piece of ⅜-inch-wide lace
- ½-inch scrap of pink felt or pink fabric paint for nose
- Curly craft hair
- Purchased 6 mm eyes
- Craft glue

Mrs. Santa Ornament

Cutting the Fabrics

1. Using the pattern on the opposite page, cut one Mrs. Santa face from flesh-colored fabric. Using the pattern from the Advent Calendar on page 132, cut two small B triangles from red print fabric for her arms.

2. Trace the dress inset pattern on the opposite page onto the paper side of a piece of fusible material, and cut loosely around the tracing. Apply the fusible material to the wrong side of a scrap of green print fabric slightly larger than the pattern piece. Cut out

the pattern piece along the traced lines. See page 153 for details on working with fusible material.

3. Using the pattern on the opposite page, cut two Mrs. Santa hats from white print fabric and one from Thermore.

Fusing and Piecing Mrs. Santa

1. Fuse the dress inset in place on the Mrs. Santa's face pattern piece.

2. Sew one red triangle to each side of Mrs. Santa's face. Open out, and press the seam allowances toward the arms.

Layering and Quilting

1. Using the small D triangle pattern on page 132, cut the backing. Use the same pattern to cut the fusible fleece, but trim off the seam allowance. Fuse the fleece to the wrong side of the backing, inside the seam lines.

2. Layer the ornament top and the backing fabric right sides together. From the wrong side, sew around the ornament, leaving the top end open. Be careful not to catch the fleece in the seam when sewing.

3. Turn the ornament right side out. Slip stitch the opening closed.

4. Machine stitch in the ditch between the face and the arms.

Making the Hat

1. Using the fusible material, fuse the Thermore to the wrong side of one hat piece. Place the two hat pieces right sides together and sew around the outside edge, leaving 2 inches open along the bottom. Clip the curves. Trim the Thermore close to the line of stitching.

2. Turn the hat right side out. Slip stitch the opening closed.

3. Add the ribbon trim to the hat. Use a 3-inch piece of ribbon to go across the top of the brim section. Wrap the ends to the back of the hat, and sew them in place. Make a tiny bow using the remaining ribbon. Glue the bow in position.

4. Mrs. Santa's hair is glued to the back of her hat. Allow her bangs to extend approximately ¼ to ⅜ inch below the hat brim, and her side curls to extend approximately ½ to ⅝ inch below the hat brim, as shown in **Diagram 1**.

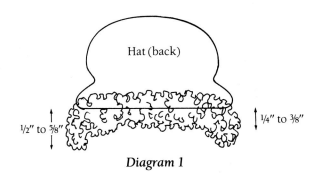

Hat (back)

½" to ⅝"   ¼" to ⅜"

Diagram 1

5. Position the hat on top of Mrs. Santa's head, and sew it in place.

Finishing the Ornament

1. Give Mrs. Santa a face by gluing two purchased eyes in place and adding a tiny dot of pink felt or fabric paint for her nose.

2. To make Mrs. Santa's collar, use a long running stitch to gather the lace to approximately 2½ inches long. Turn under the raw ends, and stitch the lace in place between her dress and face.

3. Use ribbon or invisible thread to create a loop hanger for the ornament.

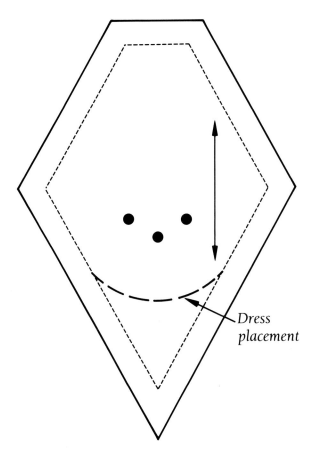

Dress placement

Mrs. Santa's Face

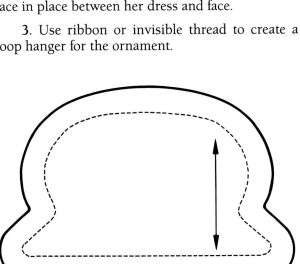

Mrs. Santa's Hat

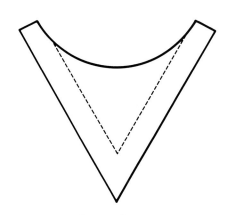

Dress Inset

REINDEER ORNAMENT

Approximate Size

7½ × 6½ inches

Materials Required

(for one ornament)

- 6 × 10-inch scrap of brown print fabric (includes backing)
- 4 × 12-inch scrap of dark brown felt
- 4-inch square of very light brown fabric
- 2-inch square of beige felt
- ½-inch square of white felt
- 6-inch square of fusible fleece
- 15-inch piece of invisible thread for loop hangers
- Dark brown thread to match felt
- ½-inch-diameter red pom-pom for nose
- 7-inch pipe cleaner or chenille stem
- ⅜-inch copper bell
- Purchased 6 mm eyes
- Craft glue

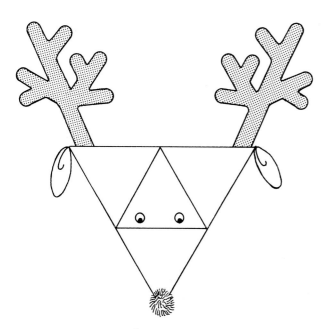

Reindeer Ornament

Piecing the Reindeer

1. Using the pattern from the Advent Calendar on page 132, cut three small B triangles from brown print fabric and one from very light brown fabric.

2. Sew the triangles together to make the reindeer head as shown in the photo. Press the seam allowances away from the center.

Layering and Quilting

1. Using the small D triangle pattern on page 132, cut the backing and the fusible fleece. Trim the seam allowances from the fleece, and fuse the fleece to the wrong side of the backing, inside the seam lines.

2. Layer the ornament top and the backing fabric right sides together. Sew around the outside edge of the ornament, leaving openings to insert the ears and antlers. Leave an opening approximately ½ inch long for each antler and ¾ inch long for each ear. Sew the corners between the openings, as shown in **Diagram 1**. Be careful not to catch the fleece in the seam when sewing.

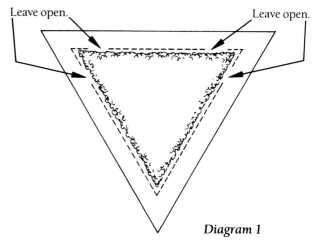

Leave open. Leave open.

Diagram 1

3. Turn the ornament right side out. Do not slip stitch the openings yet.

4. Machine stitch in the ditch around the center triangle.

Making and Adding the Ears and Antlers

1. Using the pattern on the opposite page, cut two ears from beige felt. Fold each ear in half lengthwise.

Note that the ear is not symmetrical; make sure that both ears are facing the front of the head when placing them in position. Place the ears in the open side seams. Slip stitch the openings closed, catching the ears in the stitching.

2. Cut four antlers from dark brown felt, using the pattern below. Place each pair of antlers together, and use a tiny whip stitch to sew around the outside edge, leaving the bottom open. Give the antlers body by inserting a 3½-inch pipe cleaner into the center of each one, as shown in **Diagram 2**. Place the antlers in the seam openings at the top of the head. Slip stitch the openings closed, catching the antlers in the stitching.

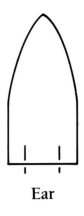

Ear

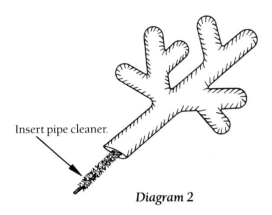

Insert pipe cleaner.

Diagram 2

Finishing the Ornament

1. Cut two ¼-inch circles from white felt to use as a base for the purchased eyes. Glue the felt circles in position, and glue the purchased eyes on top of the felt.

2. Glue the red pom-pom in place for the reindeer's nose.

3. Use approximately 3 inches of invisible thread to dangle a bell from one antler.

4. Make a loop hanger for the ornament. Secure invisible thread at the corner above each ear and through the inside branch of each antler.

Antler

SHOWER CURTAIN AND BATH ACCESSORIES

When I named this chapter "All through the House," I really meant *all* through the house. What better way to convince family and guests that you are serious about decorating for Christmas than to decorate the bathroom? (And what a fun and unexpected way to show off your sewing skills!) This grouping (shower curtain, towel ring, and tissue box cover) was designed to complement the User-Friendly Carolina Lily Quilt on page 15. This quilt and bathroom accessory combination is especially effective when the bathroom adjoins the bedroom. While any Christmas print could be used, for quilters it is nice to find a preprinted quilt pattern in Christmas colors.

SHOWER CURTAIN

Approximate Size

72 inches square

Materials Required

- 4⅝ yards of user-friendly quilt fabric
- 2 × 76-inch piece of fusible interfacing
- 72-inch-square plastic shower curtain liner
- Shower curtain hooks equal to the number of grommets in the plastic liner
- Coordinating fabric for appliqués (optional)

Cutting the Fabric

1. For a standard 72-inch-square shower curtain, cut one center panel 44 × 82 inches and two side panels 17¼ × 82 inches.

2. If you are using a nonstandard liner or making your own liner, measure the shower area from the bottom of the rod to the desired length. Add 10 inches to that measurement to get the total length needed. Measure the width of the shower area, and add 4 inches to get the total width needed.

3. To determine the number of full-width center panels needed, divide the total width by the fabric width minus 1¼ inches. (Do not include selvages in the fabric width!) Cut this number of panels to the needed length.

4. To determine the width of the side panels, subtract the width of the center panels from the total width, and divide by two. Add 1¼ inches if there is one center panel or 1⅞ inches if there are two center panels. Cut two side panels to this width and the total length.

Making the Curtain

1. Sew the panels together with ⅝-inch finished seams. A French seam or serged seam would be best, but a zigzag finish should suffice for limited holiday use. Be sure to match the design before sewing.

2. To make a double-fold hem on the bottom edge of the curtain, turn under 3 inches along the raw edge. Press. Turn under 3 inches again. Stitch along the first fold, stitching through all layers.

3. In the same manner, make a 1-inch double-fold hem on both sides of the curtain.

4. Turn under 2 inches at the top edge of the curtain, and press. Open out the fold, and align one long edge of the strip of fusible interfacing along the crease; it will be 2 inches below the top raw edge of the curtain, as shown in **Diagram 1**. Fold the top edge over on top of the interfacing, and fuse. Turn under 2 inches again to complete the double-fold hem.

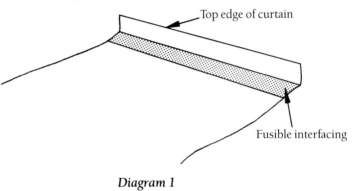

Diagram 1

Finishing the Curtain

1. Mark the buttonhole positions on the top edge of the curtain, using the holes in the liner as a guide. Position the top of the liner ¼ inch down from the top edge of the curtain, as shown in **Diagram 2**, and mark the holes with a pencil.

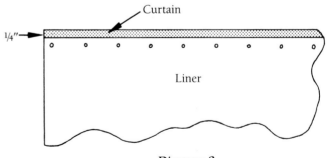

Diagram 2

2. Make a sample buttonhole, and check to make sure it works for your shower curtain hooks. A ½-inch vertical buttonhole works on most hooks, but there are several different styles. Make the appropriate buttonhole or slit at the marked locations. Apply a liquid fray preventer or clear fingernail polish to the edges of the buttonholes to limit fraying.

QUICK BUTTONHOLES

If you can't face the thought of making a lot of buttonholes for a limited-use shower curtain, take the easy way out. Paint the buttonhole area with clear fingernail polish, and make a slit with a seam ripper or scissors.

TOWEL RING AND TOWEL

Continue the Christmas decorating theme with a towel ring and hand towel that match the Shower Curtain on page 142 and the Tissue Box Cover on page 146.

Approximate Size

11 inches in diameter, including lace trim

Materials Required

- ¼ yard of fabric for hoop ruffle
- 6 × 10-inch scrap of fabric for hoop insert
- 6 × 10-inch scrap of fabric for backing
- 5 × 20-inch scrap of fabric for towel band
- Coordinating hand towel
- 6 × 10-inch scrap of batting
- 2¼ yards of lightly gathered 1-inch-wide lace trim for hoop ruffle and towel band
- 20-inch pieces of assorted-width ribbons for bow
- 5-inch piece of ribbon or plastic loop for hanger
- 8-inch wooden embroidery hoop with screw adjustment

3. Decorate the curtain, if desired. The user-friendly small block Carolina Lily fabric used for this curtain also had a complementary large block fabric. Four of these large (18-inch) Carolina Lily blocks were cut out and appliquéd from top to bottom along one side of the curtain. See **Diagram 3**. With such edge decoration, the curtain is even attractive when pulled to one side! Still not Christmassy enough? Tie bells to the curtain hooks with pretty little ribbon bows.

Diagram 3

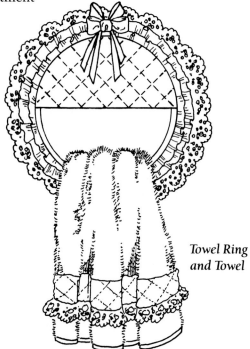

Towel Ring and Towel

Making the Quilted Hoop Insert

1. Position the outer rim of the hoop on the 6 × 10-inch scrap of fabric to take advantage of the design on the fabric. You may wish to cut and fuse sections as we have done. Using a water-erasable marking pen, lightly mark around the outer edge of the hoop, as shown in **Diagram 1**. Do not trim the fabric yet.

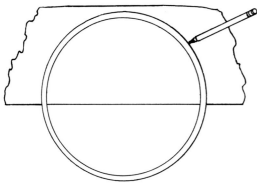

Diagram 1

2. To finish the bottom edge of the hoop insert, place the marked fabric right sides together with the 6 × 10-inch scrap of backing fabric. Sew the pieces together along the bottom edge. Unfold the pieces so that the right sides are facing out. The remaining raw edges will be hidden by the hoop.

3. Sandwich the 6 × 10-inch scrap of batting between the fabric and backing. Quilt as desired. Set aside the insert for now.

Making the Hoop Ruffle

1. Cut 3-inch strips across the width of the hoop ruffle fabric, and join them to make a strip approximately 3 × 60 inches.

2. With right sides together and long raw edges even, baste 60 inches of 1-inch-wide lace to the fabric strip.

3. Without moving the lace, make a fabric tube by folding the fabric strip lengthwise, right sides together and raw edges even. The lace will be inside the tube. Stitch the entire length of the strip with a ¼-inch seam allowance. Turn the fabric tube right side out. Topstitch ¼ inch from the lace edge of the tube.

4. Completely unscrew the outer embroidery hoop so that the tube can be threaded onto the hoop. Adjust the gathers, and turn the tube so that the lace extends off the back side of the hoop. That is, when the hoop is hung on the wall, the lace will be flat against the wall. See **Diagram 2**. The tube will fit loosely around the hoop.

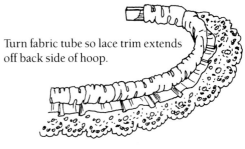

Turn fabric tube so lace trim extends off back side of hoop.

Diagram 2

5. Place the quilted insert in the hoop, with the top of the design centered at the screw adjustment of the hoop. Check the trim marks you made earlier, and make any necessary adjustments. Remove the insert from the hoop, trim the excess fabric, and reassemble.

Finishing the Hoop

1. Make a bow using the 20-inch lengths of ribbon. Sew this to the top of the hoop to cover the screw adjustment.

2. Make a ribbon loop hanger, or use a plastic loop. Attach the hanger firmly to the top back of the hoop, centered at the screw adjustment.

Trimming the Towel

1. Measure the width of your towel. Cut a fabric band this length plus ½ inch for seam allowances. The width of the fabric band will be determined by the width of the design, but approximately 4 inches wide, including seam allowances, should work nicely. You may wish to piece and fuse fabrics to create your band. Cut the band to this width.

2. Cut the remaining piece of 1-inch lace to the same length as the fabric band from Step 1. With right sides together and raw edges even, stitch the ruffle to the lower edge of the fabric band. Open the ruffle away from the fabric, and press carefully.

3. Measure and mark a guideline 6¼ inches from the bottom edge of the right side of the towel. Place the fabric band right sides together with the towel, so that the upper raw edge of the fabric band is aligned with the guideline and the ruffled edge of the band is toward the top of the towel. See **Diagram 3**.

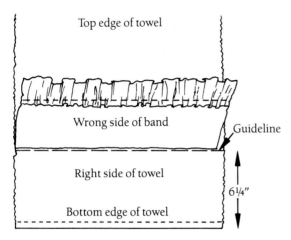

Top edge of towel

Wrong side of band

Guideline

Right side of towel

6¼"

Bottom edge of towel

Diagram 3

4. Turn the raw edges along the sides of the fabric band to the wrong side of the fabric, even with the edges of the towel. Using a ¼-inch seam allowance, sew the fabric band to the towel. Fold the fabric down over the seam allowance, and press.

5. Secure the bottom of the fabric band to the towel by stitching in the ditch between the fabric and the ruffle. Quilt the fabric band through the towel as desired.

TISSUE BOX COVER

The Tissue Box Cover is made up of four separate padded sections. Two are side panels only; the other two panels cross over at the top. Their overlapping curved edges make the tissue opening. The cover slips over the standard boutique-style tissue box from the top.

Approximate Size

4¾ inches wide × 5¼ inches tall

Materials Required

- ¼ yard of fabric (⅜ yard if fabric is directional on the lengthwise grain)
- ¼ yard of fleece, cotton batting, or Thermore batting

Tissue Box Cover

Making the Panels

1. Make templates using pattern pieces A and B on pages 148 and 149. Cut two side panels and two top panels out of fleece. To cut the fabric, place the side panel pattern on the fold of the fabric, and cut out the pattern piece; repeat for a second piece. Cut four of the top panel pieces from the fabric. To cut the fleece, cut two side panels and two top panels. It is not necessary to place the side panel pattern on the fold to cut the fleece.

2. To line the side panels, fold them in half wrong sides together, and insert a piece of fleece. Pin the layers together, and set them aside.

3. To line the top panels, place two of the fabric pieces right sides together on top of a piece of fleece. Stitch across the curved end, using a ¼-inch seam. Trim the excess fleece, and clip the seam allowance at the curves. Press one layer of fabric back over the seam allowance. Topstitch the curve ¼ inch from the edge, as shown in **Diagram 1**.

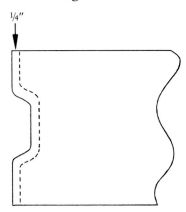

Diagram 1

4. To finish the bottoms of the top panels, cut off ½ inch of fleece along the bottom edge. Press one layer of fabric around the layer of fleece, as shown in **Diagram 2**. Turn under ⅝ inch on the raw edge of the other piece of fabric, and press. Blindstitch in place, as shown in the diagram. Make sure this becomes the inside (the wrong side) of the panel in the next step.

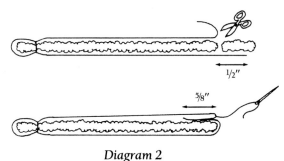

Diagram 2

Assembling the Tissue Box Cover

1. Sew the upright seam between one side panel and one top panel. Place the pieces right sides together, and start at the bottom so that the finished edges match. Stop ¼ inch from the top of the side panel, as shown in **Diagram 3**. Backstitch carefully. Stitch the second top panel to the opposite side of this side panel. At this point, one side panel is sewn between two top panels, as shown in **Diagram 4**.

OPTIONAL PATCHWORK OR QUILTING

The Tissue Box Cover shown in the photo on page 142 is made from a printed patchwork fabric; however, any of the designs in the "Sew or No-Sew Miniatures" chapter, beginning on page 175, would fit on these panels. Following the general directions for fusing beginning on page 153, center the desired designs equidistant from each panel bottom. Fuse and quilt them before joining the panels. Do any optional quilting before final assembly.

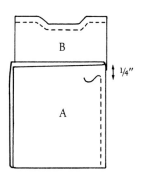

Diagram 3

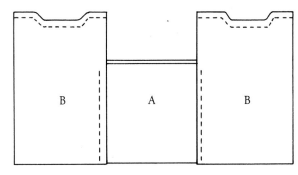

Diagram 4

2. Clip into the seam allowances on the top panels at the point where the stitching ends. Bring the raw edge of one top panel into place along the top of the side panel. Overlap the flap of the second top panel, and pin it in place. Stitch the entire top edge, as shown in **Diagram 5**.

3. Complete the other side panel in the same general manner. Trim the excess fleece from the seam allowances. Turn the cover right side out, and slip it over a tissue box.

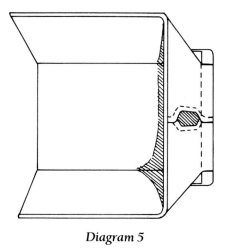

Diagram 5

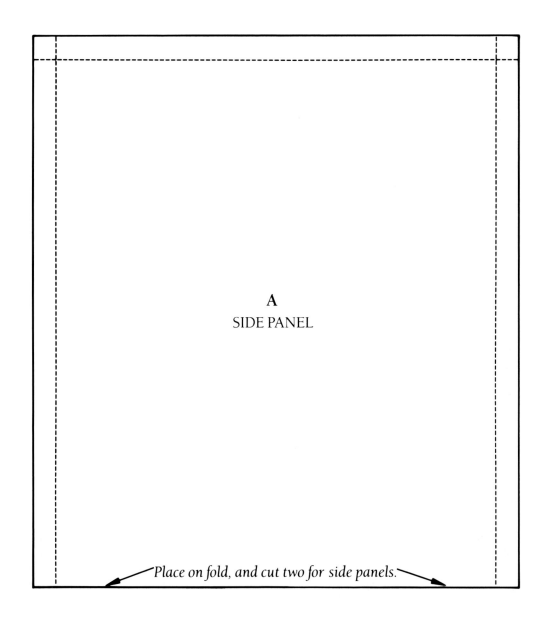

A
SIDE PANEL

Place on fold, and cut two for side panels.

B
TOP PANEL

SEW OR NO-SEW MINIATURES

Antique baby quilts and doll quilts have become very popular for country decorating. Their size makes them easy to use in small spaces, as well as perfect for grouping in larger areas. They are the ideal accent for many country collections, such as bears, dolls, and other toys. The popularity of small antique quilts, combined with their rarity, has made them expensive to purchase. As a result, there are suddenly lots of people making small quilts. Many quiltmakers enjoy making small quilts because, in addition to their decorative appeal, they let them sample many different designs and fabric combinations in less time. Small quilts also use less fabric and take less space to store.

The 3-inch blocks featured in this chapter do not meet the dollhouse manufacturers' standard miniature scale of 1 inch = 1 foot. But because these blocks are being made for people houses, not for dollhouses, I believe they qualify to be called miniature. If you have never tried small designs like these, I hope you will. Generally, people who see these projects are fascinated with them and are drawn to the miniature size just as most people are attracted to babies. And, of course, the fact that the projects are shown in Christmas fabrics here doesn't mean that you can't make them in any fabric combinations you choose.

You could, of course, piece these designs in the traditional way. But they are so much fun to make using the no-sew method, it would be a shame not to at least try it. Paper-backed fusible products, introduced to the consumer market sometime in the mid-1980s, make the no-sew fusing process possible. With these products, the heat of your iron holds the pieces of fabric together, instead of hand or machine stitches. For me, fusing is the technique that has brought miniatures into my repertoire of quilting. Some people will look down their noses at those of us who would fuse our patchwork in place and then machine quilt. But I know that just because I enjoy fusing, it doesn't mean I can't or don't sew or hand quilt. Fusing is especially appropriate when you have very little time but still want to complete a meaningful project. It's okay to want the look of complicated designs without making the time commitment.

The paper-backed fusible products used in no-sew patchwork are easy to use, flexible, machine washable, and have a secure bond. They are also readily available: Just ask for them where interfacing is sold in a fabric store. Some of the common names they are sold under include Wonder-Under and Heat 'N Bond. The cut fused edges do not have to be finished, although a small zigzag stitch or a bead of textile paint along those edges adds a nice touch. This is also a good idea if you intend to launder the project. Finishing the edges will ensure that the designs stay in place.

◀ *Shown in the photo is the Holly Basket Wallhanging, page 160.*

About the Designs

These miniatures are so much fun, it would have been easy to fill this whole book with patterns for 3-inch blocks and projects in which to use them. Instead, I'm providing 17 of my most fun and festive block patterns, beginning on page 175. You can pick and choose from these to make the ornament, wallhanging, bell pull, doll bed quilt, and stocking projects I describe beginning on page 156.

The list below divides the block patterns into patchwork and appliqué designs. To help you in planning your projects, the list also indicates which patterns should be used in a diagonal set and which can be used in either a straight or a diagonal set. In a diagonal set, the squares balance on a corner (on point). In a straight set, the squares sit flat on a side.

Patchwork Designs

Usable On Point Only
- Bow Tie
- Christmas Pine Tree
- Strip Pine Tree

Usable in Straight Sets or On Point
- Churn Dash*
- Eight-Pointed Star (two different layouts given)
- Glorified Nine Patch*
- Ohio Star*
- Pinwheel*
- Square within a Square*

Appliqué Designs

Usable On Point Only
- Folk Heart
- Holly Basket

Usable in Straight Sets or On Point
- Circle of Hearts (two different layouts given)
- Holiday House (two different layouts given)
- Holly Wreath
- Oak Leaf
- Ohio Rose
- Orange Peel

These designs can be made with miniature templates made by EZ International. See "Resources" on page 256.

About the Patterns

The block patterns should be used both to trace individual pattern pieces and as placement diagrams. So that you will not feel restricted as far as color placement is concerned, there are no shading designations in the block patterns. You may want to make copies of the blocks and use colored pencils to try different combinations. Or you can rough-cut little pieces of fabric and place them in position. Individual illustrations of projects are shaded to represent the items shown in the photos, but again, please don't feel restricted to those arrangements. All of the projects could be made differently. The full-size patterns included in this section are for the 3-inch finished-size patchwork blocks; no seam allowances are necessary when fusing.

If you choose to piece the patchwork blocks rather than fuse them, however, you need to add ¼-inch seam allowances to all the pattern pieces. Trim the seam allowances to ⅛ inch when the stitching is complete. If you choose to appliqué, use the freezer-paper method described in the Rose Wreath Pillow project on page 68. The seam allowances should be trimmed as close to ⅛ inch as possible.

Fabric and Batting Selection

The most commonly used fabrics are tiny prints and solids, but they are not the only fabrics that are suitable. Little pieces carefully cut from large-scale prints can provide just the color or shape needed. Because so many of the blocks end up on point, beware of using directional prints that may cause undesirable results.

When selecting batting for the miniature projects, choose a lighter weight than you would generally use for full-size items. A lightweight batting is especially important on something like the Christmas Pinwheels Doll Bed Quilt on page 166, where you would like to have a little drape. If you don't have lightweight batting and don't want to buy it just for a small project, it is usually possible to separate layers of medium-weight batting. Polyester fleece is an acceptable choice for many projects and is available by the yard in the interfacing sections of fabric stores.

Making the Fabric Fusible

Techniques for working with the different paper-backed fusible materials vary, so carefully read and follow the manufacturer's instructions. Generally, the material consists of one side that carries the adhesive—either a web or a film—and a nonadhesive paper side that protects your iron as you apply (iron) the fusible material to the wrong side of the fabric. Be very careful. Cleaning the adhesive off the bottom of your iron is not fun; removing it from an ironing board cover is usually impossible. In fact, if you have a spare iron, or can pick up an old one at a yard sale, devoting that one to fusing fabric can be a good safeguard.

Don't try to cut pieces of fusible material and fabric the same size and then iron them together. Instead, cut a piece of fusible material that's larger than the pattern piece to be cut. Apply it to the wrong side of a piece of fabric that's slightly larger than the fusible material. Then, using a template, mark the pattern piece and cut it out.

You can also trace the pattern piece right onto the paper side of the fusible material before cutting it. This eliminates having to make a template. Once you've traced the pattern, apply the fusible material to the wrong side of the fabric, and then cut out the pattern piece.

Cutting the Pieces

The cutting is done after the paper-backed fusible material has been applied to the wrong side of the fabric and before the paper is removed. The paper adds a nice stiffness or rigidity to the fabric that makes cutting and handling very easy. And, if you haven't already traced the pattern, the paper is available to draw the pattern on, so no marks are made on the fabric. If the piece is symmetrical, no special instructions are required. If it is not symmetrical, put the right side of the template down on the paper before tracing; or, if you're tracing directly onto the paper, trace the pattern in reverse. This is important; the pattern must be traced in reverse on the paper so that it is correct when fused in position.

Once the pattern is traced, the obvious next step is to cut every little piece individually. That certainly works, but with fusible miniatures, there are many times when construction will be simpler if you start with larger pieces and then stack or layer them to create the illusion of many smaller pieces. **Diagram 1** shows an example of this method: Two pieces (a smaller square angled diagonally on a larger square) take the place of the usual five pieces. Fusing cut pieces to a 3-inch background square eliminates much of the cutting and all of the sewing of patchwork. In other words, look for the less obvious way to cut.

   instead of

Diagram 1

Each block design has different possibilities. The same design in different fabrications might even be cut differently. This is not meant to confuse you, but to remind you to look at the designs and consider different cutting possibilities. Layering does make the area thicker and less flexible, and each layer adds to that. However, as each layer will be smaller than the last, even four layers may make sense. There is no right or wrong here; there are just different acceptable approaches.

You may prefer to substitute other blocks for those shown in a project. In any case, study the block designs carefully to determine how the patchwork pieces can most easily be cut. As stated above, sometimes it is appropriate to cut large pieces and layer smaller pieces over them when fusing. Occasionally you may decide to cut an odd-shaped piece in order to avoid gaps that may be formed when fusing numerous tiny pieces. **Diagram 2** illustrates some examples of efficient ways to cut pieces for layering.

If you are doing a small quilt or other project in which many blocks use the same background fabric, try cutting a single large piece of background fabric for the entire project. Use a lead pencil to lightly mark the positions of the block corners and centers on the background fabric, and fuse the individual block components into place within those marks. This method is used in the Doll Bed Quilt on page 166.

The finished size of all the blocks in this section is 3 inches square. Remember, if you are planning to piece or appliqué the designs, you must add seam allowances as you cut the pattern pieces.

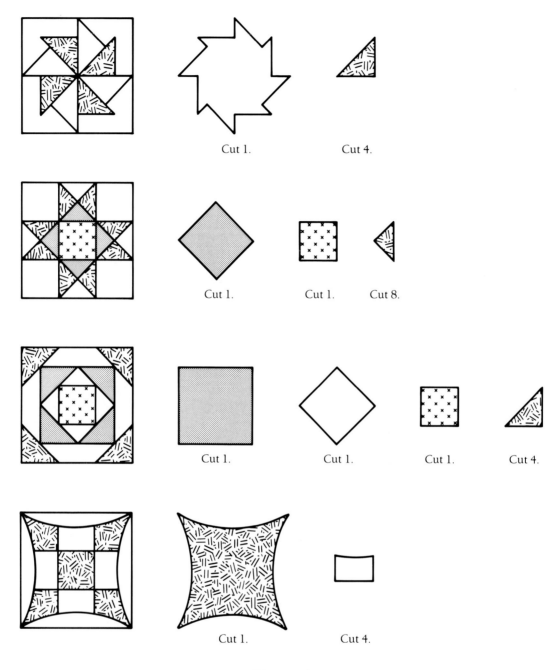

Cut 1. Cut 4.

Cut 1. Cut 1. Cut 8.

Cut 1. Cut 1. Cut 1. Cut 4.

Cut 1. Cut 4.

Diagram 2

Fusing the Designs

Reading through the instructions for the finished projects will familiarize you with the different approaches to cutting and fusing. One of the nice things about fusing miniatures is that you will not have wasted very much time or fabric if you decide you would like to cut and fuse a different way.

Because each square is different, there are no hard and fast rules. Study the block and determine a starting point. For example, for the Pinwheel block, find and mark the vertical and horizontal centers of the patchwork block background fabric. Be certain that the lines are perpendicular. Then, cut out the Pinwheel shape and align it with the guidelines. For the Holly Wreath block, make sure the circle is centered on the background, then use it as the guideline for the other pieces. For the Orange Peel block, the outside edges provide the guide. After all pieces have been cut out and positioned once to check accuracy, you can begin to fuse them in place. Generally, it's easiest to work from the center out, taking care to match straight lines and angles to the block edges, marked centers, and corners where possible.

Peel the paper backing from one or two pieces at a time. Once the paper is gone, the pieces almost stick to the fabric background. Position the pieces, and following the manufacturer's instructions, fuse them in place. I usually tap each piece with the tip of the iron and look at it again before the final fusing.

Finishing Touches

Finishing the cut edges of fused patchwork is not absolutely necessary, but it is recommended if the item will be handled or laundered. Going over the edges with a narrow zigzag stitch is an easy way to finish them. If you use "invisible" nylon thread, it isn't necessary to match the thread color to the fabric. If you apply this finishing method after the piece is layered with batting and backing, you will be quilting and finishing at the same time. This is a nice way to provide definition for the design.

An even easier way to finish the cut edges is to apply a narrow bead of fabric paint along them. Look for those paints with the tiny point dispenser. There are many brands and types of washable textile paints; follow the manufacturer's instructions for the brand you choose. This finish is especially suitable for garment embellishment.

If you want a quilted indentation with the paint finish, machine stitch through all three layers, using a straight stitch right beside the fused block design. Then run the paint along the edges. You could also outline quilt by hand before applying the paint.

Continuous Quilting

Machine quilting is easier and more attractive if it can be done with a continuous line of stitching. This is also true when finishing the edges of fused patchwork with stitching. This means planning a stitching route that allows you to move through the entire block without starting and stopping and clipping threads. Complete directions for this technique begin on page 8.

These miniatures provide the perfect opportunity to learn and practice this technique. The Doll Bed Quilt on page 166 provides an example of continuous stitching on both individual blocks and a project.

INDIVIDUAL CHRISTMAS ORNAMENT

Making individual ornaments is fast, easy, and fun. Of course,
they look great hanging on a tree, but think of other places you can
use them. How about an extra-special finishing touch for a package?

Approximate Size

3½ inches square

Recommended Design and Setting

Any patchwork or appliqué design that can be set on point.

Materials Required

- Scraps of assorted fabrics for background, design, backing, and mock binding
- Scraps of thin batting or fleece
- Paper-backed fusible material
- 17-inch piece of ⅛-inch-wide red ribbon
- 10-inch piece of ⅛-inch-wide green ribbon
- ½-inch red bell

Please read the general directions beginning on page 152.

Individual Christmas Ornament

Making the Design Block

1. Cut a 3½-inch square from background fabric.

2. Select the design for the ornament from the block patterns beginning on page 175. Study the chosen block design to determine the best way to cut and fuse the individual pieces. Cut, center, and fuse the design in place, leaving a ¼-inch seam allowance around the outside edge of the background fabric.

Adding the Mock Binding Strips

The mock binding creates the look of a separate added binding with less time and effort than what's required for a separate binding. It's added to the front of the ornament now, the way a border would be added, and finished later to resemble a·binding. This eliminates the tedious step of folding over and hand stitching a traditional binding.

1. Cut two ¾ × 3½-inch strips of fabric and two ¾ × 4-inch strips of the same fabric.

2. With right sides together, stitch the shorter strips to two opposite sides of the block, aligning the raw edges. Press the strips away from the block. In the same way, stitch the longer strips to the remaining sides. Press them away from the block. These strips become the mock binding.

Finishing the Ornament

1. Cut a 4-inch square of thin batting.

2. To make the backing, cut two 2¼ × 4-inch pieces of backing fabric that match the mock binding strips. Lay the two backing pieces right sides together. Stitch 1 inch in from each end along one of the long sides, leaving a 2-inch opening in the middle, as shown in **Diagram 1**. Open the pieces, and press.

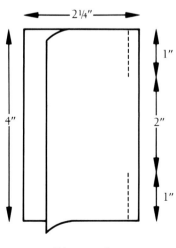

Diagram 1

Instead of a standard line-and-turn with an opening to hand stitch on the edge, this method creates a neat opening in the center back that is easier to close up.

3. Place the patchwork square and the backing fabric right sides together. Lay the batting on top of the patchwork square. Stitch around the outside edge, using a ¼-inch seam allowance. Do not trim the excess batting except at the corners.

4. Turn the ornament right side out through the center back opening. Push the corners out carefully with a blunt-ended tool such as a knitting needle. Press. Slip stitch the opening closed.

5. To complete the mock binding, stitch in the ditch on the seam that attached the narrow binding strips to the edge. Stitching through all layers creates an indentation ¼ inch from the outside and a nice rolled edge that looks like a separate binding.

6. Quilt along all cut edges with a very narrow zigzag stitch and invisible thread. An alternate finish would be to outline quilt with a straight stitch and finish the cut edges by outlining with fabric paint.

Trimming the Ornament

1. Cut a 5-inch piece of the red ribbon, and make a loop. Tack the loop to the top corner of the ornament to act as a hanger.

2. Attach the bell to the bottom corner of the ornament. Cut a 2-inch piece of the red ribbon, loop it through the top of the bell, and tack it in place.

3. Using the 10-inch piece of green ribbon and the remaining 10-inch piece of red ribbon, make a bow to go underneath the loop hanger, and tack it in place.

MINIATURE WALLHANGINGS

The miniature wallhangings are a natural extension of the Individual Christmas Ornament on page 156. They can be made with any of the designs that can be set on point. This arrangement is often called a diamond in a square setting.

CHRISTMAS PINE TREE WALLHANGING

Approximate Size

4¾ inches square

Recommended Design and Setting

Any patchwork or appliqué design that can be set on point.

Materials Required

- Scraps of assorted fabrics for background, design, backing, and mock binding

Christmas Pine Tree Miniature Wallhanging

- Scraps of thin batting or fleece
- Paper-backed fusible material
- Small dowel or miniature wire hanger

Please read the general directions beginning on page 152.

Making the Design Block

1. Cut a 4¾-inch square of dark green print fabric; this fabric creates the four corner triangles.

2. Apply a piece of fusible material to the wrong side of a scrap of tan fabric. Mark and cut a 3-inch square from the tan fabric.

3. Turn the tan square on point, center it on the larger square, and fuse it in place.

4. Cut the individual pieces for the Christmas Pine Tree block, and fuse them in place on the tan square.

Adding the Mock Binding Strips

The mock binding creates the look of a separate added binding without the time or effort of a separate binding.

1. Cut two ¾ × 4¾-inch strips of fabric and two ¾ × 5¼-inch strips of the same fabric.

2. With right sides together, stitch the shorter strips to two opposite sides of the block, aligning the raw edges. Press the strips away from the block to create a binding look. In the same way, stitch the longer strips to the remaining sides. Press them away from the block. These strips give the effect of binding along the outside edge of the block.

Adding the Batting and Backing

1. Cut a 5¼-inch square of thin batting.

2. To make the backing, cut two 2⅞ × 5¼-inch pieces of backing fabric that match the mock binding strips. Lay the two backing pieces right sides together. Stitch 1½ inches in from each end along one of the long sides, leaving a 2¼-inch opening in the middle.

3. Place the patchwork square and the backing fabric right sides together. Lay the batting on top of the patchwork square. Stitch around the outside edge. Do not trim the excess batting except at the corners.

4. Turn the wallhanging right side out through the center back opening. Push the corners out carefully with a blunt-ended tool such as a knitting needle. Press. Slip stitch the opening closed.

Finishing the Wallhanging

1. To complete the mock binding, stitch in the ditch on the seam that attached the narrow binding strips to the edge. Stitching through all layers creates an indentation ¼ inch from the outside and a nice rolled edge that looks like a separate binding.

2. Quilt along all cut edges with a very narrow zigzag stitch and invisible thread. An alternate finish would be to outline quilt with a straight stitch and finish the cut edges by outlining with fabric paint.

3. To hang your miniature wallhanging, sew loops or tabs to the top edge of the quilt backing, as shown in **Diagram 1**. Slip a small dowel or rod through the loops, or use a miniature wire hanger.

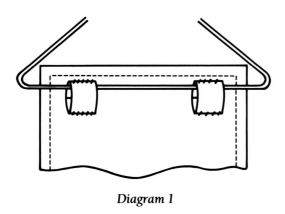

Diagram 1

HOLLY BASKET WALLHANGING

The finished Christmas Pine Tree Wallhanging pictured on page 159 was so cute, the obvious thing was to make another block in a different color scheme to show variety. I intended to make it the very same way, but when a strong dark print was chosen for the large square and a white fabric was selected for the small square, the dark print showed through the white in a very distracting way. So, I simply reversed the layers. Then, just when I thought I was finished, I realized this little wallhanging was crying out for a different border treatment. What started out as very similar actually ended up looking quite different!

Approximate Size

5¾ inches square

Recommended Design and Setting

Any patchwork or appliqué design that can be set on point.

Materials Required

- Scraps of assorted fabrics for background, design, backing, border, and mock binding
- Scraps of thin batting or fleece
- Paper-backed fusible material
- Small dowel or miniature wire hanger

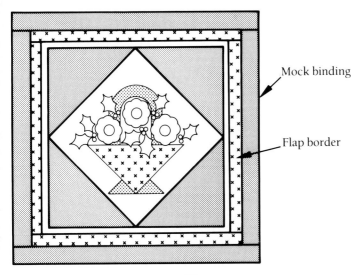

Holly Basket Miniature Wallhanging

Making the Design Block

1. Cut a 5¼-inch square of white fabric.

2. Apply a piece of fusible material to the wrong side of a scrap of dark green print fabric. Using the pattern on page 175, mark and cut four corner triangles from the fabric.

3. Position the corner triangles on the white fabric so that the points meet, leaving a white square on point in the center.

4. Cut the individual pieces for the Holly Basket block, and fuse them in place on the white background.

Adding the Borders

1. The first "border" is actually created by allowing ⅛ inch of the white background fabric to be exposed.

2. The second, red print border is a flap, created from a folded strip. The raw edges are sewn in place, while the folded edge is free. To make the flap border, cut four 1 × 4¾-inch strips. Fold the strips in half lengthwise, wrong sides together and raw edges even; press.

3. Add border strips to two opposite sides of the wallhanging. Place them right sides together with the top, and align the raw edges with the outside edges of the wallhanging. Use a ¼-inch seam allowance to stitch them in place.

4. Add the remaining two border strips to the remaining sides of the wallhanging in the same manner.

Adding the Mock Binding Strips

1. Cut two 1 × 5¼-inch strips and two 1 × 6¼-inch strips from the same fabric used to make the corner triangles.

2. With right sides together and raw edges even, sew the shorter strips to two opposite sides of the wallhanging, and press them away from the center.

3. Sew the two longer strips to the remaining sides of the wallhanging, and press.

Adding the Batting and Backing

1. Cut a 6¼-inch square of thin batting.

2. To make the backing, cut two 3⅜ × 6¼-inch pieces of backing fabric that match the mock binding strips. Lay the two backing pieces right sides together. Stitch 1½ inches in from each end along one of the long sides, leaving a 3¼-inch opening in the middle.

3. Place the patchwork square and the backing fabric right sides together. Lay the batting on top of the patchwork square. Stitch around the outside edge. Do not trim the excess batting except at the corners.

4. Turn the wallhanging right side out through the center back opening. Push the corners out carefully with a blunt-ended tool such as a knitting needle. Press. Slip stitch the opening closed.

5. To complete the project, see "Finishing the Wallhanging" on the opposite page.

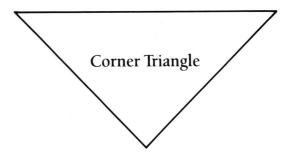

Corner Triangle

GLAD TIDINGS BELL PULL

With this festive piece, you can mix and match block designs or repeat your favorite four times. All of the block designs and borders just look time-consuming—you'll be pleasantly surprised by how quickly all the pieces in this bell pull go together, using my no-sew techniques and other shortcuts.

Approximate Size

6½ × 18 inches

Recommended Design and Setting

Any patchwork or appliqué design that can be set on point.

Materials Required

- Fabric for background, larger than 6 × 18 inches
- Fabric for backing, larger than 6 × 18 inches
- Scraps of assorted fabrics for blocks, setting triangles, and mock binding
- Batting, larger than 6 × 18 inches
- Paper-backed fusible material

Please read the general directions beginning on page 152.

Glad Tidings Bell Pull

Making the Individual Blocks

1. Choose a background fabric for the four individual blocks; one scrap slightly larger than 6 inches square will be enough for all four blocks. Apply paper-backed fusible material to the wrong side of the fabric. Cut the fabric into four 3-inch squares. Do not remove the paper.

2. Select four designs from the block patterns beginning on page 175. Analyze the block designs to determine the best way to cut and fuse the individual patchwork pieces for each block. Complete the four blocks.

Fusing the Blocks to the Background

1. Cut a 6 × 18-inch piece of fabric for the bell pull background. In the sample, the background is red, the green triangles are fused in place, and green mock binding strips are sewn to the red fabric. It is much easier to position the triangles than it would be to align strips of red on top of the green fabric.

Mark the vertical and horizontal centers on the background. Mark a second horizontal line 2⅛ inches above the horizontal center, as shown in **Diagram 1**.

2. Referring to **Diagram 2**, position the first patchwork block where the center lines cross, so that each corner touches a marked line. Fuse it in position.

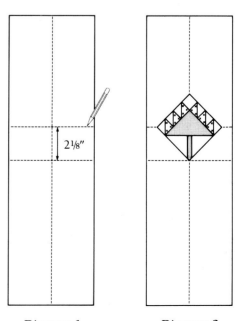

Diagram 1   *Diagram 2*

3. Position and fuse the remaining blocks, aligning them with the marked lines and the first block.

Adding the Setting Triangles

1. Apply paper-backed fusible material to the wrong side of the fabric chosen for the setting triangles. Cut six side setting triangles and two corner setting triangles, using the patterns on page 165.

2. Referring to **Diagram 3**, position the triangles on the background fabric and fuse them, leaving a ¼-inch margin surrounding the patchwork blocks.

3. Referring to **Diagram 4**, trim the lower edge of the bell pull to a point. Using a see-through plastic ruler, measure out ½ inch from the lower edge of the bottom block, and trim. Repeat on the opposite side.

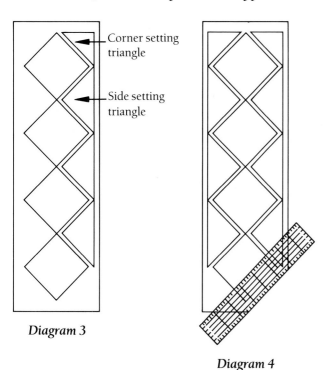

Diagram 3

Diagram 4

Adding the Mock Binding Strips

1. Cut the following strips from green fabric: two 1 × 16¼-inch strips; two 1 × 5½-inch strips; and one 1 × 7-inch strip.

2. With right sides together and edges even at the top, stitch the two long strips to the sides of the bell pull, as shown in **Diagram 5**. Press the strips away from the bell pull. Wait to trim any excess until after all the strips have been added.

3. Stitch the 1 × 7-inch strip to the top of the bell pull. Press the strip away from the bell pull.

4. Position and stitch one of the 5½-inch strips to one side of the bell pull lower point, as shown in **Diagram 6**, and press. Stitch the second strip to the opposite side, and press.

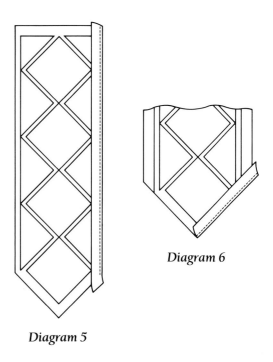

Diagram 6

Diagram 5

Adding the Batting and Backing

1. Cut a piece of batting, using the completed bell pull front as a pattern.

2. Cut the backing in two pieces, each approximately one-half. Again using the bell pull as a pattern, cut the top and bottom separately, adding a ¼-inch seam allowance to the two edges in the middle that will be joined. With right sides together, stitch these backing pieces together, leaving a 3½-inch opening in the center as shown in **Diagram 7**. Unfold the backing, and press.

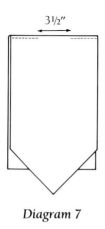

3½″

Diagram 7

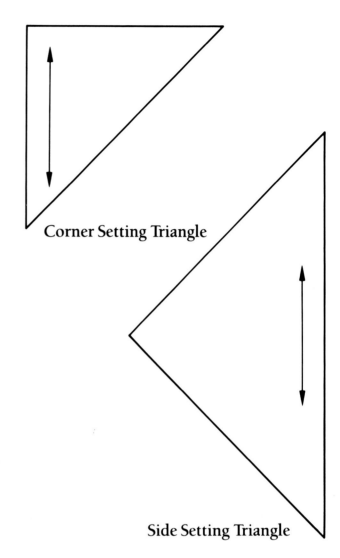

Corner Setting Triangle

Side Setting Triangle

3. Place the bell pull front and backing fabric right sides together, and lay the batting on top of the front. Using a ¼-inch seam allowance, stitch around the outside edge. Do not trim the excess batting except at the corners.

4. Turn the bell pull right side out through the center back opening. Slip stitch the opening closed.

Completing the Bell Pull

1. To complete the mock binding, stitch in the ditch through all layers on the seam that attached the narrow binding strips to the edge.

2. If you wish, finish the cut fused edges with a zigzag stitch or paint. Quilt as desired. If the fabric you selected for the triangles was a solid color, you might want to add quilting in that area.

3. Add a sleeve or loops to the top back for the dowel or hanger that you are using, as shown in **Diagram 1** on page 163.

CHRISTMAS PINWHEELS DOLL BED QUILT

In this tiny quilt, the Pinwheel shapes and the elliptical Nine-Patch blocks create a playful sense of swirling Christmas colors. Don't be fooled by the seemingly complex shapes. The Pinwheels are fused directly onto a large piece of background fabric. The background for each of the Glorified Nine-Patch blocks is cut separately.

Approximate Size

11 inches square

Materials Required

- 12-inch square of light-colored fabric for background
- Fabric for backing, larger than 11 inches square
- Scraps of assorted fabrics for blocks and binding
- Lightweight batting, larger than 11 inches square
- Paper-backed fusible material

Please read the general directions beginning on page 152.

Making the Glorified Nine-Patch Blocks

Using the Glorified Nine-Patch pattern on page 178, cut 4 background pieces from green fabric and 16 squares from red fabric. Fuse the red squares in place on the green background pieces.

Making the Quilt Background

1. Referring to the **Christmas Pinwheels Doll Bed Quilt Diagram**, lightly mark the block corners

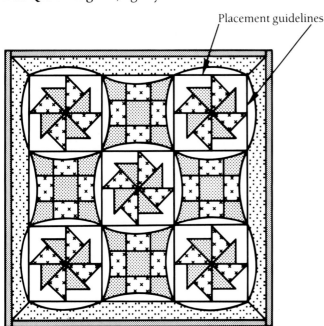

Placement guidelines

Christmas Pinwheels Doll Bed Quilt Diagram

and centers on the 12-inch square of background fabric. To find the outside edges of the blocks, measure in approximately 1½ inches from the outside edges of the background square.

2. Position the four completed Glorified Nine-Patch blocks on the background fabric, as shown in the diagram, aligning corners with markings. Fuse the blocks in place.

Cutting and Fusing the Pinwheel Blocks

1. Study the Pinwheel block on page 176 to determine the best way to cut the patchwork pieces. Cut the pieces from red and green fabric.

2. Using the Glorified Nine-Patch blocks and the marks on the background as guides, position and fuse the Pinwheel pieces in place directly on the background fabric.

Adding the Border

1. For the fused green border, cut four border pieces from green fabric using the pattern piece on page 169.

2. Position the borders on the background fabric, matching the inside straight edges to the corners of the Glorified Nine-Patch blocks. Fuse the center sections of the border strips in place first, as shown in **Diagram 1**.

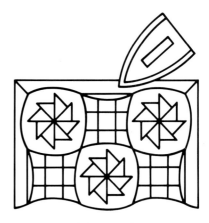

Diagram 1

3. Align the border corners, and trim any excess to create a neat mitered edge; complete the fusing of the borders.

4. Trim the background fabric to 11 inches square.

Adding the Backing and Batting

1. Layer the backing, batting, and quilt top, and pin or baste them together. Do not trim the excess backing and batting at this time.

2. Quilt using a continuous line of stitching. **Diagram 2** illustrates a continuous stitching layout. See page 8 for a complete discussion of this technique.

Completing the Quilt

1. To make the binding, cut two 7/8 × 11-inch bias strips of fabric and two 7/8 × 11½-inch bias strips.

2. With right sides together, stitch the shorter strips to two opposite sides of the quilt. Press the strips away from the quilt. Turn under a scant ¼ inch on these binding strips, and slip stitch the binding to the back of the quilt, covering the line of machine stitches. It may be necessary to trim a little of the backing and batting at this point, but don't trim too much.

3. In the same way, stitch the longer strips to the remaining opposite sides. Press them away from the quilt. Turn under ¼ inch on each end, and then bring the binding to the back of the quilt, turning under ¼ inch on the long edge. Slip stitch the binding in place.

Start here.

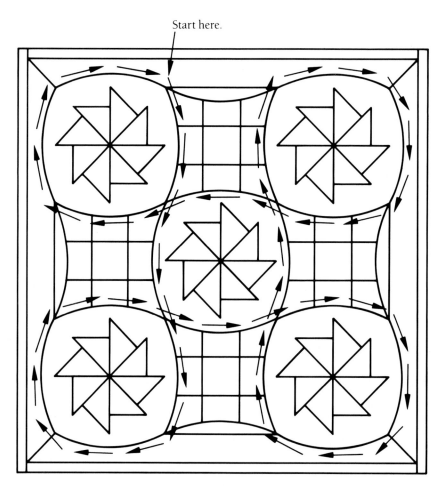

Diagram 2

CONTINUOUS STITCHING LAYOUT

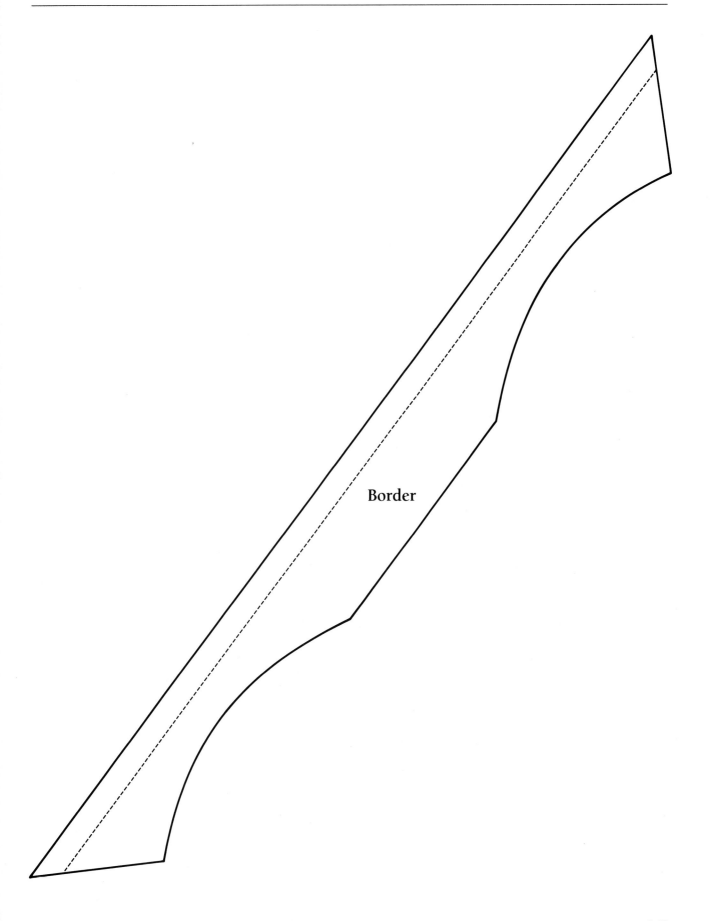

Border

LAFAYETTE
ORANGE PEEL STOCKING

Stop! Don't turn the page too fast. This is a wonderful example of looks that are deceiving. At a quick glance this seems to be a beautifully pieced Lafayette Orange Peel quilt made into a stocking. Instead, it is a fast and easy fused version. My streamlined no-sew construction calls for you to fuse all the red shapes you see onto a green background. What could be easier?

Approximate Size

12 inches wide at the toe × 18 inches long

Materials Required

- ½ yard of green fabric for background, lining, and backing
- 8½ × 19-inch piece of print fabric for cuff
- Red print fabric for stocking front, larger than 6 × 12 inches
- ½ yard of batting
- Paper-backed fusible material

Please read the general fusing directions beginning on page 153 and the Basic Christmas Stocking instructions beginning on page 77.

Cutting the Background Fabric

1. Make a template for the stocking using the basic pattern beginning on page 80. Carefully join the pattern pieces together. Using the stocking pattern as a guide, loosely cut the green background fabric for the stocking front. You will cut the background fabric to size after fusing and quilting the design area.

2. Lightly trace the stocking pattern onto the fabric. Mark the grid of 3-inch squares as it appears on the basic pattern. It may be easier to draw the grid of squares on point first, and then draw the outline of the stocking around the grid so that the center top square is right at the top of the stocking.

Cutting the Design Fabric

1. Draw a 6 × 12-inch grid of 3-inch squares on the paper side of a piece of fusible material. Trace the Orange Peel star shape on page 176 in each 3-inch square.

2. Apply the fusible material to the wrong side of the red print stocking front fabric.

3. Cut apart on all lines. Cut carefully, since the part cut away from the stars is used to create the frame on the alternate blocks.

Fusing the Design to the Background

Study the **Stocking Front Diagram** carefully. Peel the paper backing from a few pieces at a time, and fuse the stars and frames onto the stocking squares. Work from the center out. Allow pieces to extend over the stocking outline where necessary; it is better for the ends of the fused pieces to be secured in seams than to be cut off.

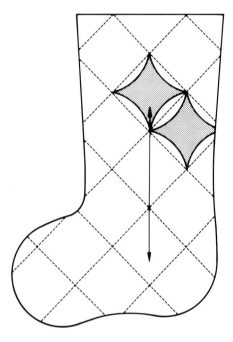

Stocking Front Diagram

Quilting the Stocking Front

1. Referring to the Basic Christmas Stocking directions beginning on page 77, cut the lining, batting, and backing pieces. For now, set aside one lining piece, one batting piece, and the stocking back.

2. Still working with the loosely cut size, layer the stocking front with batting and lining. Pin or baste the pieces in place.

3. Machine quilt along all raw edges. Add decorative quilting in the open spaces as desired. Trim the excess fabric from the stocking front.

Completing the Stocking

Layer the back, stitch the front and back together, and add the cuff to the stocking.

HOLIDAY HOUSE
SAMPLER WALLHANGING

This festive sampler is guaranteed to bring good cheer to any wall. It is small enough to be used almost anywhere, but intricate enough to command attention no matter where it is hung. Even though the design features nine different blocks set on point, the house in the center is unquestionably the focal point, as it forms the central square in the Ohio Star secondary design. While I think this sampler is delightful in the somewhat formal fabrics shown in the photo, it would be equally wonderful made up in country fabrics and colors.

Approximate Size

21 inches square

Recommended Design and Setting

Any patchwork or appliqué design that can be set on point. In the sample shown in the photo, I used (*counterclockwise from top right*) Eight-Pointed Star, Circle of Hearts, Ohio Star, Oak Leaf, Churn Dash, Holly Wreath, Strip Pine Tree, and Ohio Rose. Holiday House has the place of honor in the center.

Materials Required

- ⅝ yard of green print fabric for wallhanging background
- ⅝ yard of fabric for backing
- ¼ yard of green fabric for border and binding
- ⅛ yard of red fabric for border
- ⅛ yard of beige fabric for block backgrounds
- ⅛ yard or scraps of gold fabric for border
- Scraps of assorted fabrics for blocks
- 22-inch square of thin batting
- Paper-backed fusible material

Please read the general directions beginning on page 152.

Making the Individual Blocks

1. Apply fusible material to the wrong side of the beige background fabric. Cut nine 3-inch-square background pieces from the fabric. Do not remove the paper backing.

2. Study the block patterns beginning on page 175 to determine the best way to cut the pieces for each block.

3. Cut the pieces for each block, and fuse them in place on the beige background squares.

Making the Wallhanging Background

1. For the wallhanging background, cut one 21-inch square from green print fabric. This size includes the outside matching border. All of the other pieces are applied to this background. You may want to cut this piece a little larger and trim it before binding to allow for discrepancies or a change of plans.

2. Without removing the paper backing, position the nine completed patchwork blocks on the background fabric as shown in the **Sampler Assembly Diagram** on page 174. Measure in approximately 4⅛ inches from each outside edge, and lightly mark a guideline on the background fabric. Place the outer blocks so that the outside points are touching this line. When you are satisfied with the positioning of all the blocks, fuse them in place.

Making the Ohio Star Secondary Design

1. Cut two 3-inch squares from a red fabric scrap and one 3-inch square from a green fabric scrap. Cut each square diagonally both ways, into four triangles.

2. Referring to the **Sampler Assembly Diagram** and using the fused patchwork blocks as a guide, position and fuse the Ohio Star pieces in place on the background fabric.

Adding the Backing, Batting, and Quilting

1. Cut one 22-inch square of backing fabric.

2. Layer the backing, batting, and wallhanging right side up, and pin or baste them together to hold them in position for quilting.

3. Finish the cut fused edges, and quilt as desired.

Adding the Borders

These instructions are for the borders as shown. I believe that borders should be personalized in response to the fabrics in use. Your fabrics may require

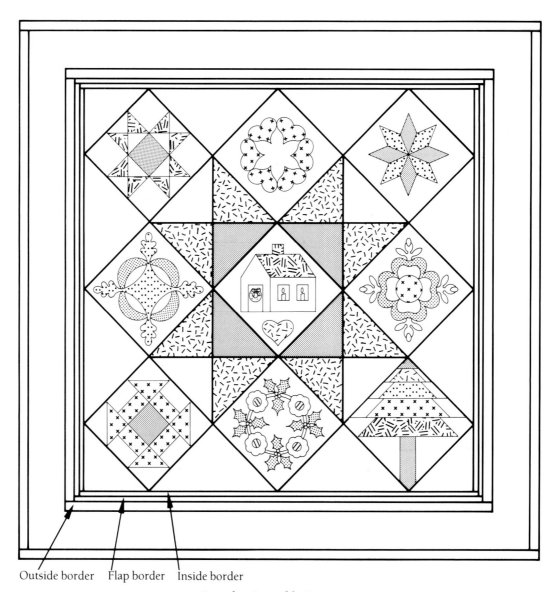

Outside border   Flap border   Inside border

Sampler Assembly Diagram

an additional border, or even one less, to look their best. So use the following as a guide, but don't be afraid to alter dimensions or quantities of borders.

1. For the inside border, cut two 1 × 13½-inch strips and two 1 × 14½-inch strips from green fabric. For the gold flap border, cut four 1 × 14½-inch strips of fabric. The outside border strips will be cut in Step 4.

2. Begin with the inside border. To find the correct placement for the border, measure out ¼ inch from the outside points of the patchwork blocks and lightly mark a placement line, as shown in **Diagram 1.** Place a 13½-inch strip right sides together with the background fabric, with the outside raw edge aligned with the placement line. Using a ¼-inch seam, stitch the strip in place. Press the border and seam

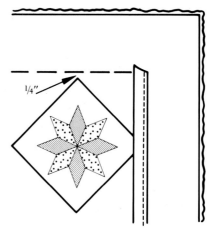

Diagram 1

allowance toward the outside edge of the wallhanging. (The remaining raw edge will be covered later.) Add the second 13½-inch strip to the opposite side. Then add the 14½-inch border strips in the same manner, with the ends extending over the shorter strips.

3. The gold flap border is simply a folded strip. The raw edges are sewn in place, while the folded edge is free. To make the flap border, fold the gold strips in half lengthwise, wrong sides together and raw edges even; press. With the raw edges of the flap border strips even with the raw edges of the inside border, stitch in place.

4. Before cutting the red fabric strips for the outside border, apply fusible material to the wrong side of the fabric. Cut two 1 × 14½-inch strips and two 1 × 15¼-inch strips from the fabric. Leave the paper backing in place until the borders are sewn in position.

5. Add the two shorter borders to opposite sides first; complete all steps for these strips before adding the 15¼-inch strips. Place the border right sides together with the quilt top, aligning the raw edges of the outside border with the raw edges of the inside and flap borders; stitch. Remove the paper backing, and press the border and seam allowance toward the outside edge of the wallhanging. The raw edges of the two inner borders will be covered by the outside border.

Stitch the two longer borders to the remaining two sides. Remove the paper backing, and press the borders in place.

Adding the Binding

1. A separate ⅜-inch French-fold binding is used. Cut four 2 × 22-inch strips from binding fabric.

2. Fold the strips in half, wrong sides together. Place a strip along one edge on the front of the wallhanging, and match the raw edges. Using a ¼-inch seam allowance, stitch the binding in place. Repeat on the opposite side.

3. Fold the binding to the back of the quilt, and hand stitch in place, covering the machine stitches.

4. Add the two remaining binding strips in the same manner. Fold over the raw ends of the strips, and hand stitch the binding in place, covering the raw ends of the first strips.

Completing the Wallhanging

1. Machine quilt a narrow zigzag stitch along the fused edge of the outside border.

2. Use beads and gold and red metallic threads to add the wreath berries and candles to the center Holiday House block.

Folk Heart

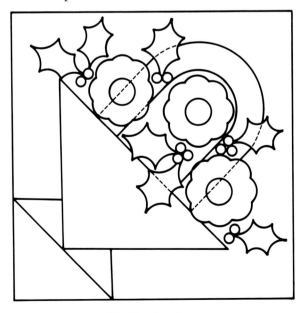

Holly Basket

Ohio Rose

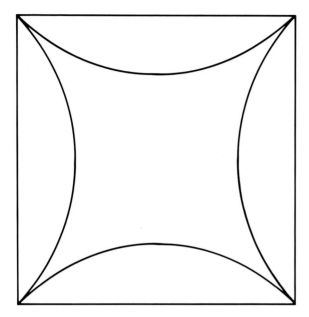

Orange Peel

Oak Leaf

Holly Wreath

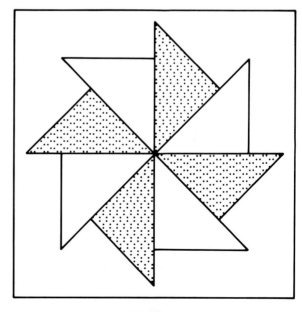

Pinwheel

Circle of Hearts,
Straight Set or On Point

Eight-Pointed Star, Straight Set

Holiday House,
Straight Set or On Point

Eight-Pointed Star, On Point

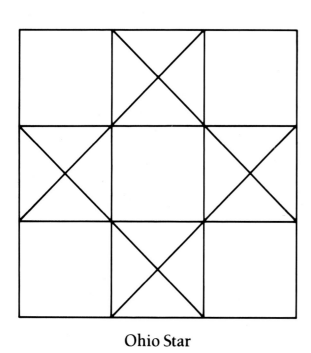

Ohio Star

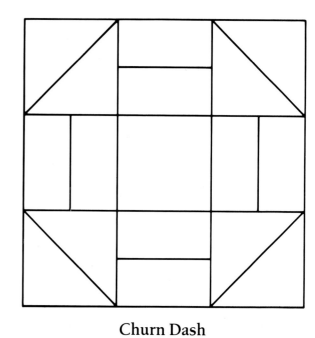

Churn Dash

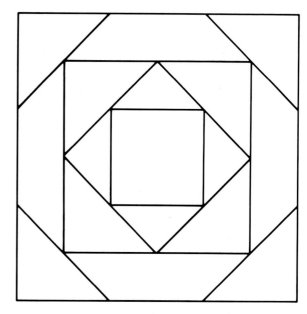

Square within a Square

Glorified Nine-Patch

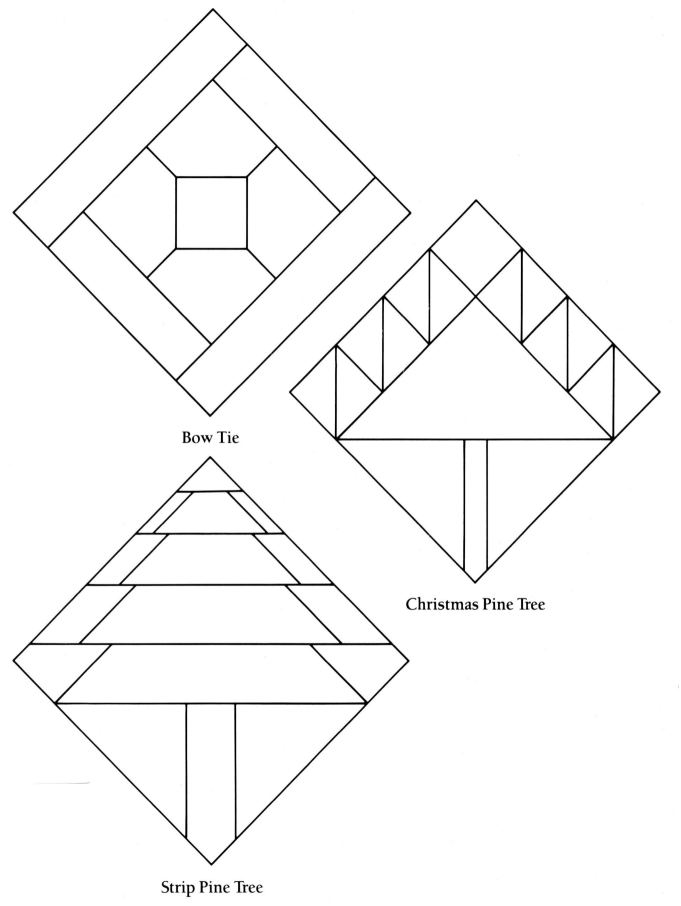

Bow Tie

Christmas Pine Tree

Strip Pine Tree

WEST BY SOUTHWEST

Eclectic decorating has freed people to combine favorite items from many different styles. Christmas decorations are the same. You don't have to live in the West or Southwest to enjoy the styles and motifs of the area. For many people, decorations in this theme are a memento of a wonderful family vacation; for others, the dream of one. Admittedly, these Western designs have been interpreted with a great deal of whimsy, but the items included still allow me to reminisce about a recent trip West.

MERRY CHRIS-MOOSE WALLHANGING

A moose for Christmas? Why not, when he's this colorful and this much fun! It's certainly a surprising twist on traditional Christmas decorating. Though he's shown here in Amish-inspired colors, he could as easily be done up in other color combinations, or even in Ultrasuede for a real Western flavor.

Approximate Size

41¼ × 55 inches

Materials Required

- 2 yards of fabric for background and binding on three sides
- ¼ yard of fabric for narrow side and top borders
- ¼ yard of fabric for wide side and top borders
- ¼ yard of fabric for bottom border and binding
- Approx. 18-inch-square pieces of assorted fabrics for body and antlers
- Smaller scraps of assorted fabrics
- 1¾ yards of fabric for backing

- 45 × 60-inch piece of batting
- 4 yards of paper-backed fusible material
- Nylon monofilament thread for quilting
- Gold variegated and purple metallic threads for quilting stars
- Freezer paper (if appliquéd)

Selecting the Fabrics

The fabrics I gathered were guided by, but not confined to, Amish colors of purple, bottle green, and red. The prints selected look like a wonderful collection of jockey silks, but are actually cotton. I collected them at quilt shops and shows in small amounts. As you can see from other projects in this book, I tend to use rather traditional fabrics, but these fabrics seemed

Diagram 1

Scale: ½″ = 2″

like pieces I should buy because someday they would be just what I needed. I think I was right, don't you?

Perhaps you love the moose, but are feeling a little more subdued. Try a forest green background, assorted brown tones for the moose, and red for the decorative parts, maybe even the antlers. Assorted Christmas prints for the Flying Geese triangles would add just the right festive touch.

Making the Patterns

1. To make the wallhanging shown in the photo, you'll need to enlarge **Diagram 1** four times. First, read through the explanation of the grid system of enlargement on page 2.

To make enlarging the pattern easier, some of the more complex parts of the design are printed as full-size pattern pieces beginning on page 187. The idea is to trace the pattern pieces, tape them in place on the grid, and then complete the rest of the enlargement around them.

The pattern pieces do not have seam allowances. If you are fusing the pieces, seam allowances are unnecessary. If you are doing freezer-paper appliqué, be sure to add seam allowances when you cut the pieces out of fabric.

2. Mark a 28½ × 37-inch area on a large sheet of paper. This area does not equal the full background of the wallhanging, but only the space shown inside the dotted line around the moose on the **Wallhanging Layout**. Mark this space off in a 2-inch grid. Each square on **Diagram 1** is ½ inch, but will equal 2 inches in the full-size pattern.

3. Trace the partial moose face pattern on page 190; this is the right half of the center of the face, as shown by the dotted line on the moose face in the **Wallhanging Layout**. Flip the pattern over, and trace the left half. Referring to **Diagram 1** and the **Wallhanging Layout**, tape the pattern pieces in the correct position on the grid.

4. Trace the two parts of the antler/ear pattern on pages 188 and 189, and carefully join them. This is the left antler pattern; flip the pattern over, and trace the right antler. Again referring to **Diagram 1** and the **Wallhanging Layout**, tape the pattern pieces in the correct position on the grid.

5. Complete the enlargement of the moose as shown in **Diagram 1**. When it's completed, I recommend leaving the enlargement in one piece to serve as a placement pattern. Trace the shapes you need for pattern pieces from the enlargement.

Making the Moose

1. Cut a piece of background fabric at least 40 × 54 inches, and lightly mark a 36 × 50-inch rectangle on it using a pencil or erasable marking pen. Do not trim to size at this time.

2. Lay out the fabrics for the moose, folded to roughly the size of the pattern pieces, to take a first look at the fabrics you plan to use. Stand back and squint, make a few adjustments if necessary, and start cutting the pieces to size.

3. If you are fusing, trace the shapes onto the paper side of the paper-backed fusible material. On asymmetrical pieces like the body, the shape must be traced in reverse so that it's facing the right way when fused on the background. The easy way to do this is to trace from the wrong side of the enlarged pattern. On mirror image shapes like the antlers, trace one in each direction.

The detail lines on the face can be handled in several different ways. On the wallhanging in the photo, the red detail lines were created by fusing the face pieces onto a red fabric, which was then fused onto the background fabric. The same pieces could have been appliquéd, which would make the face less stiff than the fused version. Either way, you'll be hand-

Wallhanging Layout

ling the face as a unit, which I believe to be the best method. If you choose this method you'll need to cut the base fabric now. Other options for the facial details include fabric paint, narrow appliqué bias strips, and a simple zigzag stitch.

4. Cut the fusible material slightly larger than the traced shapes.

5. Apply the fusible material to the wrong side of the chosen fabric, and cut the pattern piece out on the drawn line.

6. Without removing the paper backing, lay the cut pieces on the background. When satisfied with the arrangement, start with the body in the lower left corner, and fuse the pieces in place. The neck and face sections need to be fused or appliquéd to a contrasting fabric, and then fused or appliquéd as a unit. There are several places that are three or four layers thick.

7. If you are appliquéing, I recommend the freezer-paper method, including hidden machine appliqué.

EASY SCRAP REMOVAL

You may want to cut the fabric around the outside of the paper first, then cut the piece out on the drawn line. Although this means cutting twice, it also means the little scraps of fabric with fusible material attached are easily thrown away, instead of staying on the larger piece of fabric and becoming a nuisance.

See page 69 for complete directions on this technique. Proceed as described in Step 6, appliquéing instead of fusing.

Making the Flying Geese Band

Lightly mark a line 4½ inches down from the marked line at the top of the wallhanging. Cut 16 Flying Geese triangles from paper-backed fusible material or freezer paper using the pattern on page 191. Using the method suited to the material you chose, apply the triangles to the selected fabrics. Arrange the triangles as shown in the **Wallhanging Layout**, with the center points aligned with the new line and the triangles overlapping each other approximately 1½ inches. In the center, place two triangles so their long straight sides meet and the points face the top and bottom of the wallhanging. Fuse or appliqué all the triangles in place. Make heart sections using the pattern on page 187, and add them to the center two triangles.

Quilting the Wallhanging

Center the wallhanging front on a relatively low-loft batting and backing that are approximately 45 × 60 inches. Quilt this section before adding the borders. Before you start, fold the backing over the exposed areas of batting, and pin; this will cover the batting and prevent things from catching in it. When the quilting is complete, remove the pins and smooth out the batting and backing.

Quilt around the moose and the Flying Geese triangles. If you have fused these sections, part of the purpose for the quilting is to secure the edges. Using the nylon monofilament thread in the top of the machine and thread to match the backing fabric in the bobbin, zigzag the edges of the moose section.

Around the Flying Geese, either zigzag or try what I call "random edge quilting." I came up with this technique when I tried to figure out the best way to quilt around the geese. Doing a zigzag around them meant endless turning and either stopping and starting or doubling back. After thinking about it awhile, I switched to free-motion stitching, invisible thread, and a very random stipple-type movement back and forth over the edges, as shown in **Diagram 2**. I was very pleased with this new look. However, I never could decide whether, had I done the geese first and seen the effect, I would have used this random edge finish on the moose instead of the slightly more laborious zigzag.

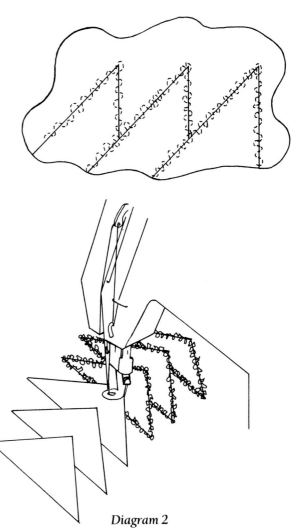

Diagram 2

Stars of assorted sizes and threads are randomly quilted in the background. The quilting can be done by hand or machine. The stars in my wallhanging were done using free-motion quilting and continuous stitching. See **Diagram 3**. For a complete discussion on continuous stitching, see page 8.

Start here.

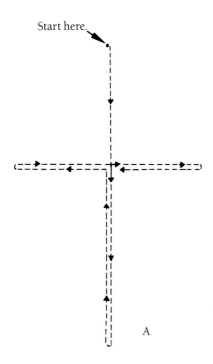

A

Start here.

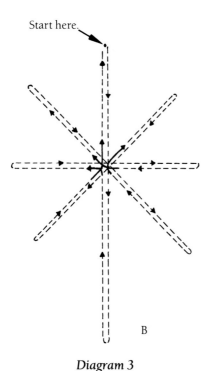

B

Diagram 3

Adding the Borders and Binding

There are two narrow borders on the sides and across the top, and one wide border across the bottom. All of the borders are added using the Quilt-As-You-Sew technique.

1. The narrow border on the sides and top is 7/8 inch wide finished. Cut two 1 3/8 × 50-inch side border strips. Piece the strips if necessary to reach the required length. Place a border strip right sides together with the wallhanging, aligning the long outside edge with the marked line on the background fabric. Using a 1/4-inch seam allowance and sewing through all layers, including the batting and backing, stitch the border in place. Press the border away from the center of the quilt. In the same manner, add the narrow border to the opposite side.

2. Measure across the top of the wallhanging, including the side borders. Cut a 1 3/8-inch-wide strip to this length. Place the strip right sides together with the wallhanging, aligning the long outside edge with the marked line on the background. Stitching through all layers, sew the border to the wallhanging. Press the border away from the center of the quilt. At this point, trim the excess background fabric on the two sides and across the top, being *very* careful not to trim any batting or backing that extends beyond the first border. Do not trim any background fabric from the bottom of the wallhanging.

3. The wider border on the sides and top is 1 3/4 inches finished. Measure the length of the wallhanging front, and cut two 2 1/4-inch-wide side border strips to that measurement. Place a strip right sides together with the wallhanging, this time aligning the long outside edge with the outside edge of the first border. Stitching through all layers, sew the border in place. Press it away from the center of the quilt. Repeat for the other side border.

4. Measure across the top of the wallhanging, including the borders you just added, and cut one 2 1/4-inch-wide top border strip to the needed length. Sew the strip to the wallhanging in the same manner as for the side borders. Press it away from the center of the quilt.

5. The bottom border is 3 1/2 inches wide finished. Cut a strip 4 inches wide and the same length as the top border strip you just added. Place the strip right sides together with the wallhanging, aligning the outside edge with the line marked on the background

fabric. Sew the border to the wallhanging, stitching through all layers. Press the border away from the quilt center. Trim any excess background fabric.

6. The wallhanging is finished with separate French-fold binding. The bottom binding, cut from the bottom border fabric, was added and finished first. The two sides were added next, and the top last. The binding for the sides and top was cut from the background fabric. Cut 2½-inch-wide strips, and join them to get the needed length. Fold the long strip in half lengthwise, wrong sides together. Place the strip right sides together with the wallhanging, aligning the raw edges. Stitch the binding to the front of the wallhanging, bring the folded edge around to the back side, and slip stitch it in place.

Decorating the Moose

1. The Christmas ornament hanging from the antler could be appliquéd in place, but I thought it would be much more fun to finish it on both sides and let it hang free. Make a template using the ornament pattern on page 191. Cut a front and a back from fabric.

2. After you've cut the front and back of the ornament, trim the seam allowance from the template. Use the trimmed template to cut one piece of paper-backed fusible material. Fuse the material to a batting scrap, and then cut the batting to size. Remove the paper, and using a pressing cloth or low-temperature iron, center and fuse the batting to the wrong side of the back of the Christmas ornament. Cut a slit in the horizontal center that will be used for turning.

3. Fuse or appliqué the decorative band and the little opening protector to the right side of the front of the ornament.

4. With the front and back of the ornament right sides together, stitch around the ornament, just outside the edge of the batting. Turn it right side out through the slit, and press. Cover the opening with a fused decorative band.

5. Make a thread loop or sew a paper clip to the back of the ornament, and then hang it with thread or very narrow ribbon from one antler, as shown.

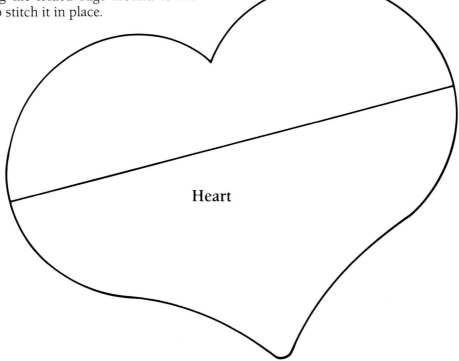

Heart

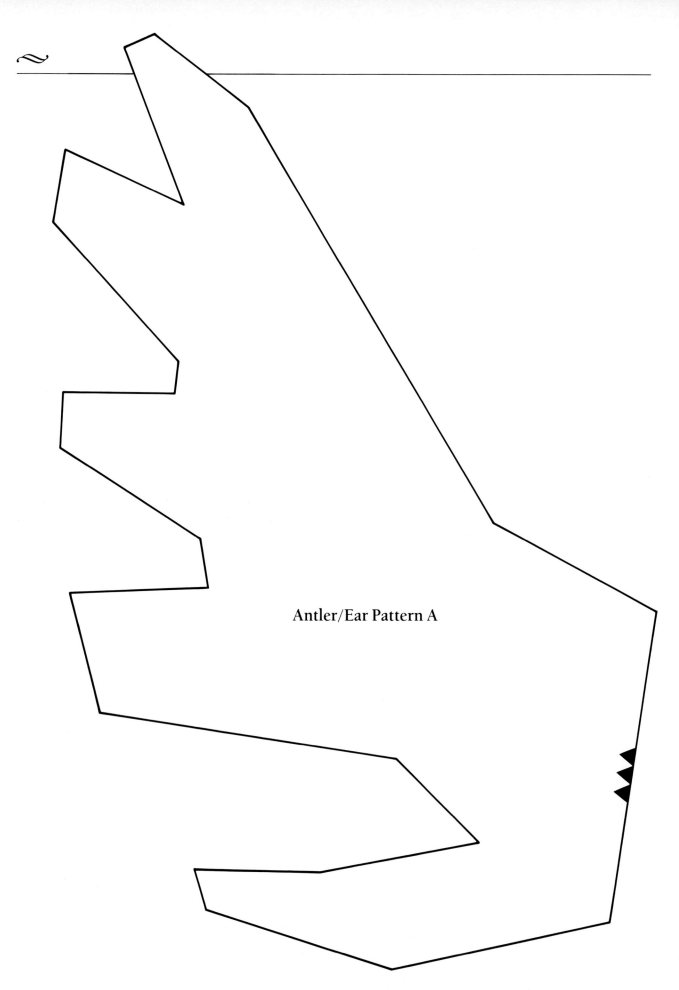

Antler/Ear Pattern A

Antler/Ear Pattern B

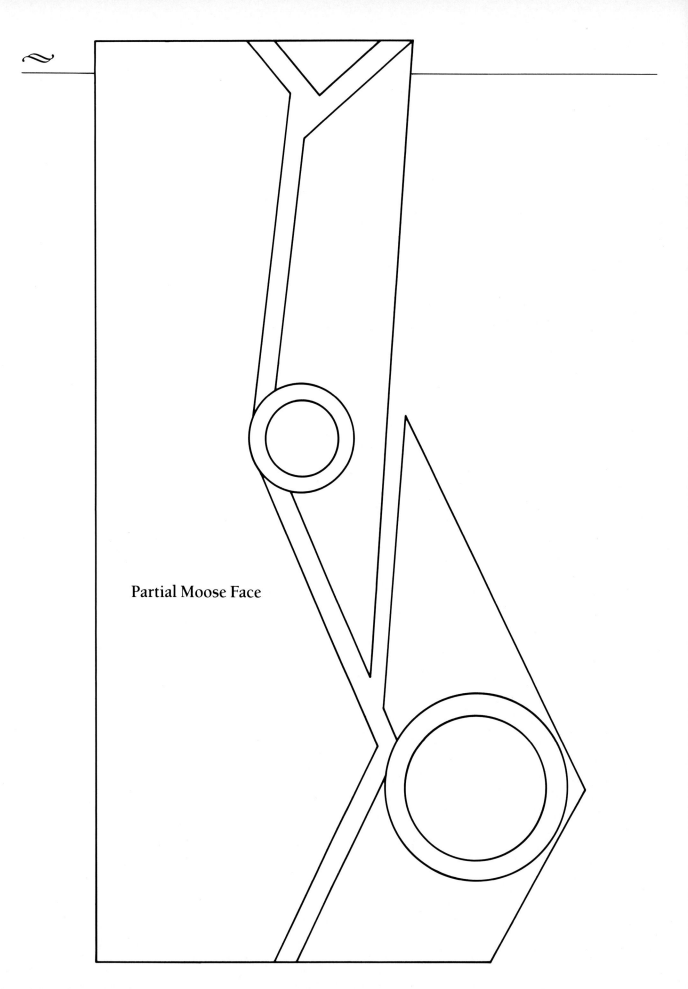

Partial Moose Face

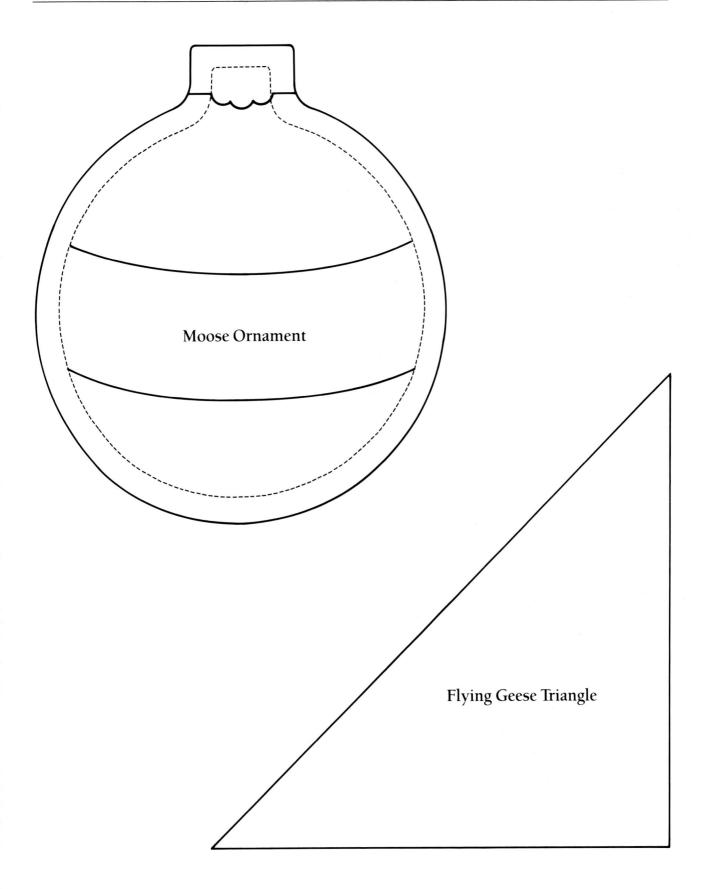

Moose Ornament

Flying Geese Triangle

MERRY CHRIS-MOOSE TWIN QUILT

The Merry Chris-Moose Wallhanging on page 180 can easily be expanded to twin-bed size with a larger background piece and some additional borders. The fabric yardages given are for the borders shown in the **Twin Quilt Layout**; each fabric was cut across the width and pieced to achieve the length needed. Any combination of borders totalling 14 inches in width will give you a twin-size quilt. If you decide on a different border treatment, or if you wish to cut the borders in one piece, adjust the yardages accordingly.

Approximate Size

65 × 96 inches

Materials Required

- 2 yards of fabric for background
- 1½ yards of fabric for fourth border
- ¾ yard of fabric for third border
- ½ yard of fabric for second border
- ⅜ yard of fabric for first border
- Approx. 18-inch-square pieces of assorted fabrics for body and antlers
- Smaller scraps of assorted fabrics
- 5 yards of fabric for backing
- ⅝ yard of fabric for binding
- Queen-size batting, approx. 70 × 100 inches

Making the Moose

Using the method described for the wallhanging beginning on page 183, enlarge the moose pattern and cut the fabric pieces. Mark a 36 × 68-inch rectangle on the background fabric. Measure in 9 inches from the bottom line, and mark a guideline across the full width of the rectangle. This marks the lower edge of the moose design area; align the bottom edge of the moose body with this line. Fuse or appliqué the pieces to the background.

Adding the Flying Geese

1. The twin quilt has Flying Geese on both the top and the bottom. To arrange them as shown in the

Twin Quilt Layout, you will need 20 triangles, 10 each for the top and bottom.

2. Lightly mark a line on the background fabric 5½ inches in from the top and bottom marked lines. Align the center points of the Flying Geese along these guidelines. Fuse or appliqué the pieces in place.

Quilting and Finishing

1. Using the same method as for the wallhanging, center the quilt top on the batting and backing, and quilt as desired.

2. All of the borders are added with the same Quilt-As-You-Sew method used for the wallhanging. For each of the four borders, you will measure and cut the side border strips first, and add them to the quilt. Then, measure and cut the top and bottom border strips, and add them to the quilt.

For the first border, cut two 2½ × 68-inch strips, and add them to the sides of the quilt. Press them away from the center of the quilt. Measure the width of the quilt, and cut two 2½-inch-wide strips to the needed length. Add the strips to the top and bottom.

3. The second border is 2½ inches wide finished. Measure the length of the quilt, and cut two 3-inch-wide side border strips to that length. Add the borders to the sides of the quilt, and press. Measure the width of the quilt, and cut 3-inch-wide strips for the top and bottom. Add the borders to the quilt, and press.

4. The third border has corner squares. Measure the length of the quilt, and cut two 4-inch-wide strips to that measurement. Add the borders to the quilt, and press. Measure the width of the quilt to the outside edge of the second border, and cut two 4-inch-wide strips to this length. Cut four 4-inch-

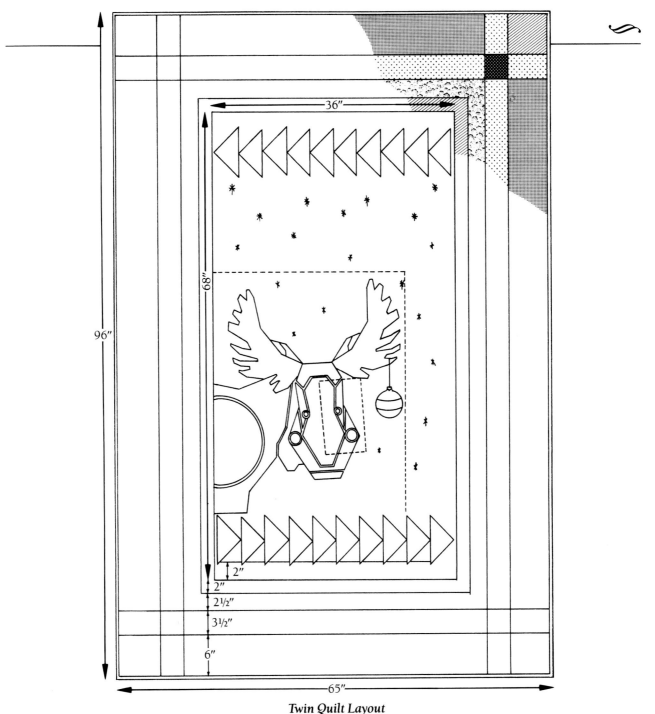

Twin Quilt Layout

Center panel 36″ × 68″ finished

square corner blocks, and sew one block to each end of the top and bottom border strips. Add the borders to the quilt, carefully matching seams.

5. The fourth border is also pieced. Cut two 6½-inch-wide strips to the same length that you cut the side border strips for the third border. Now, cut eight 4 × 6½-inch rectangles from the fabric used for the third border. Sew one rectangle to each end of the side border strips you just cut; set aside the remaining four rectangles. Sew these borders to the quilt top, carefully matching seams.

6. Cut two 6½-inch-wide strips to the same length that you cut the top and bottom border strips for the third border. Sew one of the 4 × 6½-inch rectangles to each end of these strips. Cut four 6½-inch squares from the fourth border fabric, and sew one square to each end of the border strips. Sew the top and bottom borders to the quilt.

7. Cut 2½-inch-wide strips for French-fold binding, and add the binding as described in the wallhanging directions.

BOOT ORNAMENTS

You'll get a kick out of how easily these boot ornaments go together. Why not dig around in your scrap bag and have some fun with them? Different fabrics and embellishments create a nice assortment of boot styles. The general directions for constructing the boot ornaments are given first; the pointers on how to create the different looking boots follow. Directions for the Cactus Ornaments begin on page 198.

Approximate Size

5 × 5½ inches

Materials Required

(for one ornament)

- Approx. 7 × 14-inch scrap of fabric
- 6½-inch square of batting
- Gold or other metallic thread
- Twine or cord for loop hanger

Basic Boot Ornament Directions

The ornaments shown in the photo are single boots. If you want to make pairs, double the materials. These instructions are for the basic brown boot with gold stitching.

1. Make a template for the boot using the pattern on page 197. Cut one boot front from fabric, flip the template over, and cut one boot back. Cut one boot from batting.

2. Place the fabric pieces right sides together, and place the batting on the wrong side of the boot backing fabric. Sew around the ornament, leaving 2 inches open along one side for turning. Trim the batting close to the seam. Clip the curves, and trim the corners.

3. Turn the ornament right side out, and press. Slip stitch the opening closed.

Quilting the Ornament

1. Use a water-erasable marking pen to mark the quilting lines on the front side of the ornament. If

◄ *Shown in the photo are* (clockwise from top right): *Multicolor Boot with Cactus and the Chili Pepper Boot, page 194; Cactus Ornament, page 198; quilted Ohio Star Boot, page 194; another Cactus Ornament; and a fused Ohio Star Boot, page 194. The Howling Coyote pattern, page 197, is shown fused to a real boot in the lower right corner of the photo.*

you are making pairs of boots, now is the time to reverse the direction of one boot or you'll end up with "two left feet."

2. With gold or contrasting thread, machine quilt along the marked lines. Stipple quilt inside the Ohio Star points. See page 9 for directions on stipple quilting.

Completing the Ornament

Use a loop of twine or cord to make a hanger. If you have made a pair of boots, join them with one 6-inch piece of twine that can be draped over a Christmas tree branch.

Ohio Star Boot

Make the basic boot as directed, and mark the quilting lines as shown on the pattern. Fuse the Ohio Star pieces in place on the completed boot using scraps of fabric and paper-backed fusible material. See page 153 for complete instructions on cutting and fusing. Use a narrow machine zigzag stitch along the edges of the fused fabric, stitching through all layers of the boot. Machine quilt along the marked lines.

Star Placement Guide

195

Chili Pepper Boot

1. To make chili peppers, trace the pepper shape onto a scrap of red fabric using the pattern on page 197. Layer the fabric wrong sides together with batting and backing; pin the layers in place. Stitch the layers together all the way around on the traced line; the seam allowance will remain on the outside of the pepper. Cut the pepper shape from the fabric, cutting just outside the line of stitching. Make six chili peppers.

2. Cut a star from green fabric using the pattern on page 197. Pin the star in position as indicated in the **Star Placement Guide** on page 195, with the ends of the chili peppers caught under the lower edge of the star. Machine appliqué the star in place. Machine quilt along marked lines at the boot heel and top of the foot.

Howling Coyote Boot

Use the patterns on page 197 to make the moon, coyote, and scarf. Referring to the **Coyote Placement Guide** below, fuse the pieces in place on the boot in the same manner as for the Ohio Star. Machine quilt along marked lines at the boot heel and top of the foot.

Coyote Placement Guide

Multicolor Boot with Cactus

Make a cactus using the pattern in the **Cactus Placement Guide** below. Fuse the cactus in place in the same manner as for the Ohio Star. Refer to the guide for the correct placement on the boot. Machine quilt along marked lines at the boot heel, at the top of the foot, and on the cactus.

Cactus Placement Guide

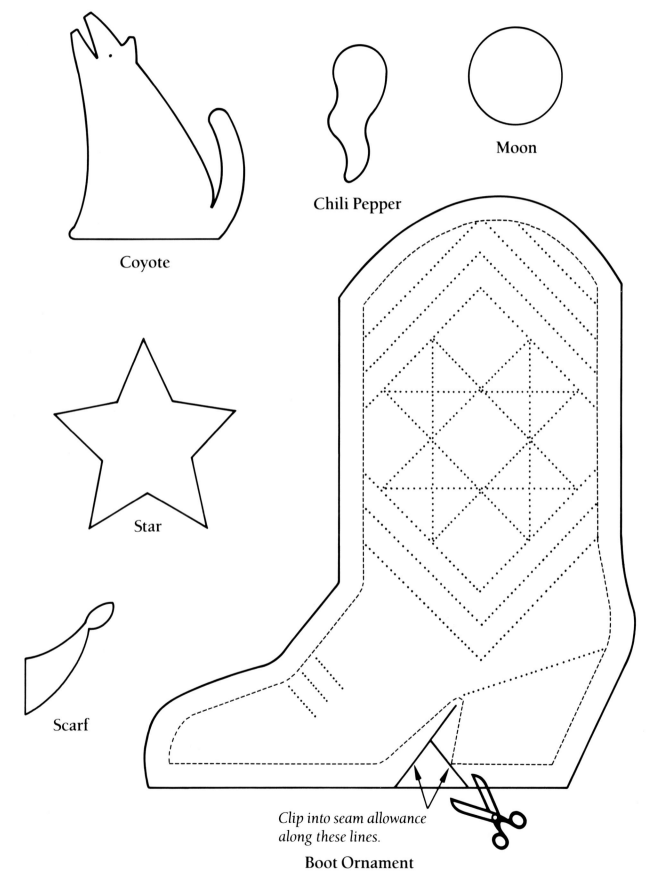

Coyote

Chili Pepper

Moon

Star

Scarf

Clip into seam allowance along these lines.

Boot Ornament

CACTUS ORNAMENT

This quick and simple ornament is a fun departure from the usual pine tree shape we see at Christmastime. Hung on a tree along with the Boot Ornaments on page 194, they help set the tone for a Southwestern holiday.

Approximate Size

3¾ × 5¼ inches

Materials Required

(for one ornament)

- Approx. 6 × 12-inch scrap of fabric
- 4 × 6-inch scrap of batting
- Green metallic thread
- Twine or cord for loop hanger

Making the Ornament

1. Make a template for the cactus using the pattern below. Cut two from scrap fabric and one from batting.

2. Layer, stitch, and turn the ornament as described in the "Basic Boot Ornament Directions" on page 195.

Finishing the Ornament

1. Use a water-erasable marking pen to mark the quilting lines on the front side of the ornament.

2. With green metallic thread, machine quilt along the marked lines.

3. Make the cactus spines by hand using a needle and green metallic thread. From the front, working along a quilting line, take a tiny stitch. Leave both ends of the thread long, and tie a tiny knot to hold the thread in place. Cut the thread, leaving the ends approximately ¾ inch to 1¼ inches long.

4. Use a loop of twine or cord to make a hanger.

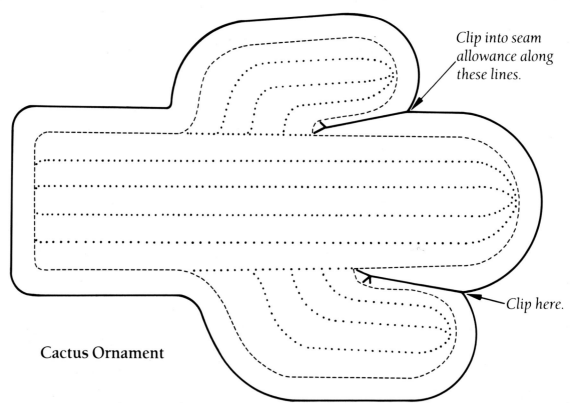

Clip into seam allowance along these lines.

Clip here.

Cactus Ornament

FUSED AND PAINTED SWEATS AND T-SHIRTS

Decorated clothes are fun and easy and very popular. The easiest way to decorate an article of clothing is to fuse a design to it. Apply paper-backed fusible material to printed fabric, cut out the design, remove the paper, fuse the design onto a sweatshirt or T-shirt, and outline and accent with paint. What could be easier?

There are so many different fabric paints available that it is impossible to detail them here. Ask at your local craft store for advice on the appropriate paints. Generally, the fabric dyes recommended for stenciling are not thick enough or opaque enough for edging fused fabric designs. Fine-tip paint applicators make edging much neater and easier.

MERRY CHRIS-MOOSE SWEATSHIRT

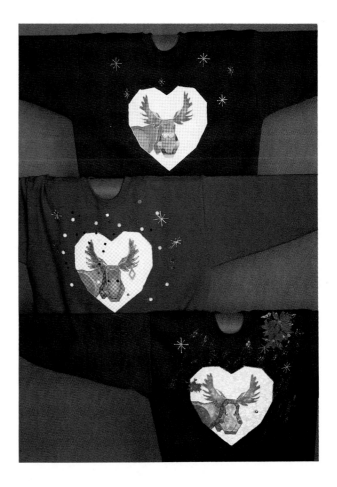

Immediately after the first Chris-Moose sweatshirt was completed, Ellen Rosintoski, one of my studio associates, stopped by the studio. She loved the Chris-Moose and begged Ann Nunemacher to stencil a moose for each Rosintoski. They had a series of parties and family gatherings to attend, and Ellen thought matching shirts would be fun.

Finally, Ann agreed and stenciled. Ellen bought sweatshirts on the way home, washed them, fused each moose in place, and embellished them, returning the next day to show them off. We had all been confident that her daughter, Erin, would love her shirt, and we were delighted to discover that her husband, Joe, not only had agreed to the sweatshirt concept but had personally picked out the sunglasses for his moose!

Materials Required

- Sweatshirt
- 11-inch square of fabric for background
- 11-inch square of paper-backed fusible material
- Stenciling supplies
- Dimensional fabric paint

Making the Pattern

Make a master pattern to work from. Trace around the half heart pattern on the opposite page, and cut it out. Trace the pattern onto a large sheet of tracing paper to get the left side of the heart. Flip the pattern over, line it up with the left side, and trace around the pattern to get the right side of the heart. Place the tracing paper over the pattern inside the half heart, and trace the left side of the Merry Chris-Moose design. To trace the right side of the face, lay the tracing paper over **Diagram 1** on page 182, match up all lines, and trace the right side of the face. Use this master pattern to make stencils or to cut patterns for appliqué. I recommend leaving it in one piece as a guide to placement of the design pieces.

Making the Sweatshirt

Appliqué or stencil the design onto a piece of muslin or other fabric. When the design is complete, cut out the heart, and fuse it onto a sweatshirt or T-shirt.

On the sweatshirts shown in the photo, the design was stenciled onto light fabric, which was then fused to the sweatshirt. Dimensional fabric paint was used between the pieces and to outline the circles. The fabric paint was also used to outline the heart, finishing the fused edges. Rhinestone eyes and a small bell ornament complete the moose design.

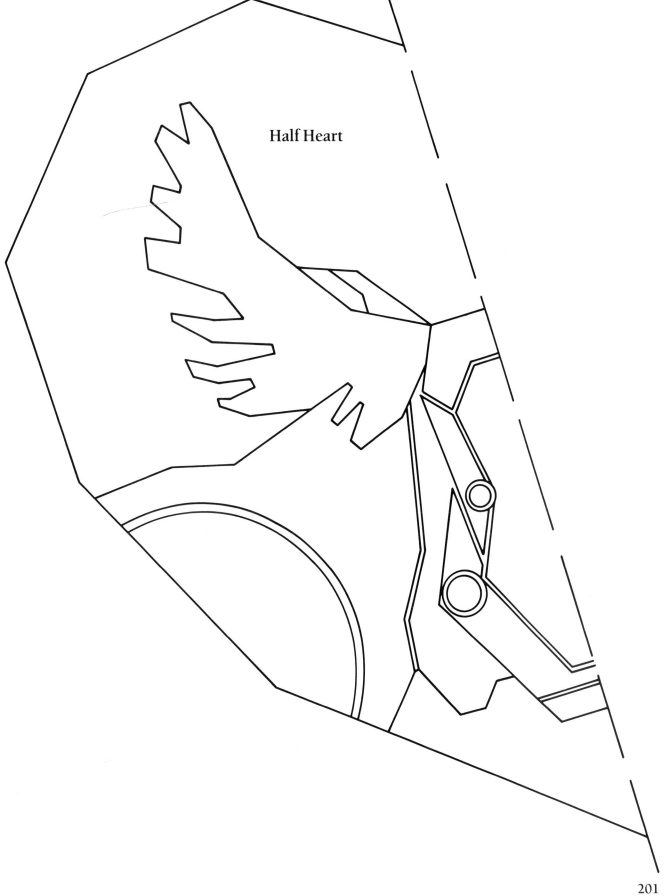

Half Heart

MY WEST BY SOUTHWEST T-SHIRT DRESS

One reason that quilters are quilters may be that they love working with fabric, but don't like to make collars or set-in sleeves or clothes that have to fit perfectly. The T-shirt dress is a great way to make an expressive outfit without that dressmaking effort. Currently, fashion dictates a wonderful selection of reasonably priced, ready-made, oversized T-shirts with a wide variety of sleeve and collar styles. They become the perfect top for a dress. Decorate them with fused fabric designs and paint, add a skirt, and you're finished!

My favorite style starts with an oversized T-shirt that is long enough and loose enough to cover the hips. The skirt can be made from just one fabric, but if you are the average quilter/fabric collector, you'll find this is a perfect place to put a little bit of every-thing that fits the theme. Most patchwork enthusiasts feel this is a good place to throw in a little piecing, too. The dress featured in the photo has an extensive collection of Western and boot fabrics, put together

in patchwork, yokes, fabric gathered to yokes, and even shirred sections. Considering the fabric collection, perhaps this dress is appropriately called "All I Want for Christmas Is Another Pair of Cowboy Boots." I usually just let the dress hang free from the shoulders. It can, of course, be belted if you prefer; if you do plan to belt the dress, be sure to allow extra length.

Materials Required

- Oversized T-shirt
- Total of approx. 2¼ yards of fabric for skirt
- Fabric scraps, fabric paint, and assorted embellishments to decorate the shirt (optional)

Making the Dress

1. Prewash the T-shirt, and decorate as desired.

2. Put the T-shirt on, and select and mark the line where the skirt will be added. Leave the existing hem alone for now. It makes the knit more stable for the sewing process.

3. Decide how long you want the skirt to be. I like the skirt to hit around midcalf. Measure from the marked line to the desired length; add ½ inch for the gathering and the seam at the top and ¾ inch for the narrow folded hem.

4. Next, cut or piece the fabric for the skirt. If I'm using a solid rather than a pieced fabric, I usually gather at least three 45-inch widths for the skirt. In other words, once I've determined the length I need, I measure along the fabric to that length, and then cut across the width. Three of these pieces, joined in one long strip and then gathered, make a nice skirt.

If you've decided to make a pieced skirt like the one shown in the photo, sew together random-size scraps to make one large piece of fabric that is approximately the length of the skirt and 135 inches wide.

5. Join the ends of the long fabric strip to make a large circle. Using pins to mark the sections, divide the circle into quarters. Measure around the bottom edge of the T-shirt, being careful not to stretch the fabric. Gather the skirt fabric to this measurement.

6. With right sides together, match the shirt side seams and center front and back to the quarter marks on the skirt. Pin the skirt securely to the shirt, and stitch.

7. Trim the seam allowance to ¼ inch. If a serger is available, serge the raw edge. If not, stitch again ⅛ inch into the seam allowance. Press the seam allowance toward the shirt.

8. Topstitch just above the seam where the skirt is joined to the shirt.

9. Hem the skirt with a narrow folded hem.

DAD'S CHRISTMAS TIES REVISITED

Because "getting another tie for Christmas" has become such a joke, I think it is appropriate to recycle some of those old ties into new gifts and decorations. Many men are very attached to their ties, and when the ties wear out or get stained or go out of style, they still don't want to throw them away. Over the years, I have made several recycled tie presents that have been very warmly received.

Christmas decorations and presents made from ties are a nice way to pass gentlemen's memorabilia from one generation to another. Christmas decorations made from your husband's and father's ties would be perfect to give to your son.

Reclaiming the Fabric

On this subject, I can pass along only what I did and what I learned. I based my plan on what I considered to be common sense. If you are as accustomed to working with cotton as I am, you'll find that the tie

Shown in the photo are "Quilted" Styrofoam Ornaments, page 213, and Grandmother's Fan from Grandfather's Ties, page 206.

fabrics seem to slither and slide. To make them a little easier to work with, I decided to sort the ties by fiber, silk being my fiber of choice. I kept a few silk/polyester blends that had the same general texture and weight.

Most of the ties in the collection I worked with had been well worn. Since I didn't want to pay for dry cleaning and I didn't want to have to cut around spots and I knew the clean narrow ends wouldn't be enough to work with, I made a difficult decision. I decided to bite the bullet and open the ties, remove the interlinings, and wash the ties.

The first 6 or 8 ties were washed very gently without mixing colors, then dried briefly in the dryer and, while still slightly damp, ironed dry. They looked great. The next 24 ties were not handled as gently; as a result, a couple faded and a few others got shiny with the ironing. Frankly, I don't know whether it was the technique or the ties, but I didn't spend a lot of time wondering, as there was now a considerable amount of clean, pressed fabric (and still more ties!).

By the way, it's a good idea to keep several of the tie interlinings—the good ones are wool—just in case you decide to make a few ties sometime. Good interlining is fairly expensive, and since it has to be cut on the bias, you have to buy a lot to make just one tie. Think about the width of the interlining when deciding whether to save it. The width of the interlining determines the width of the tie, and ties that are not the current correct width generally do not get worn. An interlining that is too wide could always be trimmed down, but one that is too narrow may not be worth saving.

GRANDMOTHER'S FAN FROM GRANDFATHER'S TIES

Grandmother's Fan is a popular quilt pattern that is perfect when made from ties. Combine it with a background of Facile or Ultrasuede for a pleasingly masculine pillow.

Approximate Size

13½ inches square

Materials Required

- ⅜ yard of brown Facile or Ultrasuede for pillow front and back
- 8 men's ties (includes material to cover cording)
- 5-inch square of coordinating fabric for fan center
- Polyester fiberfill for stuffing
- 1½ yards of ¼-inch piping cord

Cutting the Fabrics

1. Each of the seven pieces of the fan is cut from a different old tie using the fan pattern on page 208. Note that there is a V-shaped line on the wide end of the pattern piece. If you are cutting from the middle of the tie, make a template using the full pattern. If you are fortunate enough to have seven narrow finished tie ends, make a template using the dotted line marked Tie Guide. Place the point of the template on the finished tie end, and then mark the two sides and the other end of the fan segment. Neckties are cut on the bias, so handle the cut pieces gently.

2. Make a template for the fan center using the pattern on page 208, and cut the piece from the scrap of coordinating fabric.

3. The pillow cording was covered with bias binding cut from one of the ties. If you cut straight down a tie, you automatically get bias strips. Cut 1⅜-inch-wide bias strips, and join them with diagonal seams. You will need a total of 54 inches of bias binding.

4. Because Facile is very expensive and I wanted to use it efficiently, I pieced the pillow back rather than cut one large piece. Cut one 10½-inch square for the fan background and two 7¼ × 14-inch halves for the pillow back. Cut two 2¼ × 10½-inch strips and two 2¼ × 14-inch strips for the borders. The cutting layout in **Diagram 1** illustrates the most efficient use of the Facile yardage. If you are using a different fabric and don't want to piece the pillow back, buy ½ yard and cut a 14-inch square for the back.

Making the Fan

1. If you did not cut the fan segments with finished tie ends, make points at this time. Fold the broad end of each segment right sides together with edges aligned, and stitch ¼ inch from the end. Chain stitching, as shown in **Diagram 2**, speeds up this step.

2. Clip a tiny wedge off the seam allowance at the fold. Turn the point right side out so that the seam goes straight down the center of the back, as shown in **Diagram 3**. Press.

3. Using a ¼-inch seam allowance, stitch the fan segments together along the sides to form the fan. Press the seam allowances to one side.

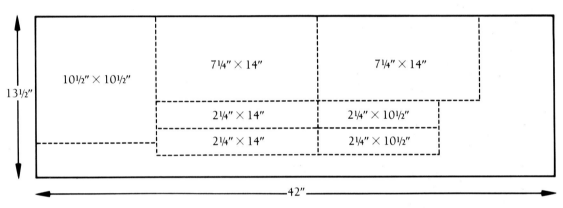

Diagram 1

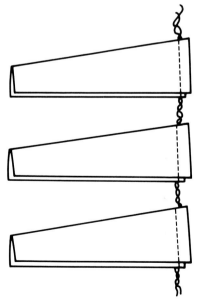

Diagram 2

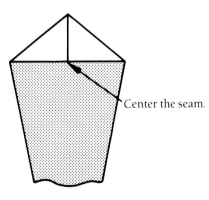

Center the seam.

Diagram 3

4. Position the fan center on the background square so that the two outside edges are even with the edges of the background. Baste the two edges in position.

5. Position the fan on the background so that the raw ends of the fan segments will be covered by the curved edge of the fan center when it is turned under. Pin the fan in place, and appliqué it. Because the tie ends are so nicely finished, you could appliqué by stitching in the ditch between fan blades with invisible thread and leaving the fan points unattached.

6. Turn under the curved edge of the fan center, and appliqué it in place.

Finishing the Pillow

1. Sew the 10½-inch border strips to the top and bottom of the appliquéd square. Sew the 14-inch strips to the sides.

2. Using the zipper foot on your machine, cover the cording with the necktie bias binding. See "Making the Piping Trim" on page 104 for complete instructions.

3. With raw edges aligned, baste the covered cording to the right side of the pillow front. Cut the cording to length where the ends meet, leaving a 1-inch section of the covering extending past the end of the cord. Turn under ½ inch of the covering to make a finished end, and baste over the other end of the cording.

4. Place the pillow back pieces right sides together, and sew in from both sides, leaving a 6-inch opening in the center of the seam. Place the pillow front and pillow back right sides together, and stitch along the edges, following the basting thread.

5. Turn the pillow right side out through the center back opening, and stuff it. Stitch the opening closed.

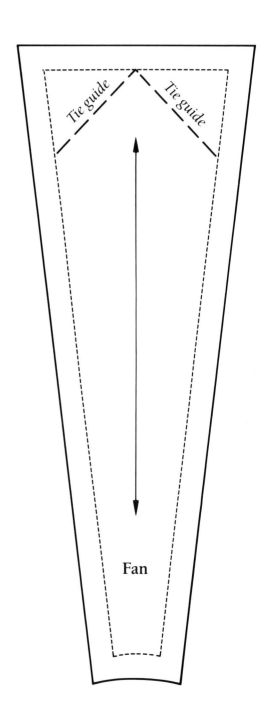

Fan Center

Tie guide   Tie guide

Fan

SUIT AND TIE STOCKING

Shown in the photo are the Suit and Tie Stocking, page 209;
the Log Cabin Suit and Tie Ornament (top right), page 210;
and the Courthouse Steps Variation Ornament (bottom
right), page 212.

Approximate Size

11 inches wide at the toe × 16 inches long

Materials Required

- ⅜ yard of fabric for lining
- 13 × 18-inch piece of men's suiting material for stocking front
- 13 × 18-inch piece of fabric for backing
- 8½ × 19-inch piece of oxford cloth for cuff
- 3 men's ties
- ½ yard of batting
- 3¾ × 18-inch piece of paper-backed fusible material
- 6-inch piece of ribbon for loop hanger
- Two ½-inch-diameter men's shirt buttons
- Assorted men's clothing labels (optional)
- Assorted men's suit buttons (optional)

Follow the directions for the Basic Christmas Stocking on page 77 to make the stocking. Use the suiting material for the stocking front and the oxford cloth for the cuff.

Add masculine finishing touches to the stocking. Cut the wide ends of three men's neckties to the following lengths: 6 inches, 8¾ inches, and 10½ inches. Arrange them on the stocking front as shown in the photo. Turn under ¼ inch on the raw edges, and hand tack the ties in place underneath the cuff. Embellish the cuff with two men's shirt buttons. Three men's suit buttons and five men's clothing labels are scattered across the toe of the stocking for additional embellishment.

LOG CABIN SUIT AND TIE ORNAMENTS

The Log Cabin is a favorite quilt block. It has a unique from-the-center-out construction technique that makes it ideal for the Quilt-As-You-Sew method used with these Christmas ornaments. The larger of the two ornaments shown in the photo on page 209 is the traditional Log Cabin design; the smaller, a variation called Courthouse Steps. For a discussion of the Quilt-As-You-Sew method used here, see page 186.

Approximate Size

Traditional Log Cabin Ornament: 4½ inches square

Courthouse Steps Variation: 3¾ inches square

Materials Required

(for one ornament)

- Scraps of men's tie fabric, oxford cloth, and men's suiting material for front, backing, and binding
- Scraps of batting
- Scraps of lightweight fusible interfacing
- Thread for loop hanger

Cutting the Materials

In these projects, I prefer to cut the batting and backing a little larger than the expected final size, and trim them to size as part of the finishing process. It's fun to vary the width of the strips and the number of strips and the arrangement, but not much fun to calculate exactly what all those different finished sizes should be. Because I don't like the finished ornaments much larger than 4½ inches square, I cut 5-inch squares of batting and backing, and trim them later.

Cut strips anywhere from ¾ inch wide to 1⅛ inches wide. The strips on the Log Cabin shown in the photo were cut 1 inch wide, and on the Courthouse Steps, ¾ inch wide. All of the strips in each ornament were cut the same width.

The center square can also vary in size. The two shown were cut 1 inch square and 1¼ inches square.

Making the Log Cabin Ornament

1. The ornament starts with a center square of tie fabric. If the tie fabric is unusually slippery, stabilize it with lightweight fusible interfacing. Check the shape of the center unit. Because everything builds around the center, it is crucial that it be truly square.

2. Place the batting on the wrong side of the backing fabric. Center the stabilized center square on the batting, as shown in **Diagram 1**.

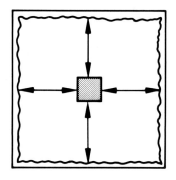

Diagram 1

3. Lay the first strip of oxford cloth on top of the center square, right sides together and raw edges aligned. See **Diagram 2**. Stitch through all four layers of material. After stitching, flip the shirt fabric away

from the center unit. The seam that holds the layers together makes an indentation. Finger press, and trim the strip to length. If all your strips of oxford cloth are going to be the same width, continue to work from one strip until it's used up, then go on to another strip.

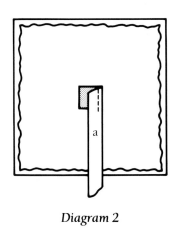

Diagram 2

4. Turn the ornament 90 degrees counterclockwise, and, in the same way, stitch a second strip of the shirt fabric to the center unit, as shown in **Diagram 3**. Notice that when you lay down the new strip, the edge that will not be sewn is a visible guide to be lined up parallel to the outside edge of the center square. (As you progress around the center, more and more seams become visible to use as guidelines for accuracy.)

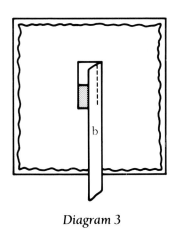

Diagram 3

5. Select a tie fabric for the next two strips, and add those strips in the same way. See **Diagrams 4** and **5**. After each complete round of strips, carefully press the piecing. Use a pressing cloth or a very low-temperature iron to press. Then, turn the ornament over,

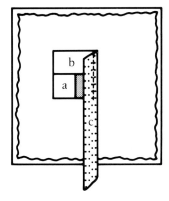

Diagram 4

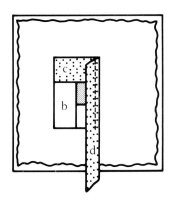

Diagram 5

and clip the threads on the back so that they will not get caught when the next strips are added.

6. Continue circling the center square for three more rounds or until the ornament is the desired size.

7. Trim the backing and batting if necessary. Finish the edges with binding strips cut from suiting material. Cut four 1 × 5-inch strips. Sew strips to two opposite sides of the ornament, right sides together and raw edges even. Fold the binding strips to the back side of the ornament, turn under ¼ inch on the edge, and hand stitch them in place. Trim the ends of the strips even with the edge of the ornament.

8. Sew binding strips to the remaining two sides, and turn under ¼ inch on the ends to enclose the raw ends of the other strips. Fold the strips around to the back, turn under ¼ inch along the edge, and hand stitch to the back of the ornament.

9. Use thread to make a loop hanger for the ornament.

Courthouse Steps
Variation

The actual stitch-and-flip sewing technique is the same as for the Log Cabin Ornament; only the arrangement of strips is different. Proceed with Steps 1 to 3 on pages 210 and 211. The first strip attached to the center square can be either shirt or tie fabric. The second strip sewn to the center square matches the first, but instead of being adjacent to the first strip, it is placed on the opposite side of the square. See **Diagram 1**.

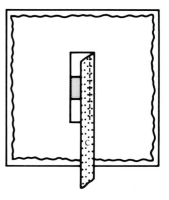

Diagram 2

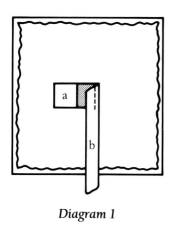

Diagram 1

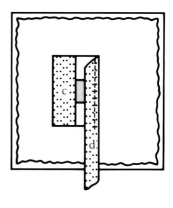

Diagram 3

The next two strips also match each other, but contrast with the first two, as shown in the photo. Add the strips as shown in **Diagrams 2** and **3**.

For the next pair of strips, go back to the first fabric. Continue to alternate pairs of matching strips, placing them on opposite sides of the center square, until the ornament is the desired size. Finish the ornament as you would the Log Cabin Ornament.

"QUILTED" STYROFOAM ORNAMENTS

This is a great way to use up small scraps of tie fabric. The no-sew technique makes these ornaments fast and fun. The basic instructions are for the eight-section ornament, which is the largest of the four shown in the photo.

Approximate Size

5 inches, including trim

Materials Required

(for one ornament)

- Scraps of men's tie fabric
- 2 yards of ⅛-inch-diameter rat tail cord
- 10-inch piece of dark thread for loop hanger
- 3-inch Styrofoam ball
- ½-inch-diameter gold shank-style blazer button
- 1 yard of lightweight string
- Tacky craft glue

Marking the Styrofoam Ball

1. Using lightweight string, divide the Styrofoam ball into four equal sections, as shown in **Diagram 1**. Mark the center of each of these sections with a pin.

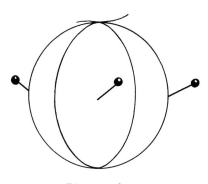

Diagram 1

2. "Quilt" the Styrofoam ball by using a plastic knife or nail file to make ⅛-inch-deep crevices in the ball along the four string lines. See **Diagram 2**. Next, make a crevice where the center of each section is marked, dividing the ball into a total of eight equal sections.

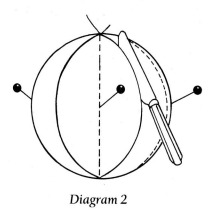

Diagram 2

Covering the Ball with Fabric

1. After making creases in the Styrofoam, wrap a scrap of fabric around the ball, and trace the creases that form one section to create a pattern for cutting the tie fabric. Cut out the pattern, allowing at least ½ inch of extra fabric around the exact size traced. Use the pattern to cut eight sections from opened, unlined scraps of men's ties.

2. Beginning at one end of a section, push the edges of the fabric into the crevices and smooth the fabric over the ball section, as shown in **Diagram 3**. Use a tiny bit of tacky craft glue at the fabric ends if needed. Trim the excess fabric.

Diagram 3

3. Cover the remaining seven sections in the same manner.

Adding the Rat Tail Trim

1. Rat tail cord is used in the crevices to cover the edges of the fabric and make the tassel. Cut six 8-inch-long pieces of rat tail.

Diagram 4

2. Decide which end of the ornament will be the top. Starting on the top of the ornament at the center point, begin gluing the rat tail cord along the crevices, holding it in place with pins until the glue dries. Begin as close to the top as possible (no more than ⅛ inch from the center point, or the ends will not be covered by the button trim), and let the excess length of each piece hang loose at the bottom. Work on opposite sides of the ornament as you glue the rat tail in place, completing six crevices. The remaining two crevices should be opposite each other. See **Diagram 4**.

Making the Tassel

1. The two remaining crevices are filled with one length of rat tail cord that is cut long enough to complete the tassel. Cut one piece of rat tail 18 inches long.

2. Thread the rat tail through the shank of the blazer button. Position the button 8 inches from one end, leaving 8- and 10-inch lengths of rat tail on either side of the button.

3. Push the button shank into the top center of the ornament, as shown in **Diagram 5**, and glue if necessary to hold it in place.

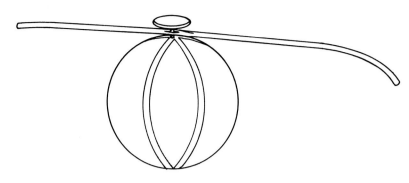

Diagram 5

4. Glue the rat tail into the remaining two crevices of the ornament, pinning it in position. Let the excess length remain loose at the bottom. Allow the glue to dry thoroughly.

5. Gather all the rat tail ends, except the longest, into a neat bunch, holding them tightly against the bottom of the ornament. Tie the bunch with thread if necessary. Wrap the remaining longest strand of rat tail around the bunch three times, but not too tightly. Push the end up through the three twists, as shown in **Diagram 6**. Tuck the loose end out of sight, using a dab of glue to hold it in place.

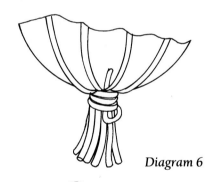

Diagram 6

Completing the Ornament

Make a hanger for the ornament using a 10-inch piece of dark thread. Wrap the thread around the button, and make a loop for hanging.

Other Design Ideas

You can use the same "quilted" Styrofoam technique with different-size balls and different crease designs, as shown in the photo and in the illustrations below. After making creases in the Styrofoam, wrap a scrap of fabric around the ball and trace the creases to create a pattern for cutting the tie fabric.

To make the ornament with the flat sides, cut off the top and bottom of a Styrofoam ball. To make a loop in the rat tail for hanging, cut the piece slightly longer, twist it into a loop in the middle, and glue it to the top center of the ornament.

Once you start sewing with tie fabrics, you are likely to keep going. For example, look at the String-Pieced Ornaments in the photo on page 216; they would be wonderful made from tie scraps.

Cut off two sides to flatten.

Ornament Variations

215

QUILTING BAG OF TRICKS

At quilt shows, there are almost always categories for Patchwork and Appliqué, and then there is that category called Other or Special Techniques. Things as diverse as yo-yo quilting, puff quilting, string piecing, whole-cloth quilting, and crazy quilting might all come under that same heading. Another name for this chapter could be "A Tribute to Other," since I've gathered some of those fun but sometimes forgotten techniques and featured them in a host of holiday projects.

STRING-PIECED ORNAMENTS

There have already been several groups of ornaments sprinkled through this book, but I couldn't resist adding some more that use the fun and fast technique of string piecing. A quilter who string pieces can always come up with a quick Christmas ornament for a teacher gift, package trim, or just a nice thank-you. The heart and star ornaments shown in the photo on the opposite page are the basic shapes from page 83, string pieced in homespun fabrics. But these ornaments could be made from any recognizable silhouette shape and from any other collection of fabrics, such as calico, Christmas prints, or Dad's ties. Make a stocking ornament in a coordinating fabric, or string piece that, too! (Directions for the stocking ornament can be found on page 84.)

Approximate Size

Heart Ornament: 4½ × 4 inches
Star Ornament: 4½ × 5 inches

◄ *Shown in the photo are String-Pieced Heart and Star Ornaments in homespun fabrics, page 217; a homespun Small Stocking Ornament, page 84; and a homespun Trip Around the World Tree Skirt, page 118.*

Materials Required

(for one ornament)

- Two 7-inch squares of muslin for lining and backing
- Scraps of assorted fabrics for ornament front
- 6-inch square of batting
- Polyester fiberfill for stuffing
- 15-inch piece of raffia, ribbon, or invisible thread for loop hanger

What Is String Piecing?

String piecing and stitch-and-flip are both terms that describe the technique of covering a foundation by placing two pieces of fabric right sides together on a backing, stitching along one side, then flipping the top piece open. This process is usually repeated many times with small pieces of fabric. Many people use the terms string *piecing* and string *quilting* interchangeably. I think I do sometimes, but it is unintentional. When I am being careful with my words, I use string piecing to refer to the stitch-and-flip process when it is being done with no batting. String quilting is the same process being done on a batting and backing fabric base. The technique is basically the same as Quilt-As-You-Sew, but in my mind, Quilt-As-You-Sew refers to more organized sewing, like borders or Log Cabin strips, while string quilting is very random. I consider these ornaments to be string pieced even though the strips are being sewn to a batting and lining base, because the actual back of the ornament is added later. You could just as easily make these without the thin batting layer; simply sew the strips to the lining fabric.

The reality is that no matter what you call this technique of stitching together little bits of fabric, string piecing is fun, quick, easy, and a wonderful way to use small pieces of fabric. String piecing may be done with even-width strips of fabric, but I prefer using irregular shapes. Even the smallest scraps of fabric can be utilized. If you enjoy the technique, you may want to explore using even more-irregular shapes than were used in the ornaments shown in the photo.

SEE-THROUGH TEMPLATES

Use see-through template plastic to make templates for the ornaments. That way, when you place the template on the string-pieced fabric, you'll be able to move it around and position it so that the finished ornament shows off an interesting portion of the string piecing.

Making the Ornament Front

1. For each ornament, make a template using one of the basic patterns on pages 85 and 86.

2. Place the batting on top of the wrong side of the lining fabric. Use the stitch-and-flip technique to cover the ornament batting with scraps of fabric. Start at the center and work out, or begin on one side and work across. Position the first scrap of fabric right side up on the batting. Put the second scrap right side down on top of the first, aligning the edges along one side. Stitch a straight line along the edge of the two scraps, sewing through the batting and lining fabric. Flip the top scrap open so that it is right side up. See **Diagram 1**.

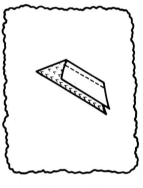

Diagram 1

Continue to add scraps until the ornament batting is completely covered, as shown in **Diagram 2**. The sizes of the scraps will determine how many are needed to make the ornament front.

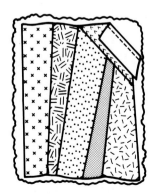

Diagram 2

Finishing the Ornament

1. Position the template on the right side of the string-pieced fabric. Move the template around until you're pleased with the placement of the strips on the body of the ornament. Trace around the template, and cut out the ornament.

2. To make a pieced back for easy turning and finishing, fold the remaining 7-inch piece of muslin in half. Using a ⅜-inch seam allowance, stitch in from each side along the fold, leaving a 2-inch open-ing in the center. Trim the seam allowance to ¼ inch, cutting off the fold. Press the seam allowance to one side.

3. Layer the backing and the string-pieced front right sides together. Stitch around the outside edge of the ornament. Trim the seam allowance, and clip the curves. Turn the ornament right side out through the center back opening. Stuff the ornament, and slip stitch the opening closed.

4. Make a loop hanger from raffia, ribbon, or invisible thread, and tack it to the top of the ornament.

QUILTED DIAMOND ORNAMENTS

You may recall a discussion back in the "Start with Some Basics" chapter on page 1 about decid-ing how much time you want to spend and choosing projects and techniques that will correspond with your time commitment. These pretty ornaments illus-trate that point beautifully. You can spend a little time or a lot of time on them: either way, the result will be pleasing. Of the four diamonds shown in the photo, the first three are a hand-quilted version (*bottom left*), a machine-quilted version (*center*), and a painted version (*top*). Of the three, the hand-quilted took the longest and is my favorite. The painted one was the fastest, and its design is the most visible. Personally, I think the machine-quilted single line isn't really acceptable, but it's shown so that you can compare it with the others. Using a heavier thread, or even a double thread, would be a definite improvement.

The fourth ornament, on the bottom right in the photo, is an enhanced machine-quilted version. To me, it is even more attractive than the hand-quilted ornament. As a bonus, the machine stipple quilting that covers the entire background took less time than the hand quilting.

While only one quilting design (pattern A) is shown completed, there are patterns for two additional designs included on page 222. In addition, there are many colors of metallic thread and lamé available that could be used to create a wide variety of ornaments. If you like the look of these ornaments, you might also like the Gold and White Wreath on page 239 and the Elegant Trapunto Stocking on page 240. Both projects are actually machine quilted, but could also be interpreted in any of the techniques shown here.

Approximate Size

4½ inches high, not including tassel and loop hanger

Materials Required

(for one ornament)

- 6 × 8-inch scrap of gold lamé for mock binding and backing
- 6 × 8-inch scrap of woven fusible stabilizer for lamé
- Two 5 × 6-inch scraps of muslin or ecru fabric for ornament front and lining
- 5 × 6-inch scrap of batting
- Polyester fiberfill for stuffing
- 5-inch piece of ⅛-inch gold cord for loop hanger
- 2-inch tassel
- Gold metallic thread or gold fabric paint with fine-point applicator

Making the Ornament Front

1. Using one of the patterns on page 222, center and trace the quilting design and the cutting line onto the right side of one piece of muslin. Layer with batting and lining, and pin the layers together. Don't cut the diamond shape yet.

2. Use gold metallic thread to hand or machine stitch along the design lines. Add additional decorative stitching if desired. As an alternative, create the design using gold fabric paint in a fine-point applicator tube. If you are using paint, the batting and lining are not necessary, but will make the binding more attractive. Another option is to machine quilt with regular thread and then outline with paint. This creates the depth of quilting, with the bonus glitter and texture of paint.

Making the Mock Binding

1. The mock binding is made from gold lamé. To prepare the lamé, fuse it to the woven stabilizer. Then cut four ¾ × 3½-inch strips. With right sides together and the raw edge of the lamé even with the marked cutting line on the muslin, sew a mock binding strip to each of two opposite sides of the ornament. Fold the lamé strips over, and, using a pressing cloth, press them down on top of the seam allowances. Try not to let the iron touch the metallic side of the lamé. In the same manner, sew a mock binding strip to each of the remaining sides of the ornament, catching the ends of the first strips in the seams. See **Diagram 1**. Again, fold the lamé strips over the seam allowances, and press.

2. Trim the excess muslin, batting, and lining, using the outer unstitched edge of the lamé mock binding as your guide, as shown in **Diagram 2**.

Adding the Backing

1. Using the ornament with mock binding as the pattern, cut the ornament backing from gold lamé.

2. Place the ornament front and back right sides together. With raw edges even, stitch around three sides of the ornament, leaving the fourth side open for turning. Trim the corners, and turn the ornament right side out.

3. Stuff the ornament lightly with loose polyester fiberfill.

4. Turn the open edge seam allowance to the inside, and slip stitch the opening closed. If you have any trouble getting a crisp edge finish, you might want to try the finishing method described in "Finishing the Ornament" on page 219. There, the back is made with a center back seam for turning and stuffing.

Completing the Ornament

1. Give the ornament dimension by using gold metallic thread to take a tiny stitch through the center front of the ornament to the back side.

2. Complete the mock binding by stitching in the ditch between the binding and the ornament.

3. Tack the tassel to the bottom of the ornament from the back side.

4. Create the loop hanger by folding a 5-inch length of ⅛-inch gold cord in half and tacking the ends to the back side of the ornament.

Diagram 1

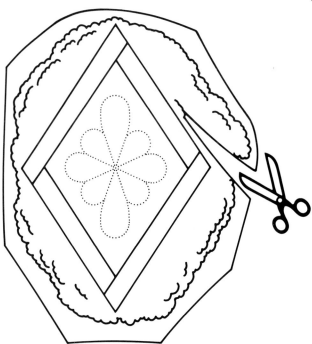

Diagram 2

YO-YO THIMBLE ORNAMENTS

What's the size of a sewing basket, cute as a button, and chock-full of thimbles? How about a quilter's thimble tree! This tree is appropriate for all thimble collectors, whether or not they are also quilters. A small tabletop Christmas tree is the perfect scale for thimbles. In addition to the Yo-Yo Thimble Ornaments I feature here, the tree can be decorated with little spools, miniature scissors, and buttons. When completed, the thimble tree is perfect as a decoration on a mantle or on an antique sewing machine table.

The easy-to-make Yo-Yo Thimble Ornaments are a wonderful way to showcase a collection of thimbles at Christmas. The thimbles are held in place without glue when set snugly on top of the pom-poms. Another fun idea is to glue an inexpensive thimble to the pom-pom and clip the clothespin to your collar or lapel for the holiday season quilt guild meetings.

Approximate Size

1¾ inches long, not including ribbon streamers

Materials Required

(for one ornament)

- 3½-inch squares of assorted fabrics
- ½-inch-diameter pom-pom
- 10-inch pieces of assorted ⅛-inch-wide ribbons
- Thimble
- 1¾-inch-long clothespin
- Craft glue
- Ribbon rose (optional)

Making the Yo-Yos

1. Three yo-yo sizes have been included in the pattern on the opposite page. You may choose to layer two or three yo-yos, or use just one. Cut the smallest circle if you will use only one; graduate sizes if you decide to layer. The finished yo-yo will be 1 inch smaller than the cut diameter of the circle. Cut fabric circles from scraps as desired.

2. Hand sew a long running stitch around the circumference of the fabric circle, ¼ inch from the outside edge. It is not necessary to turn under the raw edge of the circle, as it is never exposed.

3. Make a yo-yo by gently pulling this thread until the outside edge is gathered into a small circle in the center. The raw edge of the circle is actually pulled to the inside. Be sure that the right side of the fabric is visible. The yo-yo is now a smaller circle two layers thick, as shown in **Diagram 1**. Tie the thread to secure the yo-yo.

Assembling the Ornament

1. Referring to **Diagram 2**, glue the yo-yo to the flat side of the clothespin with the gathered edge facing up. If you are layering several yo-yos, glue the largest in position first; additional yo-yos are layered and glued in the same manner.

2. Center a pom-pom over the gathered edge of the top yo-yo, and glue it in position.

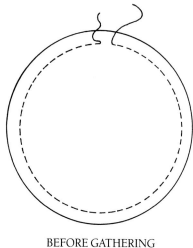

BEFORE GATHERING

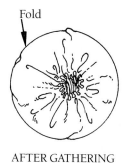

Fold

AFTER GATHERING

Diagram 1

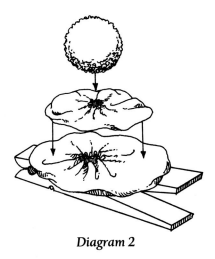

Diagram 2

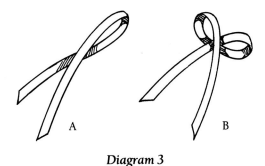

Diagram 3

Adding the Trim

The ribbon trims shown in the photo vary. Some are 4- to 5-inch lengths of ribbon in a single loop, as shown in **Diagram 3A**, and some are figure-eight loops, as shown in **Diagram 3B**. Some are several loops stacked together, and some have ribbon roses on top. Other trims may work just as well. The important thing is to glue the trim to the yo-yo and not to the pom-pom. Gluing the trim to the pom-pom keeps the thimble from sitting flat. After adding the trim, place the thimble on the pom-pom.

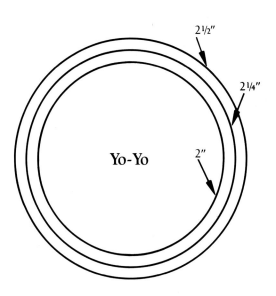

QUILTER'S GREETING CARDS AND GIFT TAGS

Although it's hard to believe, quilters sometimes need to take a break from the sewing machine or quilting hoop and dabble in another creative outlet. I'm including these designs for greeting cards and gift tags because they give you the opportunity to play with quilt designs and scraps of fabric to create something other than a quilt. These cards make a great winter afternoon project with the kids, and of course, they are absolutely perfect to accompany any quilts you're planning to give as gifts.

The patterns for all the designs shown in the photo are provided beginning on page 228, but these are just a few of the many possibilities. Mix and match the patterns, or make up your own. For example, the block pattern shown on the center right in the photo is a hybrid of two other block patterns, the Weather Vane and 54–40 or Fight. Elements were taken from both blocks to create a whole new one. See how creative you can be. Even a cookie cutter can become a pattern for a Christmas card!

Painted Cards

The painted greeting cards shown in the photo were made with very basic materials: tempera paints, sponges and sponge brushes, stamps cut from art gum erasers, even freezer-paper stencils. Make your own cards from folded construction paper, or purchase ready-made blank cards and envelopes from local art supply or stationery stores.

In the Merry Chris-Moose Wallhanging project on page 181, freezer paper was used to make appliqué easier. Here, project designer Sally Paul discovered its value as a stencil. It is easy to cut and will stay in place when lightly ironed (with the shiny side against the card). In some areas, Sally placed plastic screen over the freezer paper and stenciled through both layers for extra texture.

The stencils are cut to contain paint in certain shapes, but when the stencil is complete, you may want to use a small sponge, a sponge brush, or fabric softener foam to dab extra color onto the card. The cards at the top of the photo benefited from that idea.

Check for consistency and evenness of coverage by testing your paint on scraps of the paper you are going to use for the finished card. Be careful not to let the surface of the sponge, brush, or stamp become too loaded with paint. Too much paint is a common pitfall in stenciling. Details can be added with felt-tip pens or small brushes and tempera paints.

To make your own rubber stamps from art gum erasers, trace a pattern onto an eraser, and cut away the background. This technique works well for shapes like the star and the snowman's arms. Since an art knife works best for cutting the erasers, I'd recommend that an adult make the stamps, and let the children have lots of fun using them.

Fused Cards

We have fused almost everything else, so why not Christmas cards? You can fuse any design to construction paper or card stock using paper-backed fusible material. The tree and mitten cards on the bottom left in the photo were fused using the patterns on pages 228 and 229, but of course, any design could be substituted. Before you begin, test the papers you will be fusing onto; if there is any adverse reaction to the heat of the iron, attach the fabric pieces with rubber cement instead of fusing them.

1. Draw or trace your design onto the paper side of the fusible material, but don't cut out the design yet.

2. Using a dry iron, apply the fusible material to the wrong side of the chosen fabric, and cut out the design.

3. Peel off the paper backing, and fuse the design to the construction paper or card stock. Remember to always use a dry iron on paper. Add stitch marks around the edges with a fine-point marking pen.

The designs in the "Sew or No-Sew Miniatures" chapter, beginning on page 151, can also be adapted to these techniques; however, they generally have smaller pieces and are more appropriate for older children or adults.

MAKING SIMPLE FOAM STAMPS

An easy and inexpensive way to make stamps is to cut simple shapes from foam fabric softener dryer sheets. Cut at least two layers, and glue them to a scrap piece of corrugated cardboard.

Mitten

Tree

Star

Star Hat

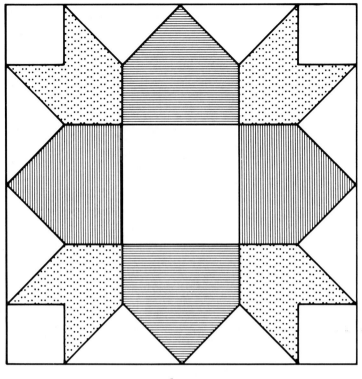

Weather Vane

Snowman

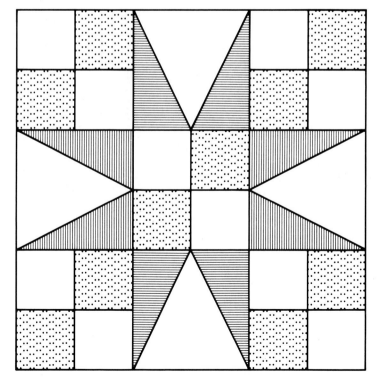

54–40 or Fight

Small Star

WELCOME HOME PUFF WREATH

The puff wreath shown in the photo is made in homespun squares, with a few of the design blocks from the "Sew or No-Sew Miniatures" chapter included for additional quilting accents. Try to picture the wreath in other fabrics, as well. Assorted Christmas or calico prints are extremely effective. Cotton tartans are very appealing to men and, of course, perfect for anyone with an affection for things Scottish. Any color theme selected to coordinate with your room or house is nice. No matter what fabrics you use, the directions are the same. Please read them carefully before proceeding.

Approximate Size

21 inches in diameter, not including bow

Materials Required

- 27 × 45-inch piece of muslin for backing
- Forty-one 6-inch squares of approx. 10 to 20 different fabrics for wreath front
- Scraps of contrasting fabrics for design blocks
- Long fabric strips and/or contrasting ribbon for bow
- Approx. 8 ounces of polyester fiberfill for stuffing
- ¼ yard of paper-backed fusible material
- Two 1½-ounce bags of raffia or equivalent for bow
- 15-inch piece of string, piping, or ribbon for loop hanger
- 18-inch-diameter wreath form *or* cardboard or Foamcore to cut a wreath base

Cutting the Fabrics

1. Cut forty-one 4½-inch squares of muslin backing. With a seam ripper or scissors, make a slit approximately 1½ inches long in the center of each square. You will insert the polyester fiberfill through this slit after the puffs are made.

2. Make a template for piece A using the pattern on page 233. From the selected fabrics, cut 41 assorted A pieces. Some of the A pieces in the wreath shown were cut from string-pieced scraps of homespun.

3. If you are using fused design blocks from the "Sew or No-Sew Miniatures" chapter, cut, center, and fuse your favorite designs on at least five of the A pieces before assembling the puffs. The design blocks begin on page 175.

Making the Puffs

1. Place the *wrong* side of the A piece on top of the muslin backing. Make the long edges of the fabric fit the smaller muslin piece by folding the corners. Fold the fabric so that points A and B meet and the pleat in the fabric is on the right side (the top). See **Diagram 1**. Match the folded corner to the corner of the muslin backing, and pin it in place. Fold all four corners in the same way. This forms the puff. Using a

¼-inch seam allowance, stitch around the *entire* puff. The fiberfill will be inserted later through the slit in the backing fabric. The seam allowance stays on the outside of the puff and will be used later to sew the puffs together.

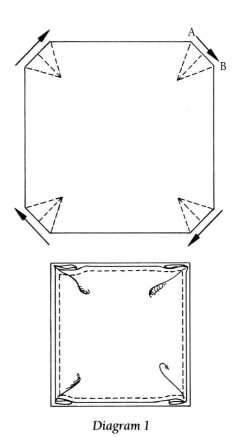

Diagram 1

2. Complete all 41 puffs in the same manner.

Making the Wreath

1. Arrange the completed puffs into one row each of 11, 14, and 16 puffs. The middle row of 14 puffs will be the most visible in the finished wreath, so it should be arranged carefully and is definitely where any squares with fused designs should be placed.

2. When you've arranged the rows to your liking, machine stitch the puffs in each row together. Place two puffs right sides together, and stitch just inside the existing line of stitches to prevent any stitching from showing on the finished wreath.

231

3. When all the rows are complete, place the 14-puff row and the 11-puff row right sides together, and pin, easing the longer row to fit. Baste, then machine stitch the rows together. Pin the 16-puff row to the other side of the 14-puff row, ease to fit, and stitch. See **Diagram 2.** For more even easing, it is helpful to fold each row into halves and quarters, and mark the row with pins. Then match the pins as you join the rows.

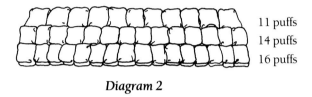

11 puffs
14 puffs
16 puffs

Diagram 2

4. From the back, stuff each puff lightly but completely. Filling in the corners will help the puffs to maintain the square look. But don't pack the fiberfill too firmly; it should not extend or stretch the puffs in any way. Filling the wreath too tightly will give the wreath a hard look. It is not necessary to sew the slits in the backing fabric unless you intend to wash or fluff the wreath.

5. When stuffing is complete, sew the ends of the rows together. You now have a flared doughnut shape, as shown in **Diagram 3.**

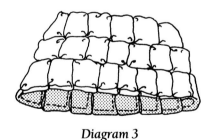

Diagram 3

Finishing the Wreath

You will need a form for the wreath. Any straw, wire, or Styrofoam ring would be fine, provided it has an outside diameter of 18 inches.

You can also make a ring from cardboard. Find a sturdy shipping box or two. Cut an 18-inch-diameter circle, and cut a 16-inch-diameter circle out of the middle of it. This is the least amount of stiffness that will hold the shape of the wreath. For a sturdier cardboard frame, also cut two 17¾-inch circles, and cut a 16¼-inch circle from the center of each. Glue one of these rings to each side of the original 18-inch ring. If desired, you can continue to add smaller rings until you get a rounded effect.

1. Place the wreath on top of the form so that the shortest row is toward the center. Slip this row into the center of the wreath form, and bring the longest row around so that the raw edges of the two rows meet at the center back. Start easing the longer edge under the shorter one. This can be finished as neatly as you wish; you can either fold under a seam allowance on the edges or leave the raw edges exposed. In most cases, the back of the wreath will be against a wall or door, and the raw edges won't show.

2. Before stitching this seam shut, make a loop hanger using about 15 inches of string, piping, or ribbon. The hanger will be slipped under the puffs and around the wreath form and tied in place. To find the right spot to position the hanger, look for the seam that brought the two ends together into a doughnut. This seam should be at the bottom of the wreath, where the bow will be placed. The hanger should be placed on the opposite side of the wreath. Slide the hanger material around the form, and tie it in place. Then make a small loop on the outside of the puffs that will hold the wreath, but will not extend above it and show. Finish closing the wreath seam.

3. The packaged raffia will vary in length, from too short to use to at least 6 feet. Sort it so that the centers of the usable long pieces are all together. Add

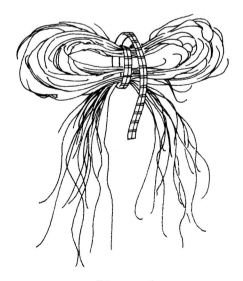

Diagram 4

some long pieces of fabric or ribbon for color and texture variation. Holding the bundle at the center, form two loops to create a bow shape. Where the loops overlap, wrap a 1 × 15-inch piece of fabric around the center, and tie it securely. See **Diagram 4**. Use the rest of that strip to tie the bow securely on the seam line at the bottom of the wreath.

The wreath can be fluffed over the years by taking it off the wreath form and putting it into the dryer on the air cycle. If the wreath is used outside the house, make sure it is in a well-protected area.

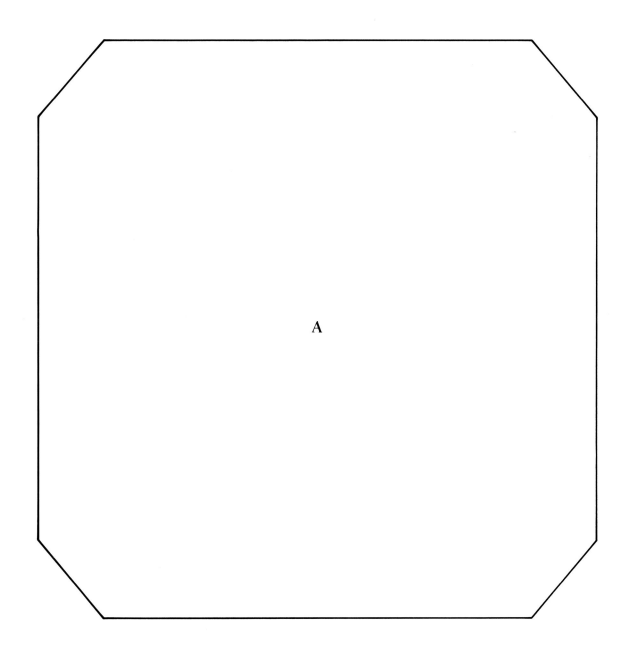

A

FEATHERED AND FESTIVE HOLIDAY "WREATHS"

Since the feathered wreath is an all-time favorite motif for quilting, and since wreaths are such a traditional decoration for the holidays, I had fun joining the two themes to create this cheerful holiday decoration. I've borrowed the feather design and adapted the wreath part to accommodate the seasonal greeting. The pattern is interpreted in two very different styles. The Country Appliqué Wreath below has a mock double ruffle in down-home red and green fabrics that looks more difficult to make than it really is. The Gold and White Wreath on page 239, with its very elegant gold metallic stitching and lace trim, creates a very different look.

COUNTRY APPLIQUÉ WREATH

Approximate Size

24 inches in diameter, including ruffle

Materials Required

- 1⅝ yards of green fabric for appliqués, bow, and ruffle
- ¾ yard of fabric for backing
- ½ yard of dark red print fabric for appliqués and ruffle
- 24-inch square of light red print fabric for background
- 15 × 18-inch piece of ecru fabric for appliqués
- 24 × 32-inch piece of lightweight batting
- Polyester fiberfill for stuffing
- 15 × 18-inch piece of paper-backed fusible material
- 18-inch wooden hoop
- Tacky craft glue
- 4-inch piece of ribbon for loop hanger (optional)
- Large safety pin (optional)

Cutting and Preparing the Fabrics

1. The feathers, letters, and small heart with decorative trim are fused to the background fabric. Using the patterns on pages 236 and 237, make templates for the feather and the letters; for the small heart and its trim, you can either make templates or trace directly onto the paper side of a piece of fusible material. (If you prefer to appliqué rather than fuse, you'll need to make templates for all the pieces. Be sure to add seam allowances when cutting the pieces from fabric.)

2. Trace the feather shape onto the paper side of a piece of fusible material. Reverse the template, and trace a second feather shape. Apply the fusible material to the wrong side of the ecru fabric, and cut out the feathers.

3. Trace the letters N,O,E,L in reverse onto the fusible material. Apply the fusible material to the wrong side of the green fabric, and cut out the letters.

4. If you haven't already done so, trace the small heart and its trim onto the fusible material. The heart is cut from dark red print fabric, and the trim from green fabric.

Making the Layered and Quilted Heart

1. Make the green background heart first. Using the pattern on page 238, cut one large heart each from backing fabric and green fabric. Make a 2-inch slit in the center of the backing heart for turning. With right sides together, sew the green heart and the backing heart together. Clip the curves and trim the point, and turn the heart right side out. Set it aside for now.

2. The red heart is quilted. Cut one medium heart each from backing fabric, batting, and dark red print fabric. As before, make a 2-inch slit in the center of the backing fabric. Place the front and the backing fabric right sides together, and place the batting on top of the front. Sew around the outside edge. Clip the curves and trim the point, and turn the heart right side out through the slit in the backing. Lightly mark the grid quilting design, or follow the print of your fabric, and machine quilt the heart.

Adding the Design to the Background

1. Place the inner ring of the hoop on the light red print background fabric. Lightly trace around the inside of the ring to mark the design area.

2. Using the photo for reference, position the feathers, hearts, and letters on the background fabric. The bottom point of the large heart is approximately 5½ inches from the traced line at the bottom of the design area; the outside edges of the feathers are approximately 1¼ inches from the line on the lower part of the ring. These measurements are not set in stone; they are simply to give you approximate guidelines. When you are satisfied with the arrangement of all the elements, lightly mark placement lines for each of the pieces.

3. Fuse the feathered wreath, letters, small heart, and decorative trim in place. With a pencil or erasable marking pen, lightly mark the center lines and arcs of the feathers for quilting later.

4. Place the green heart right side up on the background fabric, along the placement lines. Stitch it in place.

5. Place the red quilted heart right side up and centered on the green heart. Stitch it in place with a hidden stitch.

Layering and Quilting the Wreath

1. Layer 24-inch squares of backing fabric (wrong side up), lightweight batting, and the appliquéd top (right side up) on a flat surface. Pin or baste the layers together.

2. Hand or machine quilt. On the wreath shown, the outside edges of the fused pieces were finished with a tiny machine zigzag stitch. A tiny machine straight stitch was used to quilt the individual feathers and center lines on the feathered wreath. Free-motion machine quilting and hand quilting are also very suitable alternatives.

Making the Ruffle

1. A mock double ruffle is used around the hoop. Cut the dark red print fabric crosswise into 3-inch-

wide strips; join them to make one strip 145 inches long. Cut 4½-inch-wide strips crosswise from the green fabric, and join them to make a 145-inch-long strip.

2. Place the red and green strips right sides together, and using a ⅜-inch seam allowance, sew along one long edge to make a strip 6¾ × 145 inches. Press the strip open, pressing the seam allowance toward the red fabric.

3. Fold the fabric strip wrong sides together, with long raw edges even. Gather the raw edges to make a ruffle approximately 58 inches long.

Completing the Wreath

1. Center the quilted top in the wooden hoop, with the screw adjustment at the bottom of the wreath. Assemble the hoop. Trim the excess fabric from the wreath to ¼ inch, and glue the edge to the inside ring on the back of the hoop.

2. Use tacky craft glue to glue the ruffle in place on the back of both rings of the hoop.

3. Make the bow to complete the wreath. Cut and piece green fabric to make a 14 × 96-inch strip. Make a fabric tube by folding this strip in half, right sides together. Sew the long raw edges together, leaving a 4-inch opening for turning. Sew across each end of the tube at a 45 degree angle, as shown in **Diagram 1**, and trim the excess fabric. Turn the tube right side out, and slip stitch the opening closed. Press the seam edges of the tube. Tie the tube into a large bow like the one shown in the photo.

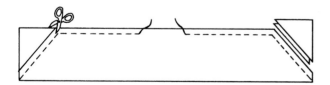

Diagram 1

4. Hand stitch or use a large safety pin from the back to hold the bow in place on the background fabric. Stuff the loops of the bow with polyester fiberfill for extra dimension; the loops are very full, and small amounts of fiberfill will stay in place without being visible.

5. Often the hoop will just rest on a nail for hanging. If not, use ribbon to make a loop hanger for the wreath.

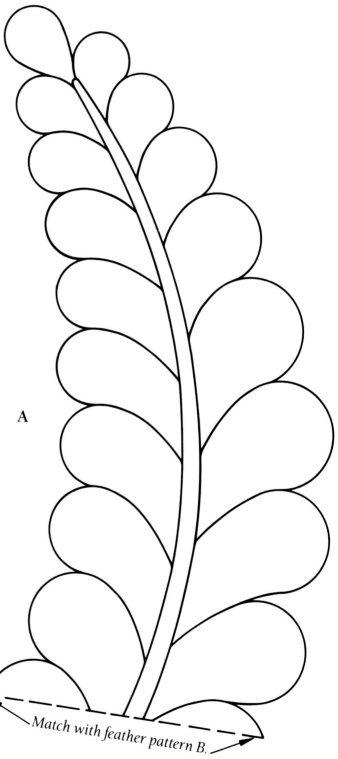

A

Match with feather pattern B.

Match with feather pattern A.

B

Small Heart

Tracing line for large heart

Tracing line for medium heart

Large and Medium Hearts

GOLD AND WHITE WREATH

Gold is such a wonderful color to use in holiday decorations. It shimmers and catches the light and has that out-of-the-ordinary feeling that makes anything seem more festive. In this version of the feathered wreath, gold metallic thread and gold lamé in the ruffle and bow create a more elegant effect. The machine stipple quilting used generously on the background helps the feathers look padded or stuffed.

Approximate Size

21 inches in diameter, including ruffle

Materials Required

- 24-inch square of muslin for wreath front
- 24-inch square of fabric for backing
- 24-inch square of lightweight batting
- 2 yards of 2⅝-inch-wide gold ribbon for bow
- 1¾ yards of purchased 1½-inch gold lamé ruffle
- 1¾ yards of purchased 1¼-inch lace ruffle
- 1¾ yards of purchased ¼-inch gold lamé piping
- Gold metallic thread
- Nylon monofilament thread
- 18-inch Foamcore circle
- Tacky craft glue
- Large safety pin (optional)

Preparing the Fabrics

1. Use the pattern pieces from the Country Appliqué Wreath, beginning on page 236, and a water-erasable marking pen (test first) to lightly trace the wreath design and outside circle dimension onto the muslin.

2. Layer the backing fabric (wrong side up), batting, and muslin (right side up) on a flat surface. Baste the layers together.

Quilting the Design

1. Using gold metallic thread, machine quilt the center heart with its quilting lines, the small heart and decorative trim, the feathers, and the word *NOEL*.

2. Use invisible thread to machine stipple quilt the background of the entire wreath front. See page 9 for directions on machine stipple quilting.

Completing the Wreath

1. Make two rows of long machine stitching, 1 inch and 2 inches outside the circle you've drawn on the fabric. Trim the fabric to ¼ inch from the outer row of machine stitching. Gather lightly so that the outside edge just begins to cup.

2. Stretch the circle of fabric firmly, but not too tightly, over the Foamcore circle, first at the top and bottom and then at opposite sides. Be sure that the design is centered and that the feathers are an equal distance from the outside edge. Continue gathering

to flatten the fabric at the back. Glue the fabric in place, making a ½-inch band of glue along the back outside edge of the Foamcore. Anchor the fabric with straight pins until the glue dries, if necessary.

3. Make a thread loop hanger, and attach it to the back of the wreath.

Embellishing the Wreath

1. Glue the gold lamé piping around the outside edge of the wreath, overlapping the ends at the bottom.

2. A gold and lace ruffle completes the outside edge of the wreath. Sew the lace ruffle on top of the gold lamé ruffle, having outside edges even. Glue the ruffle in place around the outside edge, overlapping folded ends at the bottom.

3. Double gold bows finish the wreath embellishment. Cut two 1-yard lengths of gold ribbon. Working with both lengths as though they were one, tie a large bow. Hand stitch or use a large safety pin from the back to hold the bow in place on top of the feathers at the bottom of the wreath. Separate the loops of the bow, and trim the ends as shown in the photo.

ELEGANT TRAPUNTO STOCKING

The addition of trapunto, lace, and some fun trimmings transforms the Basic Christmas Stocking on page 77 into a Victorian delight. For years I have done trapunto, or stuffed quilting, by machine stitching and adding the filling by hand. My friend Ellen Rosintoski, who believes if you can't do it by machine, it may not be worth doing, came up with a clever method of trapunto-type design that uses a double needle and adjusted tension to create a trapunto look. This technique eliminates entirely any yarn or hand stuffing. Although the stocking shown in the photo was made using Ellen's technique, both techniques are presented in the directions. Read through both techniques and decide which you prefer. If you are hand quilting rather than machine quilting, the traditional method is the only option.

Approximate Size

11 inches wide at the toe × 18½ inches long, including ruffle

Materials Required

- 1 yard of muslin or ecru fabric for stocking front, back, lining, ruffle, and hearts
- ¾ yard of batting

- 2¼ yards of purchased gold lamé piping *or* 15-inch square of gold lamé and 2¼ yards of ⅛-inch-diameter piping cord
- 2⅛ yards of ⅛-inch-wide ecru ribbon
- 1 yard of 2½-inch-wide ungathered (flat) lace
- ⅞ yard of ⅛-inch-wide gold braid
- ⅝ yard of ¼-inch-wide picot-edged ecru ribbon
- ½ yard of 1-inch-wide gathered lace
- 16-inch piece of flat gold cord
- Gold metallic thread
- 1-inch gold rosette

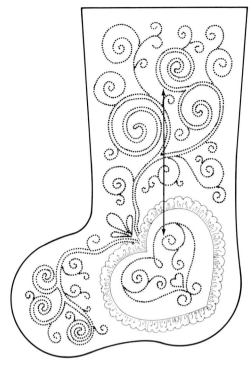

Trapunto Stocking Diagram

Additional Requirements for Traditional Method of Trapunto

- 13 × 18-inch piece of muslin for lining
- Yarn
- Tapestry needle

Additional Requirements for Double-Needle Technique of Trapunto

- Lightweight embroidery thread for machine bobbin
- Double needle to fit your machine
- Walking foot (optional)

Preparing the Fabric

1. Cut a 23-inch length from the 1-yard piece of muslin. Fold the fabric in half, wrong sides together. This double layer of fabric will be used for the outside and the lining of the stocking front and back, as well as for the heart front and lining.

2. The stocking and heart patterns begin on page 80; the design lines for the trapunto are printed right on the pattern. Trace the patterns from the book onto a large sheet of paper, being careful to line up the different sections of the stocking pattern. Darken the lines of the patterns with a felt-tip pen. The **Trapunto Stocking Diagram** shows what the completed pattern should look like.

3. Place the traced patterns under the top layer of muslin, and lightly trace the patterns onto the fabric, leaving sufficient space for seam allowances when the pieces are cut out later. Use a pencil or removable marker to make the lines. Be sure to trace the heart as a separate pattern, that is, outside of the stocking outline. The heart is made up separately and stitched to the front of the stocking later.

If you choose the traditional method of trapunto, trace double lines to indicate the areas of trapunto and a single line for the remaining areas of quilting. If you choose to make the trapunto by the double-needle technique, instead of marking the double lines for stitching the trapunto channel, trace a single solid line between the double lines. Use a single dotted line for the remaining areas of quilting. After all the design lines have been traced, pin the two layers of fabric together.

Traditional Trapunto

If you've chosen the traditional method, follow these instructions for the trapunto, then skip to "Quilting the Remaining Areas of the Stocking and Heart" on page 242.

1. Thread the top of your machine with gold metallic thread, and use a lightweight thread in the bobbin to match the stocking fabric. Use a small machine stitch (single needle) along each trapunto line, stitching through both layers of fabric (batting will be added later).

2. Make a tiny slit in the backing fabric between the stitching lines, being careful not to cut through to the top fabric.

3. Fill the channels with cord using a tapestry needle and yarn. Insert the needle into the slit between the layers of fabric, and pull the yarn through the channel, leaving a short tail outside the back of the fabric, as shown in **Diagram 1**. As you progress with the cording, make additional slits as necessary. Hand stitch the openings closed.

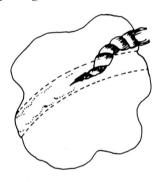

Diagram 1

Double-Needle Trapunto

1. Place a 23-inch square of batting between the layers of stocking fabric, and pin or baste all the layers together.

2. Prepare your sewing machine. Thread the top of your machine with two spools of gold metallic thread, unwinding in opposite directions. In the bobbin, use a lightweight machine embroidery thread that matches the stocking fabric. Use the widest double needle that will fit your machine. A double needle will produce two parallel rows of stitching on the top and a zigzag on the back. You may want to use a walking foot attachment, if you have one; it will help to keep the back from puckering.

3. Practice stitching on a scrap of fabric layered with batting and backing, loosening the top tension until you can see that the top threads are being pulled to the back. For best results, the bobbin tension will

need to be tightened. If your machine's bobbin case has a finger with a hole in it, run the bobbin thread through the hole. See **Diagram 2**. If not, see your sewing machine manual for the exact way to adjust the bobbin case screw to tighten the tension. The tension adjustments force the top to pouf up, and create the corded "trapunto" look without the second step of adding the yarn in the channel. Adjust the stitch length to about 14 per inch. When taking the first few stitches, hold the bobbin thread and two top threads to prevent knotting.

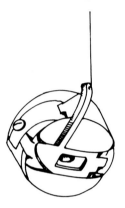

Diagram 2

4. As you begin stitching the trapunto areas of the stocking, stitch very slowly, following the gentle curve. As curves become tighter, stop stitching with the needle down, raise the presser foot, and slightly turn the fabric. In the tightest curves, it will become necessary to stitch, stop, and turn for every stitch. This method produces smoother curves and minimizes chances of breaking a needle.

5. As each section of trapunto is completed and the work is removed from the machine, leave long threads on the back and the top. Use a hand needle to hide these thread tails in the batting.

Although it may sound complicated, the actual sewing of the "corded" areas will not take much longer than it took to read these directions.

Quilting the Remaining Areas of the Stocking and Heart

1. If you used the traditional trapunto method, you must now add the layer of batting and additional lining fabric to the stocking front in order to quilt the remaining areas. If you used the double-needle method,

another layer of batting and lining is not necessary. Also layer batting between the front and lining of the heart.

2. Use gold metallic thread to machine quilt the stocking along the marked quilting lines. Using a single needle, loosen the top tension and lower the feed dogs.

3. Machine quilt the scrolled-bottom inner heart and the inside of the heart, going over the lines twice to simulate the look of couched thread. Machine quilt the remainder of the heart in the same manner as for the stocking.

Sewing the Stocking

1. Referring to the instructions for the Basic Christmas Stocking beginning on page 77, cut out the lined stocking front from the quilted fabric; cut out the back and back lining from the remaining muslin.

2. Pin the gold lamé piping to the right side of the stocking front, matching raw edges. Baste in place. Use a zipper foot attachment to stitch close to the piping. Save extra piping to complete the stocking opening and quilted heart. If purchased piping is not available, follow the directions in "Making the Piping Trim" on page 104.

3. Complete the stocking body in the same manner as for the basic stocking, except do not add the cuff.

4. Instead of a cuff, a 2¼-inch ruffle with lace and gold lamé piping is used around the stocking top. Cut a 5 × 36-inch strip of muslin; fold the strip wrong sides together with raw edges even. Machine baste the 2½-inch-wide lace to the folded fabric strip, matching raw edges. Gather the fabric and lace to 18 inches.

5. Baste an 18-inch length of gold lamé piping around the stocking opening. With right sides together and raw edges even, pin the ruffle in place over the piping; stitch. Cut a 2 × 18-inch strip of muslin to cover the raw edges of the ruffle. Press under ¼ inch along one long edge. Match the raw edge of this fabric strip to the ruffle edge, and machine stitch. Fold the fabric down over the seam allowance, and slip stitch the turned-under edge to the inside of the stocking. See **Diagram 3**.

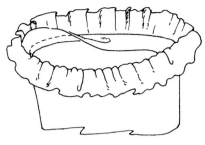

Diagram 3

Making the Heart

1. Cut out the quilted heart front from the layers of fabric, adding the seam allowance as you cut. Loosely cut the backing fabric for the heart. Make a small slit in the center of the backing for turning.

2. Pin the remaining gold lamé piping to the right side of the heart front, matching raw edges. Baste in place.

3. Complete the heart by placing the front and back right sides together and sewing around the outside edge. Trim the excess backing, clip the curves, and trim the point. Turn the heart right side out through the back slit. Sew around the outside edge of the scrolled heart, stitching through all layers. Do not stitch around the inside loop. See **Diagram 4**. Lightly stuff the scrolled heart through the back slit. Whip stitch the back slit closed.

Stitch around outside edge of scrolled inner heart.

Diagram 4

4. Baste the finished heart to the stocking heel, leaving the outside edge loose so that lace may be added.

5. Finish the heart with the ½ yard of 1-inch-wide gathered lace. Sew the lace to the outside edge of the heart between the heart and the stocking. Sew through the heart and the stocking front, being careful not to sew through the stocking back.

Trimming the Stocking

1. Ribbon and gold braid are used to tie a bow at the top of the stocking. Cut the ⅛-inch-wide ecru ribbon into two 20-inch lengths and one 36-inch length. Combine these with the ¼-inch-wide picot-edged ribbon and the ⅛-inch-wide gold braid to make a bow. Tie knots at the ends of the braid and along the braid and ribbon streamers as desired. Tack the bow in place at the top of the stocking.

2. Two tiny hearts are attached to ribbon streamers. Cut four small hearts from muslin using the pattern at right. For each heart, sew the front and back right sides together, leaving a small opening along one side for turning. Clip the curves, and trim the point. Turn the heart right side out, and loosely stuff it. Slip stitch the opening closed. A purchased gold rosette is tacked to one heart; the other has a double bow of flat gold cord. Use two 8-inch lengths of gold cord to tie a double bow, and tack it in place.

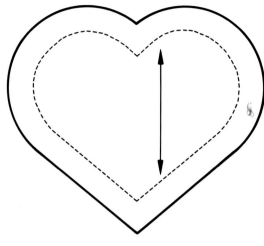

Small Heart

Sew a heart to the end of each of the two longest ribbon streamers.

SCRAPPY SPIRAL SKIRTS

When I was selecting the projects for this book, I saw someone wearing a skirt like this and thought it would be fun for Christmas. A special thank-you to the gals at Tomorrow's Heirlooms for granting permission to include their basic pattern. The festive spiral scrap skirt features slightly curved fabric rectangles that are sewn together into a long strip; the strip is then sewn in a continuous spiral. This unique spiral piecing technique creates a tiered-look skirt without the effort of creating separate tiers and gathering each tier to fit another. If you have a fabric collection, this skirt is great fun; if you have a serger and a fabric collection, this project is ideal. With all the little seams, serged edges are wonderful and make the skirt easy to care for. Rather than traditional garment seam allowances, use ¼-inch seams throughout.

Size

Size to fit

Materials Required

- 3 to 6 yards total of assorted fabrics *or* scant ¼ yard *each* of approx. 25 fabrics *or* 5 × 8-inch scraps
- 2 pieces of ½-inch-wide nonroll waistband elastic to fit your waist measurement
- Template plastic for pattern

Choosing the Style and Fabrics

The possibilities for fabric selection are endless. While all three skirts shown in the photos have a Christmas theme, this skirt is a great showcase for any type of fabric collection or any type of color scheme. It could be called a fabric collector's dream skirt. Just don't make it boring! This skirt is most attractive when made with fabrics of varied textures, styles, and print sizes (large- and small-scale). Slightly clashing colors are okay, too.

Only one pattern piece, the curved rectangle on page 249, is required to make this skirt, but two options of the pattern piece are included, A and B. Pattern B is longer than pattern A; use it if you are taller, would like fewer "tiers" in the skirt, or wish to cut fewer rectangles.

The fullness of the skirt is also variable. Because of the pattern shape, the basic skirt is not straight, but flared. Additional fullness can be added in two ways: Either you can make the spiral loops larger in diameter, or you can lightly gather one edge of the pieced fabric strip before sewing the spiral. Each method gives a different look. Do not use both methods together; the skirt will be too full and bulky.

Be aware that the method you choose affects the number of fabric rectangles you'll need to cut! To make a longish (30 inches from the waist) skirt from the smaller pattern (A) with added gathers, you may need to cut as many as 150 pieces of fabric. If, however, you make the basic skirt with pattern B and no extra fullness, you could cut as few as 80 pieces.

The all-red skirt shown in the photo is made with pattern B, and the starting loop was just large enough to go over the hips. The homespun skirt is also made with pattern B, but is extra full because the starting loop was about 10 inches larger than the hip measurement. It is also extra long. The bright red and green skirt is made from pattern A. In addition, the lower tiers were gathered before they were sewn into the spiral. (Don't worry if you're a little confused at this point. This will all make perfect sense when you are about halfway through making your first skirt.)

Cutting the Fabrics

Trace the pattern to make a template. Layering the fabric to cut four to six pieces at once will speed the cutting process. For directional fabrics, it is critical to keep the template facing the same way, as shown in **Diagram 1**. If the print is not directional, consider saving fabric by alternating the direction of the template. See **Diagram 2**. Since the actual number

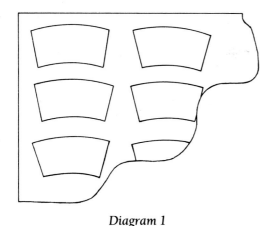

Diagram 1

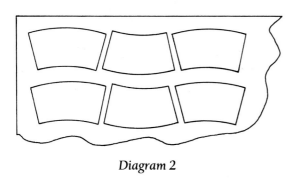

Diagram 2

of pieces needed is not definite, you may choose to cut awhile, then sew awhile.

Beginning the Spiral

1. Begin sewing the pieces together, end to end, to make a long, curving strip. Sew at least 30 to 40 pieces together before moving to the next step. (You'll add more rectangles later, as needed to lengthen the skirt, when you begin sewing the spiral together.)

2. Use a measuring tape to make a circle large enough to pull up over your hips. Because this skirt is a pull-on, this measurement will be used for the skirt waist. If you want a fuller skirt and do not plan to add gathers, add several inches of ease to the skirt waist measurement; this increases the diameter of the spiral loops. For example, 10 inches was added in the homespun sample skirt.

Starting at one end, measure along the pieced fabric strip to a point equal to half of the chosen waist measurement. With wrong sides together, fold this segment of the strip over the next segment, so that the bottom edge of the first piece of the strip meets

the top edge of the piece underneath it, as shown in **Diagram 3**. Use a straight pin to mark the strip at this point.

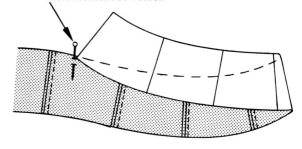

One-half of skirt waist measurement should equal at least ½ of hip measurement of wearer.

Diagram 3

3. Referring to **Diagram 4**, fold the remainder of the strip around the marked point to begin making a spiral. By the very nature of a spiral, the technique will create a slight diagonal line at both the top and bottom of the skirt. These uneven sections will eventually be cut off in a tapered manner; do not trim them at this time.

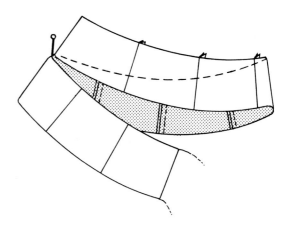

Diagram 4

Sewing the Spiral

1. Fold the top row over the adjacent row, right sides together, as shown in **Diagram 5**.

2. Beginning at the pin, sew the strip in a *continuous* spiral, using a ¼-inch seam allowance. This step seems especially weird. However, it is very easy to confirm, after stitching only a few inches, whether the spiral is going together without an extra twist and with the right sides of all fabrics showing on the outside of the skirt. Continue sewing the spiral, adding pieces to lengthen the strip as necessary, until the

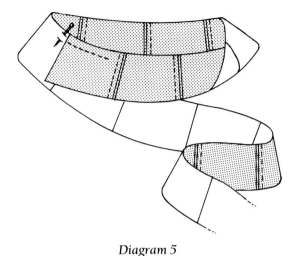

Diagram 5

skirt looks approximately the desired length. (The length will be measured more accurately later.) Press the spiral seam toward the waist.

3. If you have decided to add fullness with gathers, sew the first four "tiers" with an ungathered strip. Then, without cutting the strip, sew a line of machine basting stitches ¼ inch from the raw edge of the top (shorter) edge of the strip, gather the strip very lightly, and continue to sew the spiral. See **Diagram 6**. Starting to gather at the fourth tier prevents the skirt from being bulky at the waistline. How much to gather the strip? The ungathered top edge of the rectangles is 6¾ inches; with gathers, ours measured about 5½ inches. Keep in mind that the more you gather, the more rectangles you'll need.

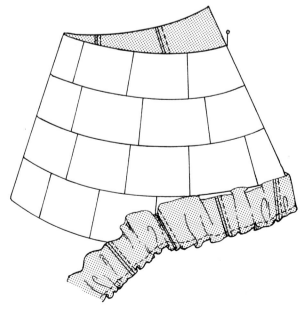

Diagram 6

If you are repeating fabrics, as you sew the spiral you may find that two pieces of the same fabric are too close together for your liking. You can fix this by opening the seam and inserting a different fabric in the spiral, but don't let this make you crazy. The homespun skirt has only 10 different fabrics, and the same fabrics often touch. It would be worse if it only happened once or twice.

4. Lay the skirt out on a flat surface. At the top, one side will extend unevenly above the other. Cut the high skirt edge even with the lower edge, using the lower edge as a guide, as shown in **Diagram 7**.

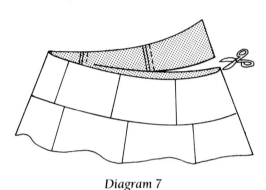

Diagram 7

Making the Waistband

1. Cut a strip of fabric for the waistband that is 4½ inches wide and the length of the waist measurement plus ½ inch. The finished double-elastic waistband will be 2 inches wide.

ADJUSTING THE LENGTH

Don't even up the top until you know the skirt is long enough; it takes many fewer pieces to add a few inches of length there than at the bottom. Although you will not be able to add a great deal at the top because of the waist measurement you began with, you should be able to add at least half a round if necessary, which would result in several inches of additional length.

2. Fold the waistband in half crosswise, bringing the short ends right sides together and matching raw edges. Sew ½ inch in from one edge and 3 inches in from the other edge, leaving a 1-inch opening for inserting the elastic. Press the seam open.

3. Fold the waistband in half lengthwise, wrong sides together, and press. Open the band up. Press under a scant ¼-inch seam allowance along one edge. See **Diagram 8**.

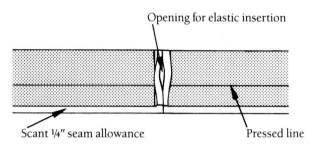

Opening for elastic insertion

Scant ¼″ seam allowance   Pressed line

Diagram 8

4. With raw edges even, stitch the unfolded right side of the waistband to the wrong side (the inside) of the skirt. Grade the seam allowances to eliminate bulk. Press the band over the seam allowance.

5. Fold the waistband in half along the center pressed line, and bring the edge over to the right side of the skirt, enclosing the seam allowance. Topstitch the waistband edge in place, keeping the line of stitches very close to the edge. Stitch around the waistband ¾ inch from the topstitching line to make the first casing. Stitch again ¾ inch from the first casing line to make the second casing. Stitch around a third time, ¼ inch from the top of the band.

6. Cut 2 pieces of ½-inch nonroll waistband elastic to fit your waist comfortably, allowing ½ inch extra on each for overlap. Insert one piece of elastic into each casing through the waistband opening. Stitch the ends of the elastic together, and close the opening.

Finishing the Skirt

1. Check the skirt one more time to determine if the shortest point of the skirt is as long as desired. If not, add more pieces to the end of the strip, and continue sewing the spiral as necessary.

2. To even up the skirt hemline, measure down from the waistband seam. Determine the desired length of the skirt, and add ½ inch for a hem allowance. Measure this distance from the waistband seam to the skirt bottom, all around the skirt, marking the hemline. (It may be helpful to place the skirt on the ironing board to measure and mark the hemline.) Trim excess fabric along the marked line.

3. Press the hem up ¼ inch, then fold and press again. Stitch by machine with one or two rows of stitching. It is most flattering to wear the skirt with the tapered row in the front.

Matching Homespun Vest

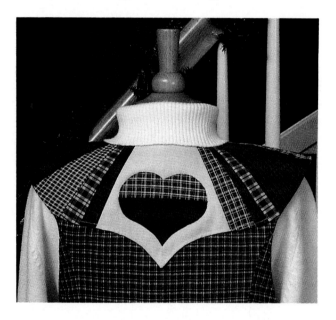

The homespun vest shown with the homespun skirt was made using the basic vest pattern beginning on page 92. The front sections and the optional back yoke were string pieced. (See page 218 for complete directions for string piecing.) The heart appliquéd on the center back is borrowed from the Merry Chris-Moose Wallhanging, using the pattern on page 187.

To add the yoke, press the seam allowance to the wrong side, and topstitch the back yoke in place after the lower back sections are joined. The vest is layered with very lightweight batting and lined. Complete directions for lining and finishing the vest are provided beginning on page 89.

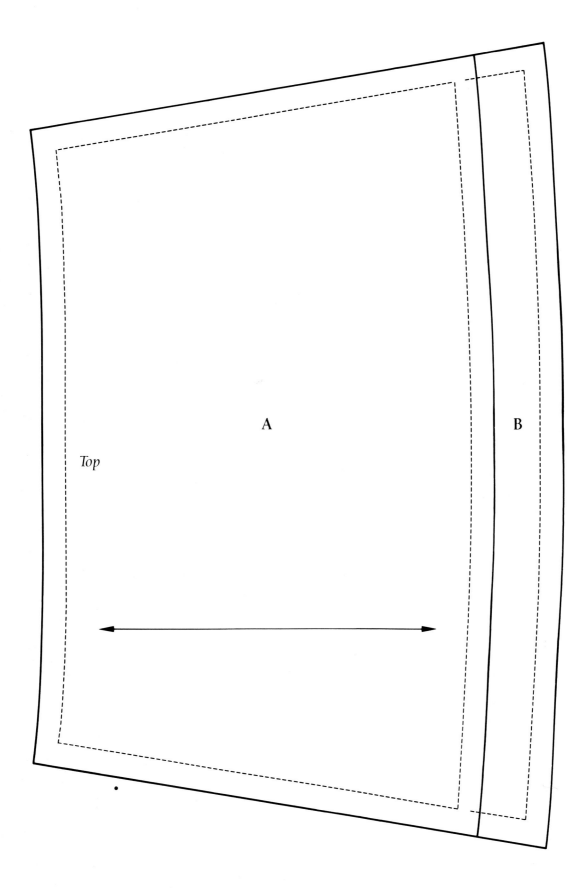

CRAZY QUILTING BY MACHINE

Even though I absolutely love crazy quilts, the idea of making crazy quilted items never crossed my mind until I met Iris Lee and saw her beautiful machine crazy quilting. Before you jump to the conclusion that I made these beautiful items, let me set the record straight. Now that I have met Iris Lee, her methods have made me believe that I *could* make items like this, but I did, in fact, commission her to make the projects shown.

Do you know all those decorative stitches on the sewing machine that you think you'll never use? Iris carefully sorts through them, looking for those that most resemble stitches that can be done by hand, and she uses those stitches to do wonderful machine crazy quilting. See what wonderful choices your own machine has to offer. Put a beautiful shiny rayon embroidery thread in your machine, and make a sampler of the stitches. You will probably be pleasantly surprised—they are usually much prettier than the drawings. Check your sewing machine manual for tips on machine settings for decorative stitches.

Iris also loves thread and has lots of fun changing threads, combining threads, and selecting threads to add more interest to the projects. She then finishes her projects off with embellishments and just enough hand embroidery to give the illusion that it is all done by hand.

Crazy quilting requires the development of a personal style, which makes it impossible to give complete directions for all of these projects. Instead, these are designed to give you lots of inspiration. Study the pictures, determine what you like most, and go for it.

CRAZY QUILTED ORNAMENTS

You have to look closely to see that these ornaments were done without hand embroidery. Use the basic patterns on pages 85 and 86 for the star, heart, and stocking shapes. The directions that follow are general and apply to all of those shapes.

Materials Required

(for one ornament)

- Scraps of assorted Ultrasuede or Facile for ornament front
- Scraps of muslin for background and backing
- Assorted rayon embroidery threads and metallic threads
- 10-inch piece of invisible thread for loop hanger
- Assorted trims and embellishments
- Fabric glue stick

Assembling the Patchwork

Assemble the patchwork pieces on the muslin background fabric. Use enough fabric glue stick on the corners of each piece to hold them in their appropriate places on the muslin background, and make sure there are no gaps between the pieces. Let the glue dry thoroughly before continuing.

Quilting the Patchwork

1. Thread your machine. Use two spools on the top, threading the machine as if they were a single thread. Schmetz needles in sizes 80 to 110 have a larger eye than the typical needle and are useful with multiple threads, metallics, and heavier threads. A size 100 topstitching needle works well with Facile. The size of the needle you use depends upon the fabric you are sewing.

Using two threads together makes decorative stitches show up better. Avoid breakage by not mixing rayons and metallics together.

Preparing the Base Material

1. Make templates using the patterns on pages 85 and 86. Trace around each template onto a piece of prewashed muslin. The muslin should be large enough to allow seam allowances around the shape plus at least an inch all around for handling. Do not cut the shape out yet.

2. Using a pencil or erasable marking pen, make a patchwork design inside the outline on the muslin. Draw interesting geometric, straight-edged shapes. Vary the sizes and shapes, but don't make them too small. **Diagram 1** shows the shapes used in the stocking.

3. When you're satisfied with the patchwork shapes, mark each shape with the color to be used. Make sure no two pieces of the same color are touching.

4. Trace the marked pattern onto a sheet of paper, and cut apart the individual patchwork pieces. Use these as patterns to cut corresponding colors of Ultrasuede or Facile. Since the edges of Ultrasuede and Facile do not have to be finished, it is not necessary to add seam allowances when cutting these pattern pieces.

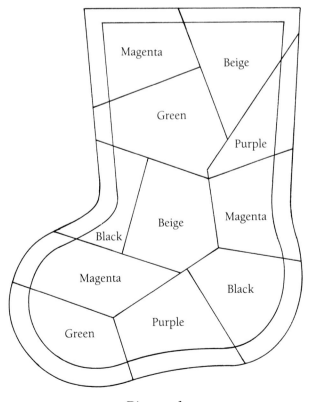

Diagram 1

MAKING A SPIDER WEB

Iris includes a hand-stitched spider web and spider on her projects, almost like a signature.

1. *To make a spider web, first make five or six spokes for the foundation using a long outline stitch. These should be the same length and radiate from a center point.*

2. *Beginning at the center, make stitches around and under one spoke, then carry the thread to the next spoke and repeat, going farther out as you go around the circle. See **Diagram A**. When the web is large enough, bring the thread straight down, and secure the end.*

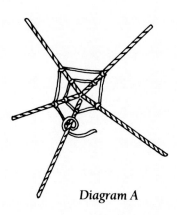

Diagram A

3. *Make the spider. Using a small bead for the head and a larger bead for the body, sew the spider in place at the end of the thread. The eight spider legs are made with doubled thread. Take two straight stitches at an angle away from the body for each leg.*

2. Using the decorative stitches you've selected, stitch exactly between two pieces of patchwork so that the stitches extend onto each piece. This keeps the muslin from showing through between the pieces. It will probably be necessary to lower the needle tension. Be sure that the bobbin thread is not showing on top of the fabric; it is better for the decorative thread to show slightly on the underside. Experiment with your stitches. Make some stitches longer or wider than normal. Cover all the lines between the patches.

Assembling the Ornament

Each ornament is finished as described in Trio of Ornaments, beginning on page 83. Referring to the complete directions provided there, add a backing, turn, and stuff the ornament.

Embellishing the Ornament

Add buttons, jewels, or small charms to the piece. Also experiment with hand embroidery stitches inside some of the shapes, using silk buttonhole twist or embroidery thread. Some examples of embroidery stitches are French knots, feather stitches, buttonhole or blanket stitches, stem or outline stitches, bullion stitches, bullion roses, lazy daisy stitches, and spider webs. See the opposite page for some examples of embroidery stitches.

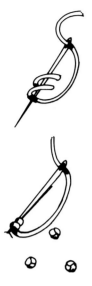

French Knot

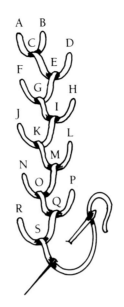

Feather Stitch

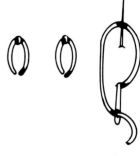

Lazy Daisy Stitch

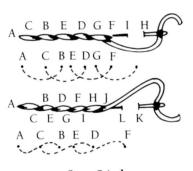

Stem Stitch

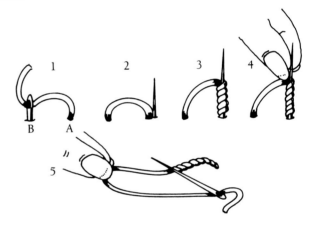

Bullion Stitch

Bullion Rose

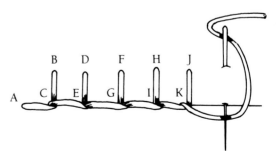

Buttonhole or Blanket Stitch

CRAZY QUILTED STOCKINGS

Iris made three stockings using the basic stocking pattern beginning on page 80. We wanted to get across the idea that you can invest varying degrees of time and labor, and so two of the stockings are made from a preprinted fabric and the third is made from scratch. As this book goes to press, there is a readily available, preprinted crazy quilt fabric. If luck holds, it will still be available when the book is printed, or at least some of you will have bought some and not used it yet.

Even if you don't have preprinted crazy quilt fabric, you can make a beautiful, crazy quilted stocking from scratch. Once again, you can invest a minimum of time and embellish only lightly, or invest a great deal of time and labor by covering the stocking with elaborate stitches and sparkling trims. Either way, the result will be lovely.

Materials Required

- ⅜ yard of muslin for lining
- 13 × 18-inch piece of preprinted crazy quilt fabric for stocking front
- 13 × 18-inch piece of fabric for backing

- 8 × 36-inch piece of coordinating fabric for cuff
- ½ yard of batting
- 18-inch piece of eyelet lace, approx. 2¾ inches wide
- 18-inch piece of ribbon to weave through eyelet lace
- Metallic threads, buttons, charms, ribbons, beads, and other embellishments, as desired

Basic Printed Stocking Directions

The first stocking, shown in the center in the photo, was made from the user-friendly crazy quilt print. It was machine quilted and embellished lightly with purchased ribbon roses, buttons, and other trims.

1. Make a template using the basic stocking pattern beginning on page 80. Cut the stocking shape from the crazy quilt fabric. Refer to the directions for the Basic Christmas Stocking beginning on page 77 to cut the necessary lining, batting, and backing pieces.

2. Layer the stocking front with batting and lining fabric, and baste. Machine quilt and embellish the stocking front as desired.

3. Follow the directions for the basic stocking to complete the construction of the stocking.

4. The cuff on this stocking is a 3¾-inch-wide gathered band. To make the cuff, cut an 8 × 36-inch piece of fabric. Place the short ends right sides together, and stitch across the end. Fold the long edges in, wrong sides together, so that they meet in the center. Sew a row of gathering stitches along each side of the center, as shown in **Diagram 1**.

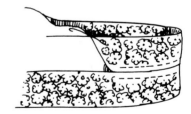

Diagram 1

5. Gather the band to fit the stocking, and baste it in place. Weave the ribbon through the eyelet lace. Center the eyelet on top of the band, and topstitch it in place as shown in **Diagram 2**.

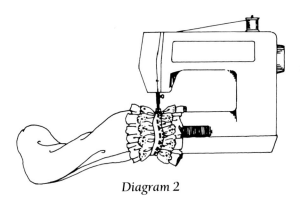

Diagram 2

Embellished
Printed Stocking

The second stocking, shown on the left in the photo, was made from the same user-friendly fabric as the first, but you would barely know it. Iris let the print inspire heavy machine-stitching embellishment and added many trims and buttons. The materials needed are the same as for the Basic Printed Stocking on the opposite page. The construction, including the cuff, is also the same.

Patchwork
Stocking

The third stocking, shown on the right in the photo, was made from Facile scraps and a muslin base, using the same technique described in the Crazy Quilted Ornaments project on page 250. This stocking combines patchwork, machine crazy quilting, hand embroidery embellishment, and other trims.

The cuff is made in the same manner as for the Basic Christmas Stocking, but it is only one layer, and so it is cut half as wide, or 4¼ × 19 inches. It is embellished with decorative machine stitches and braided narrow ribbon. See "Adding the Cuff" on page 78.

CRAZY QUILTED VEST

All I can say about this vest is that no matter how good it looks in the photo, it is much prettier in life. It uses the basic vest pattern with the optional yoke back beginning on page 92. The front panels and the yoke have just the right amount of space for crazy quilting. Using the same technique as for the Crazy Quilted Ornaments on page 250, work each crazy quilted section individually. Then, construct the vest according to the directions beginning on page 88. It is a classic that can and will be worn for Christmas and holiday seasons for years.

Of course, the same preprinted crazy quilt fabric used in the stockings could be added to the vest. Embellish in the same way as for the stockings, and you have a beautiful vest in no time at all!

RESOURCES

A heartfelt thank-you to all of the fabric companies that are making the lives of quiltmakers so much fun and giving us the opportunity to create from the most wonderful palettes of fabric. While most of the projects were created from collected fabrics, there are several projects in this book in which all or most of the fabrics came from a single company.

Thanks to:

Fabric Traditions, 1350 Broadway, Suite 2106, New York, NY 10018: For most of the fabrics used in the Holiday Tablecloth with Star Topper on page 103 and in the matching Eight-Pointed Star Pillows on page 111, as well as for the user-friendly Carolina Lily fabric used in the quilt on page 15 and in the Shower Curtain and Bath Accessories on page 142.

FASCO/Fabric Sales Company, 6250 Stanley Avenue South, Seattle, WA 98108: For the woven fabrics used in all of the homespun projects.

Springs Industries, Inc., Diversified Products Division, 104 W. 40th Street, New York, NY 10018: For Facile, an Ultrasuede Brand Fabric, used in the Grandmother's Fan from Grandfather's Ties pillow on page 206 and in the Crazy Quilting by Machine projects beginning on page 250.

V.I.P. Fabrics, 1412 Broadway, New York, NY 10018: For the print fabrics used in the Holiday Trip around the World Quilt on page 35 and in the Double Irish Chain Wallhanging with User-Friendly Pan-

els on page 46; for the preprinted crazy quilt fabric; and for the fabric door panel used in the Christmas Tree Quilt on page 22.

Alexander Henry Fabrics/Central Textile Company, 2501 S. Grand Avenue, Los Angeles, CA 90007: For most but not all of the fabrics used in the "West by Southwest" chapter on page 181, and definitely for my first Southwestern fabric, the chili peppers.

Shades, 585 Cobb Parkway South, The Nunn Complex, Studio O, Marietta, GA 30062: For the hand-dyed fabric used in the Merry Chris-Moose Wallhanging on page 181.

Thanks to these additional contributors:

EZ International, 95 Mayhill Street, Saddle Brook, NJ 07662: For templates suitable for some of the miniature block designs.

Michell Marketing/Ackfeld Mfg., 3525 Broad Street, Chamblee, GA 30341: For wire hangers.

Sulky of America, 3113-D Broadpoint Drive, Harbor Heights, FL 33983: For metallic threads used in crazy quilting.

Tomorrow's Heirlooms, 2801C Justin Road, Flower Mound, TX 75028: For sharing the pattern used in the Scrappy Spiral Skirts on page 244.

Plum Fun Wood Products, 5427 S.E. 72nd Avenue, Portland, OR 97206: For the little clothespins and miniature spools shown in the photo on page 223.

GLOSSARY

In this section, there is only a brief description of each term listed. In many cases, you'll find a cross-reference to a project or section where you can find the complete instructions.

Appliqué. The process of applying one layer of fabric on top of another. See the discussion on hand versus machine appliqué, as well as instructions for freezer-paper appliqué, in Appliqué Quilts on page 67. See the "Sew or No-Sew Miniatures" chapter on page 151 for a fusible, or no-sew, appliqué technique.

Batting. The broad general name for the material sandwiched between the quilt top and the backing. For a more detailed discussion, see "Batting Selection" on page 3.

Bias. In woven fabrics, any line that runs across both lengthwise and crosswise threads. True bias is at a 45 degree angle to the selvage. Cutting at this angle creates very stretchy edges, which is sometimes desirable, as when a binding must go around a curve. In patchwork, however, bias edges can sometimes cause problems with distortion or stretching and must be handled carefully.

Binding. As a verb, it is the term used to describe finishing a raw edge, especially on a quilt. As a noun, it is the finish. My favorite quilt binding is a separate French-fold binding, usually cut on the straight grain. See "Adding a French-Fold Binding" on page 10 for complete directions.

Borders. Strips of fabric or pieced fabrics that surround the central part of a quilt. They serve the same function for a quilt as a frame does for a picture. Just as it is hard to select mats and a frame without the picture, in my opinion it is difficult to select the actual fabrics and widths of borders before the interior of the quilt is complete.

Corner Squares. The contrasting squares pieced into corners where borders meet are called corner squares or, more interestingly, cornerstones. They are used on several projects in the book, but see the Christmas Tree Quilt on page 22 for complete construction techniques.

Cylinder Method. A special technique for keeping squares in the proper order when joining rows. See Strip Technique Quilts on page 25 for complete directions.

Diagonal Seams. Recommended when borders or binding needs to be pieced. They are less conspicuous than straight seams and prevent bulky layers. The shirred, corded ruffle on the Holiday Tablecloth with Star Topper on page 103 is pieced with diagonal seams.

Diagonal Set. The term used when quilt blocks are set on point and the rows move diagonally across the quilt. The sides and corners must be completed with side setting triangles and corner setting triangles. The Cardinals in the Pines Quilt on page 59 is an example of a diagonal-set quilt.

Flap Border. A unique way to add a narrow touch of color to sewn projects. This technique is used on the Holiday House Sampler Wallhanging on page 172.

Foamcore. Lightweight, rigid material available at art supply stores; very usable in fabric craft items. The Gold and White Wreath on page 239 has a Foamcore base.

Free-Motion Machine Quilting. A method of quilting that combines the use of the darning or embroidery foot with covered or disengaged feed dogs. The purpose is to be able to change the direction of the quilting without turning the quilt. For a complete discussion, see "Free-Motion Machine Quilting" on page 9.

French-Fold Binding. My favorite style of binding, it is durable, easy-to-apply, double-fold binding. See "Adding a French-Fold Binding" on page 10 for complete directions.

Fusible Material. In general, an item that has an adhesive that can be activated by heat and permanently fused to another surface. A paper-backed fusible web or film can be used to make almost anything fusible. The "Sew or No-Sew Miniatures" chapter on page 151 explains and explores this more fully.

Grainline. Exists in woven fabrics. *Lengthwise grain* refers to threads that run parallel to the selvage, or woven edge, of the fabric. They are the firmest threads in the fabric.

Crosswise grain refers to the threads that are perpendicular to the selvage. They have considerably more give than lengthwise threads. *See also* **Bias.**

In the Ditch. Stitching along the seam line, or in the case of appliqué, very close to the edge of the appliqué piece.

Layering. The process of combining the quilt top or design surface, the quilt batting, and the quilt backing fabric.

Loosely Cut. Instead of cutting an item exactly to shape, it is often appropriate to approximate the size of material needed—that is, to loosely cut it. Usually another step, such as sewing on the stitching line, is completed before the final cutting to the exact shape and size needed.

Mock Binding. A simplified way to get the look of a separate binding without the work. The technique is used throughout the "Sew or No-Sew Miniatures" chapter on page 151.

No-Sew Patchwork. The technique in which pattern pieces are fused rather than sewn to a background fabric using a paper-backed fusible material. The technique is used throughout this book; see the "Sew or No-Sew Miniatures" chapter on page 151 for the most complete discussion.

One-Way Design. Fabrics in which all of the design motifs need to point in the same direction to look correct or to match.

Piecing. The process of sewing pieces of fabric together into a patchwork pattern. Piecing can be done by hand or machine.

Chain piecing refers to continuous machine piecing. Pieces are fed through the machine one after the other without cutting threads or stopping between pieces.

String piecing is a method of piecing scraps by sewing them to a foundation or background fabric. See String-Pieced Ornaments on page 217 for further details.

Strip piecing means sewing strips of the appropriate widths together into a set and then making a cut across the strip set to create patchwork. See Strip Technique Quilts on page 25.

Pressing. Not optional. Careful, nonaggressive pressing is a must for precise patchwork.

Quilt-As-You-Sew. A technique in which the stitching of the piecing process goes through the batting and backing layers so that the quilting is completed at the same time as the piecing. The Double Irish Chain Quilt on page 38 and the Merry Chris-Moose Wallhanging on page 181 present two different Quilt-As-You-Sew techniques.

Quilting. The actual process of stitching together the three layers that make up a quilt: the top, batting, and back. Quilting can be done by hand or machine.

Right Side, Wrong Side. As opposed to right side and left side. Printed fabrics have a right and a wrong side. In this book, as in most other sewing texts, the right side refers to the more clearly printed side of the piece of cloth. "Right sides together" refers to placing the more clearly printed side, or the right side, of one fabric so that it is face down on the right side of another piece of fabric. Some woven fabrics also have a right side and a wrong side, but it is more difficult to establish them.

Rotary Cutter. A cutting wheel that is very effective for making fast, accurate cuts. The rotary cutter is generally used in conjunction with a see-through acrylic ruler and must always be used on a protective mat. See "Rotary Cutter Systems" on page 5 for further details.

Sashing. Strips of fabric that separate blocks in a quilt. The Temperance Tree Quilt on page 48 is an example of a quilt set with sashing.

Seam Allowance. The distance between the cut edge of fabric and the stitching or seam line of a project. In quilting, the seam allowances are generally ¼ inch and are pressed to one side rather than open, as in dressmaking or other sewing. See "Seam Allowances" on page 2 for additional information.

Sew-Before-You-Cut. Any technique in which some of the piecing is done before the cutting. The technique is explained fully in Strip Technique Quilts on page 25 and in the Homespun Sunshine and Shadows Throw on page 29. It is also used to make pieced squares in the Temperance Tree Quilt on page 48.

Stitch-and-Flip. Another term for string piecing. Generally, random-width strips are sewn one at a time to a foundation, then flipped open and pressed. See String-Pieced Ornaments on page 217 for further details.

Straight Set. Refers to the arrangement of blocks in a quilt. In a straight set, the blocks are placed so that the bottom edge is parallel to the bottom edge of the quilt. This is in contrast to a diagonal set, in which the blocks are turned so that they rest on a corner.

Tied Quilt. The term used when the sandwich of quilt top, batting, and backing is held together by a series of tied knots, instead of a quilting stitch, going through all the layers.

Trapunto. Refers to padded or stuffed quilting. The technique involves inserting yarn or small amounts of polyfill into certain quilted areas to create a raised surface. For an example, see the Elegant Trapunto Stocking on page 240.

INDEX

Note: Page references in **boldface** indicate photographs. *Italic* references indicate illustrations.